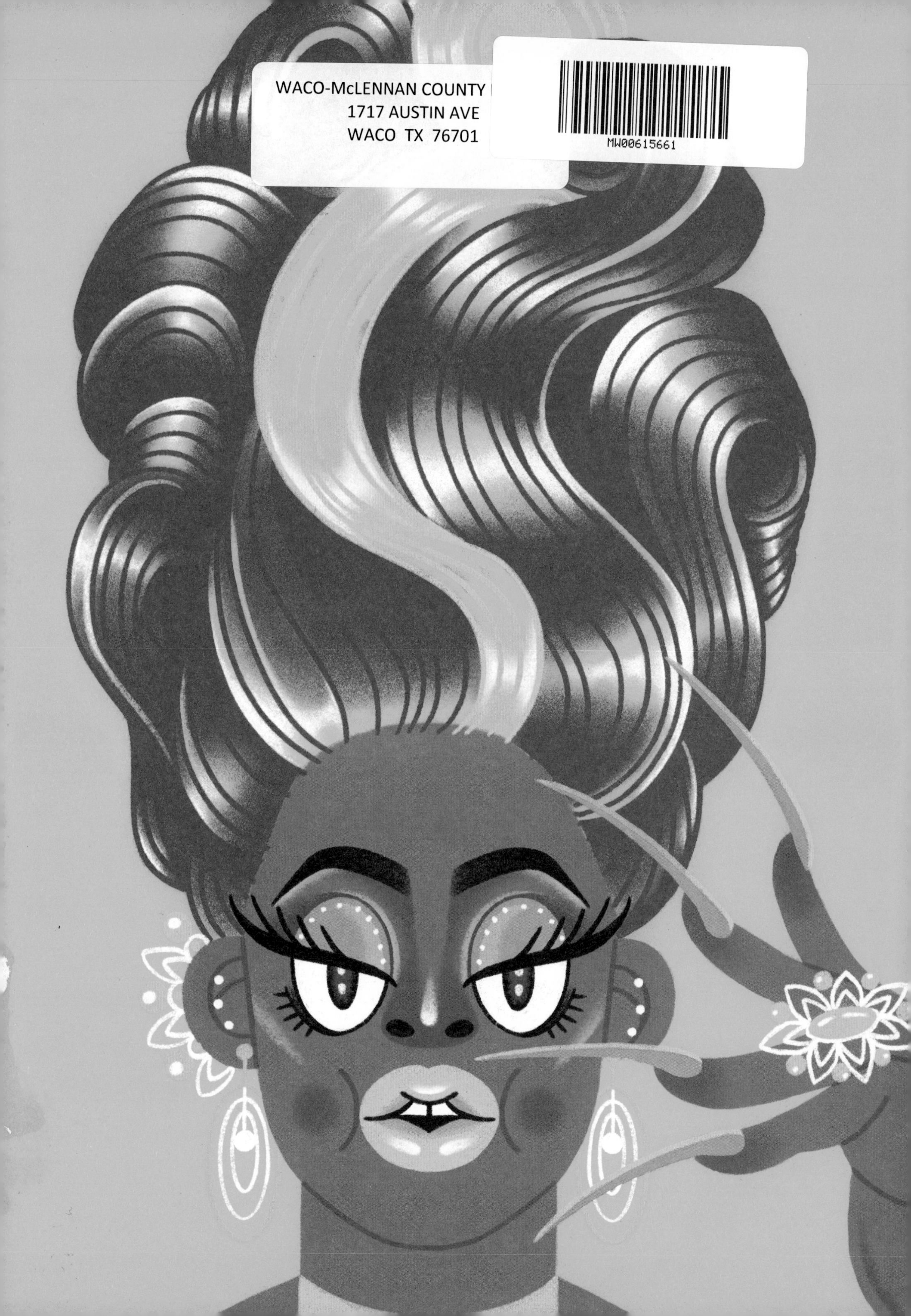

The Art of Drag © Nobrow 2020

First published in 2020 by Nobrow Ltd.
27 Westgate Street, London E8 3RL.

Text by Jake Hall.
Illustrations by Sofie Birkin, Helen Li and Jasjyot Singh Hans.

Additional artists: Eero Lampinen, Salome Papadopoullos, Noa Denmon, Nada Hayek and Marcos Chin.

Consultant: Joe E. Jeffreys

Editor: Ayoola Solarin
Design: Lilly Gottwald

1 3 5 7 9 10 8 6 4 2

Published in the US by Nobrow (US) Inc.

FSC
www.fsc.org

MIX
Paper from responsible sources
FSC® C002795

Printed in Latvia on FSC® certified paper.
ISBN: 978-1-910620-71-7

www.nobrow.net

written by Jake Hall

The ART of DRAG

artwork by Sofie Birkin, Helen Li, Jasjyot Singh Hans & more.

NOBROW

London / New York

CONTENTS

The Art of Freak 56

The Art of Charisma 76

The Art of Influence 98

The Future of Drag 114

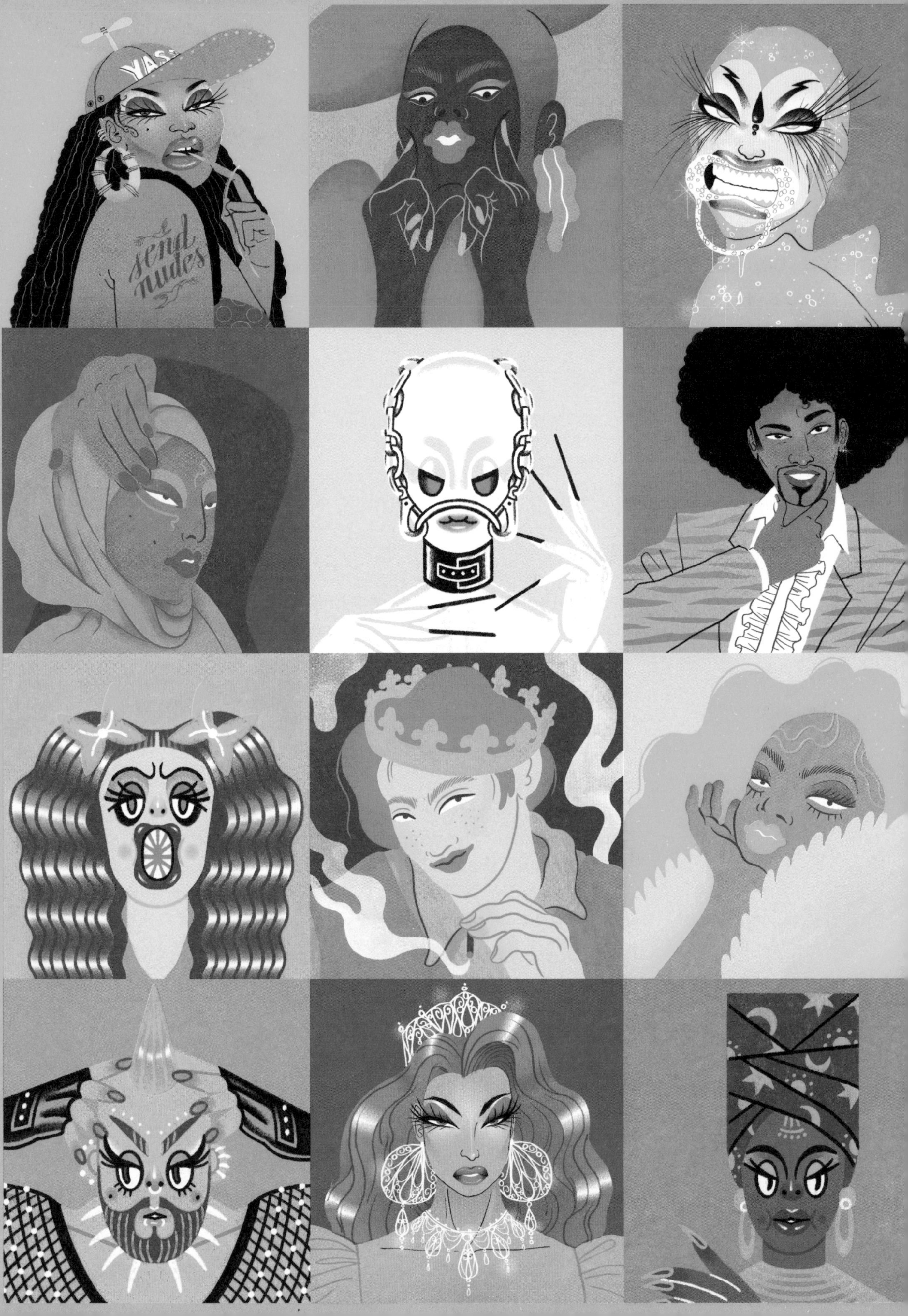
send nudes

INTRODUCTION

While cross-dressing has been around for hundreds of years, it wasn't 'drag' until an 1870 edition of the UK's *Reynold's Newspaper* printed a fabulous-sounding event invitation: "We shall come in drag, which means men dressed in women's costumes." It is now one of the world's most glamorous, hilarious and rebellious art forms. Not only does drag set out to subvert society's norms, it delights at poking fun at the world around us. Every day, artists across the globe dig deep into their dressing-up boxes, using lavish costumes and make-up to magic up larger-than-life alter-egos that dazzle and amaze. It's exciting, liberating and deliciously queer, so it's no wonder that drag has fast become a global phenomenon.

In this book, we take a look beyond the wigs and sequins to delve deep into the long, fascinating history of drag. Each chapter encapsulates a key element of drag, as seen through different snapshots in time.

First, we travel back to the stadiums of Ancient Greece and the stages of Victorian England to look at theatre as a precursor to drag, before entering the underground world of the flappers and cabaret performers of the Jazz Age. We then consider the politics of drag in the 1960s and the growing acceptance of drag in the 1970s, and, finally, go into detail on the more recent years of global domination.

Drag has come a long way over the centuries and undergone countless transformations. Every artist in this book has made key cultural contributions. Their pronouns have been carefully selected (some use different pronouns in and out of drag), and the word queer has been used not just as an umbrella term for different LGBTQ+ identities, but also as a synonym for 'radical' or 'disruptive'. Drag ticks both boxes. So, from pantomime dames and kabuki queens to avant-garde club kids, it's time to pay homage to drag legends and explore just how drag became the glitzy, queer phenomenon we all know and love today.

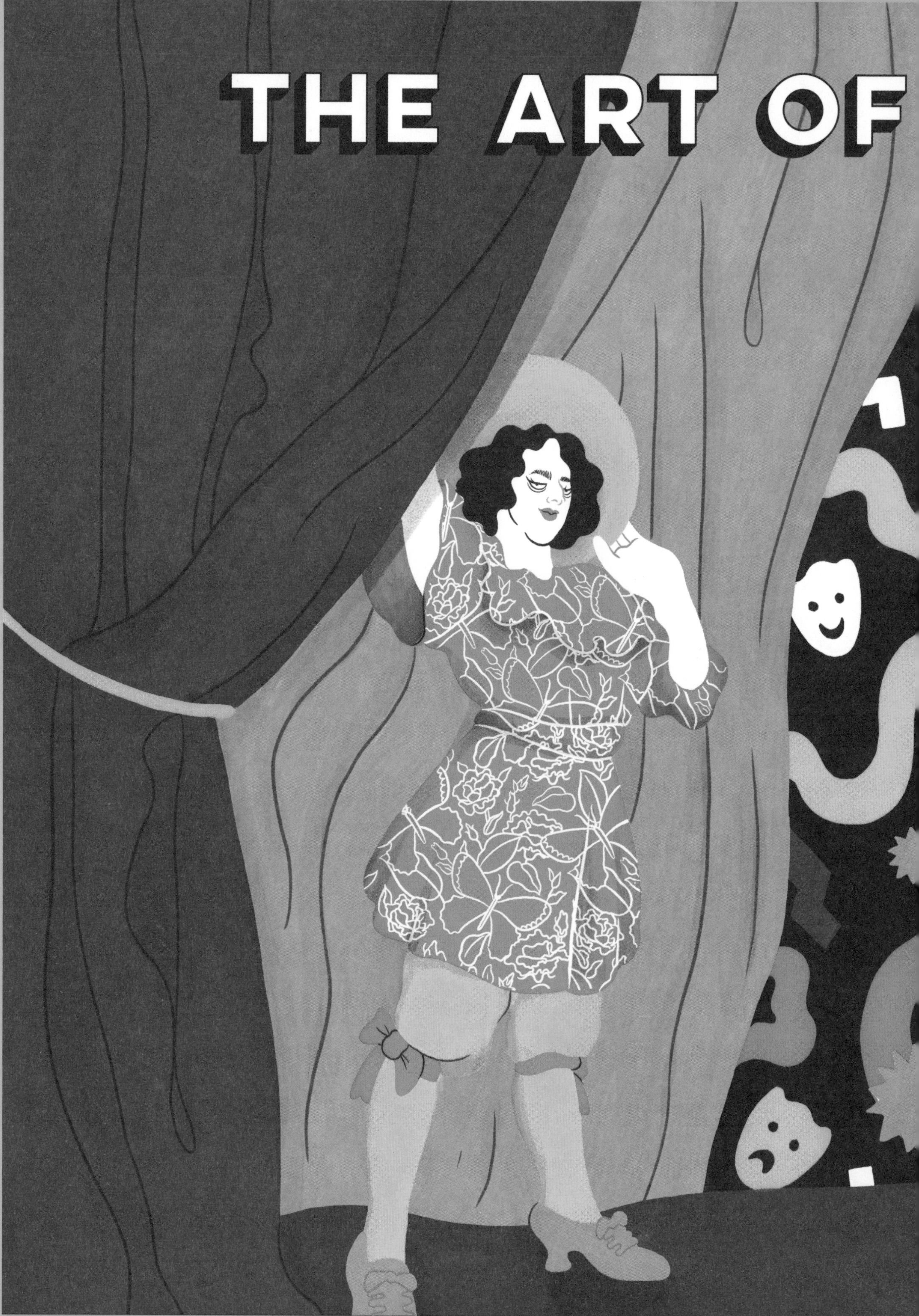
THE ART OF

PERFORMANCE

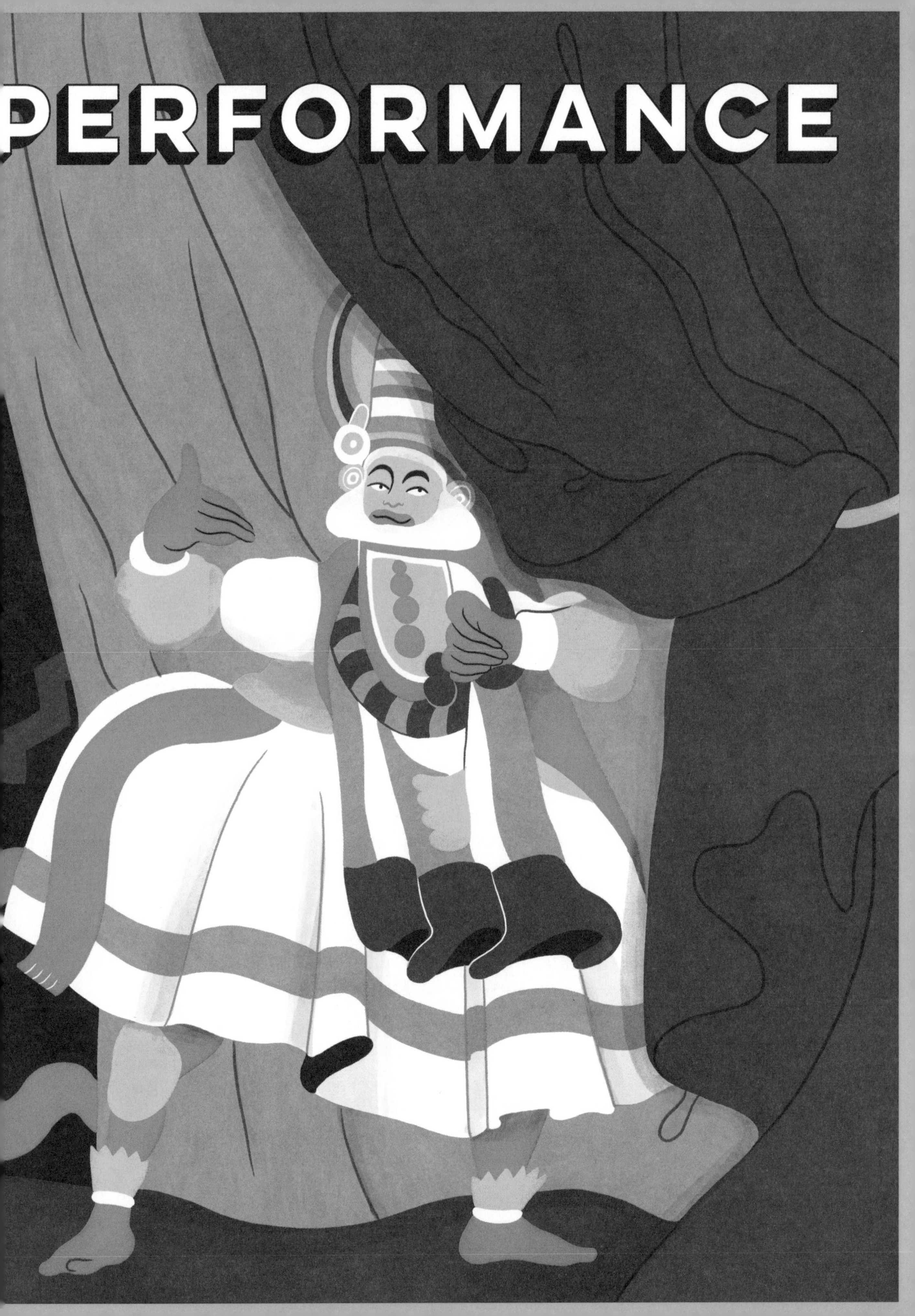

400 BCE – 1900s

From theatrical lip-syncs to slapstick skits, it's impossible to think of drag without also thinking of performance – the two have always gone hand in hand. Cross-dressing on stage dates back centuries. It is thought that the term 'drag' was first used informally in the late 1800s to describe the motion of ballgown trains and petticoat hems – worn by male actors, who often played female roles – 'dragging' along theatre floors.

Then there's the element of character creation, as integral to drag as it is to theatre. Drag performers create campy, over-the-top, glamorous alter-egos not just to poke fun at the world around them, but also to engage their audiences. In the same way that theatre often relies on crowd participation, drag stars have long used their characters to help viewers relate to them and get lost in the magic of their illusion.

Kings also had their moment in the spotlight, particularly in the late 19th century. The rise of vaudeville theatre made stars of male impersonators like Vesta Tilley and Florence Hines, whose tongue-in-cheek musical parodies of masculinity tickled fans. This winning combination of rousing sing-song and quick-witted comedy has withstood the test of time; even now, it's a beloved formula in drag shows.

MIME

Mime, a famed art form born in ancient Greece, can be considered one of history's earliest iterations of drag. Using a combination of dance and audience interaction, mimes acted out plays in ancient Greek festivals, enacting elaborate stories. While they all shared an affinity for decorated tunics and often ghoulish-looking masks, the most famous mimes were best-known for their charm, not their costumes. Telestes, the earliest known mime, was noted for his tendency to break away from the chorus and act out on his own, stealing the limelight and winning the hearts of the adoring audience.

With white face paint, striped jumpers and eerily fixed smiles, the modern mime remains an instantly recognisable persona and a trusty Hallowe'en costume staple. So although mimes aren't exactly conventional drag artists, their comedic exaggerations and over-the-top gestures have informed drag as we now know it, laying its campy, three-inch-thick foundations.

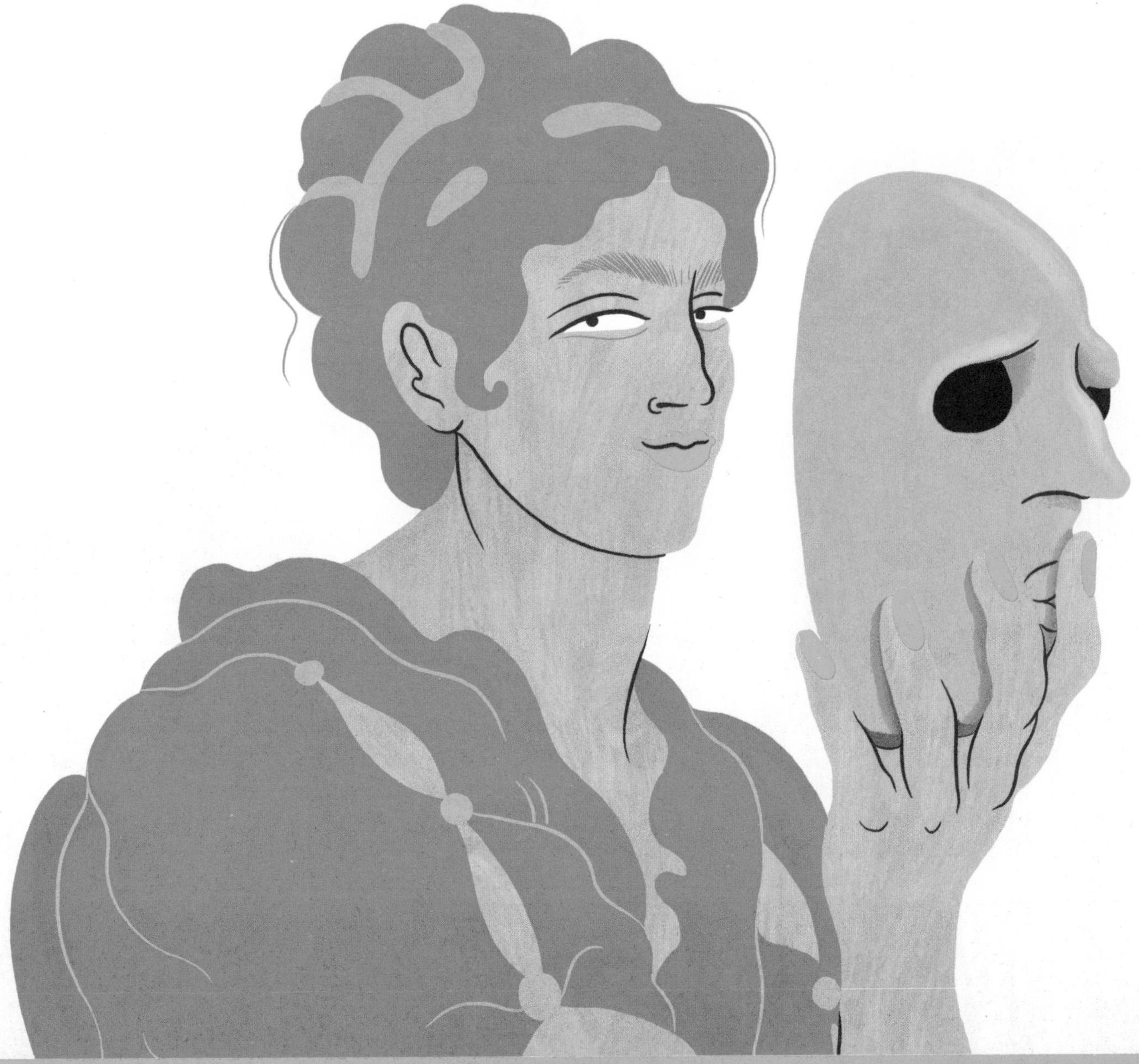

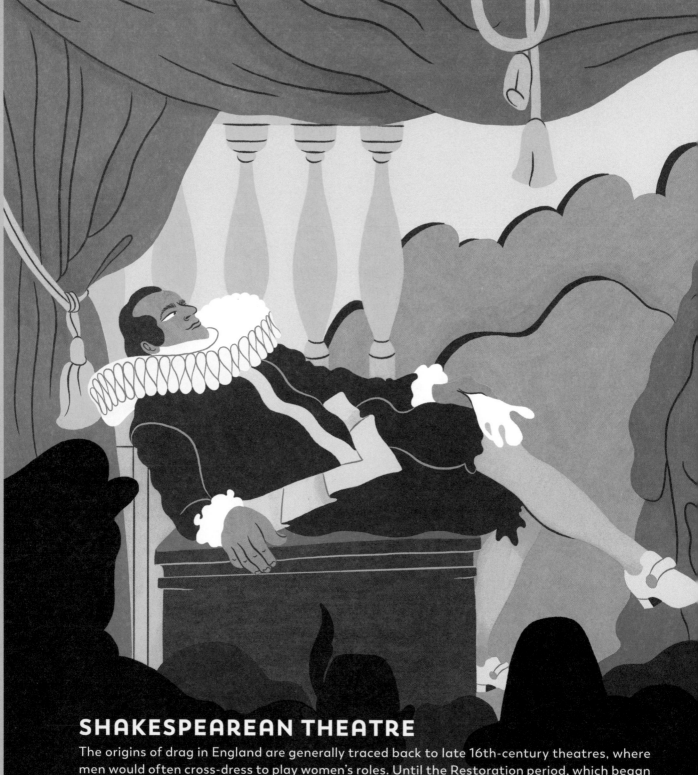

SHAKESPEAREAN THEATRE

The origins of drag in England are generally traced back to late 16th-century theatres, where men would often cross-dress to play women's roles. Until the Restoration period, which began in 1660, women were barred from stage by puritans who believed it was an inappropriate profession. The few radical actresses that did continue to perform were heavily stigmatised.

In the absence of women, male actors took over. They slicked their faces with white paint, lipstick and rouge, donning the elaborate, full-skirted, flouncy gowns popular at the time. A lot of these roles were given to young boys whose voices hadn't yet broken, particularly romantic leads like Cleopatra and Juliet. With their slender limbs, softer features and more petite bodies, these so-called 'boy players' were deemed more 'feminine' than their older counterparts.

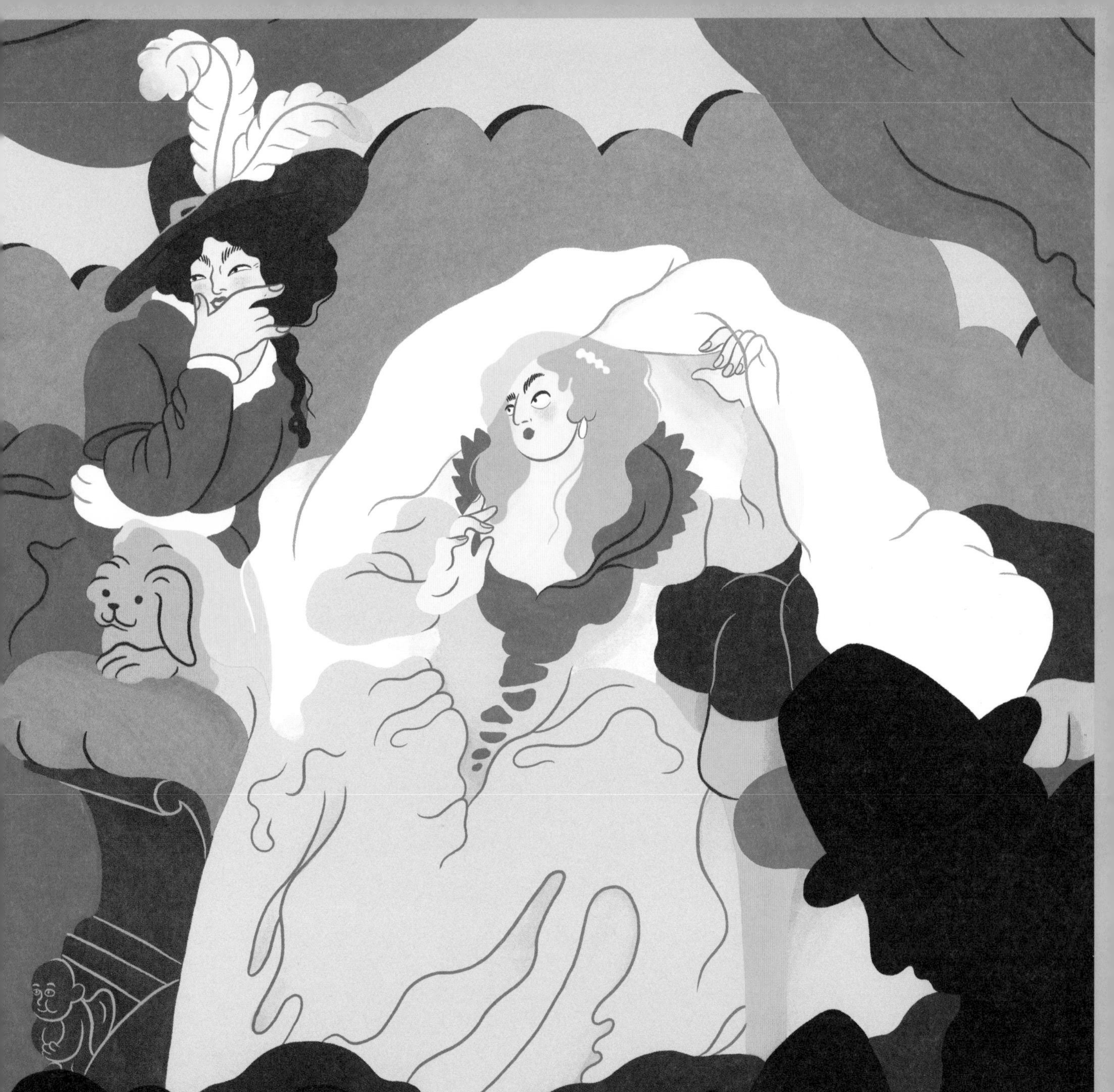

Some roles did require older actors – like the nurse in *Romeo & Juliet* and Emilia in *Othello* – but they were few and far between. Meaty female roles are generally thin on the ground in Shakespeare's work, and in fact his heroines become more central characters when they cross-dress as men. A key example comes in *Twelfth Night*, when Viola – a young woman born into an aristocratic family – seizes an opportunity presented by a shipwreck to reinvent herself as a man named Cesario. By cross-dressing, she escapes her fate and takes control of her life.

Stories like these exemplify the complicated role of gender in Shakespearean theatre. Even when women were allowed back on stage in 1660, critics wrote harsh reviews of their performances, complaining that they were no longer used to seeing actresses at work. It's true that on-stage cross-dressing has a complicated history and was often far from progressive, but at the very least, it gave the world some key early examples of drag in practice.

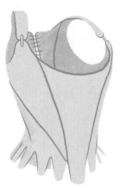 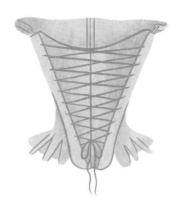 

THE CORSET

There are few garments more unforgiving than the corset, still used by women and drag artists to force the body into an idealised feminine shape, no matter the toll.

The 16th-century corset has become the quintessential example: punishing steel boning and thick laces to pull it tight. This type of corset first became popular in Italy, but it wasn't until Italian noblewoman Catherine de Medici moved to France in the 1530s and became the country's queen that the corset craze spread across Europe.

Every variation of the corset has sought to enhance the female body, so it makes sense that styles have changed to keep up with changing beauty standards. Bodices were always constricting but, while early corsets deliberately flattened the chest, the design was altered by the 1800s to accentuate the breasts, giving a more hourglass shape. Although steel boning had been briefly replaced with whale bone in the 1700s, it once again gained popularity in the Victorian era, when lacing corsets became an extreme sport. Women would 'tightlace' to get their waists as small as possible, a trend which lives on in the waist-training belts of social media fame.

For drag artists, the corset remains an important tool in their arsenal, especially when teamed with sponge padding and lavish, tight gowns. Luckily, today's designs tend to be a little more forgiving than Catherine de Medici's – more mesh and satin, and a lot less steel.

1950s   1990s   2000s

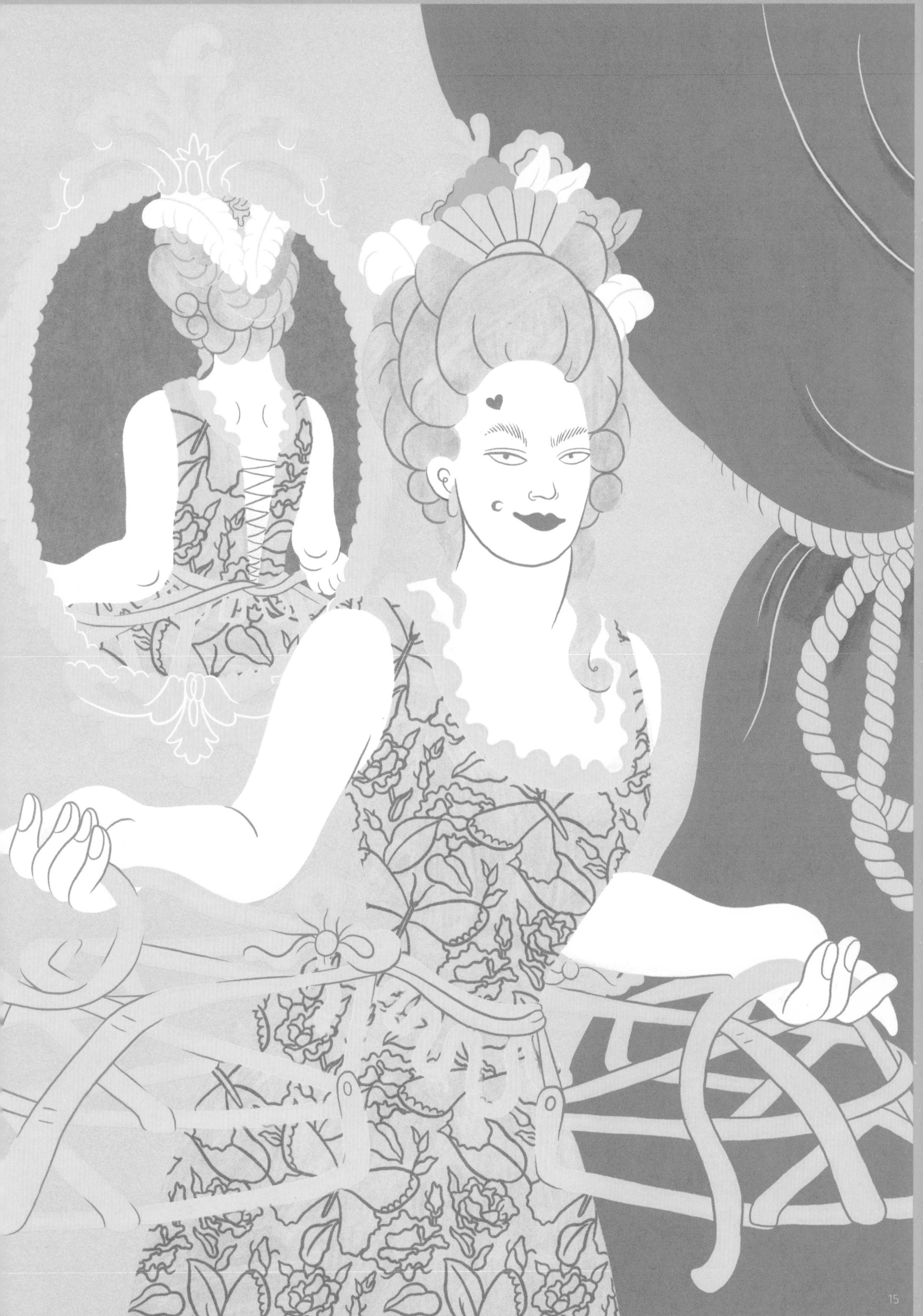

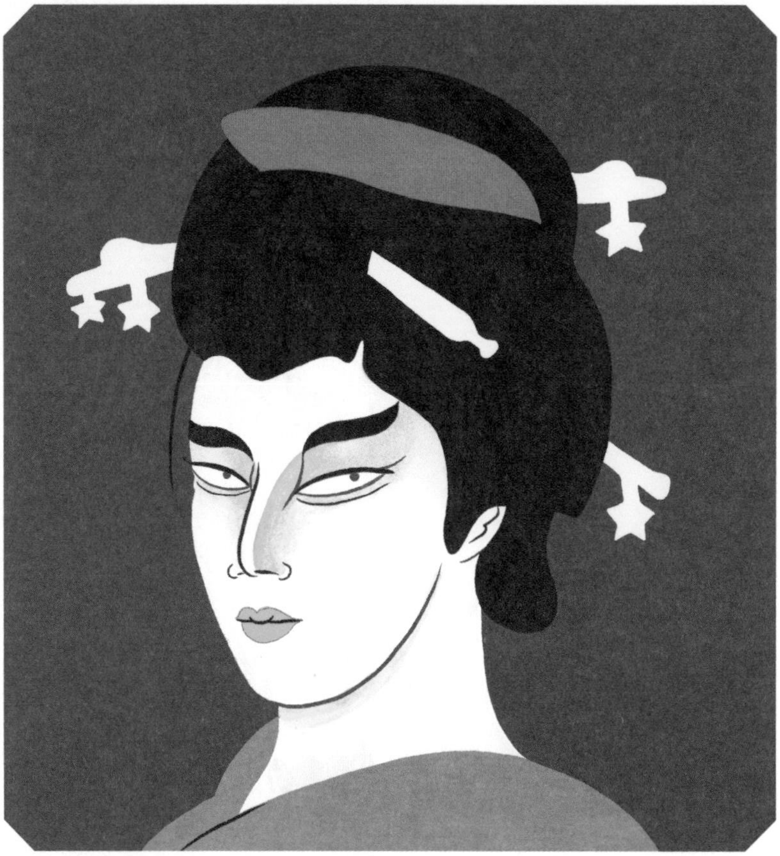

KABUKI THEATRE

Kabuki, one of Japan's most revered art forms, has been transformed over the centuries, but the essence of using costume, character and music to tell stories remains. The origins of kabuki can be traced back to one woman: Izumo no Okuni. In 1603, she gathered a troupe of young women to perform a new style of dance on a makeshift stage, nestled by Kyoto's Kama River. They dressed in typically 'male' clothing of simple kimonos.

Under Okuni, the troupe's popularity rose until 1629, when stigma, and the government's fear that performances were too erotic, led to women being banned from kabuki. It subsequently became a male-only art form, although some *wakashū* (young men, often sex workers) were also banned. This facilitated the rise of the *onnagata*, a term used to describe male actors playing female roles. These men were dedicated to femininity, mastering soft, delicate movements and mannerisms. Today's actors tend to be older men, who decorate their faces with white paint. They wear traditional geisha wigs strewn with ornate accessories, and wear long, flowing kimonos.

Kabuki stories tend to be highly emotional and laden with drama. Performances are divided into various acts over several hours. *Chūshingura* – a popular play where 47 ronin (masterless samurai) seek to avenge the murder of their master – is one of the lengthiest, running to almost eight hours. Over time, plotlines have become more complex and spectacular, but the elegant dances and traditional costumes remain largely unchanged after 400 years.

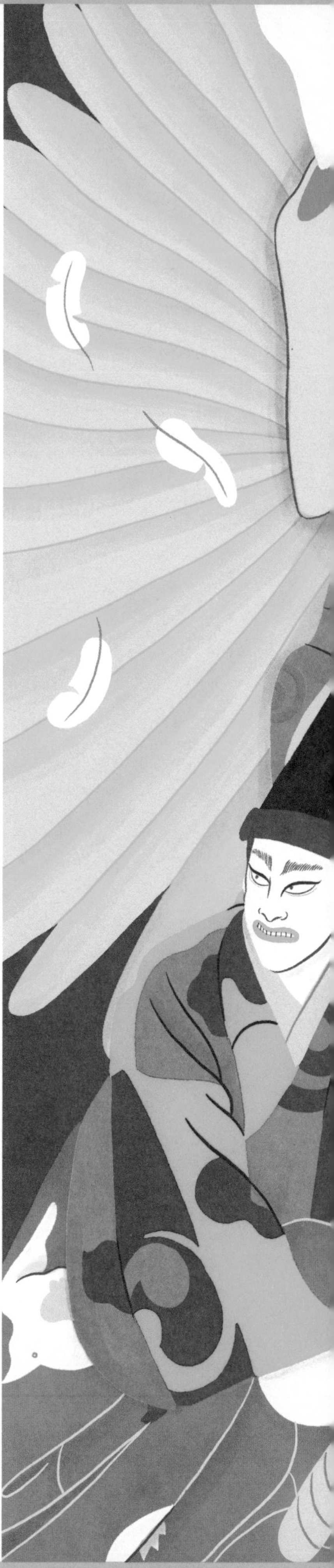

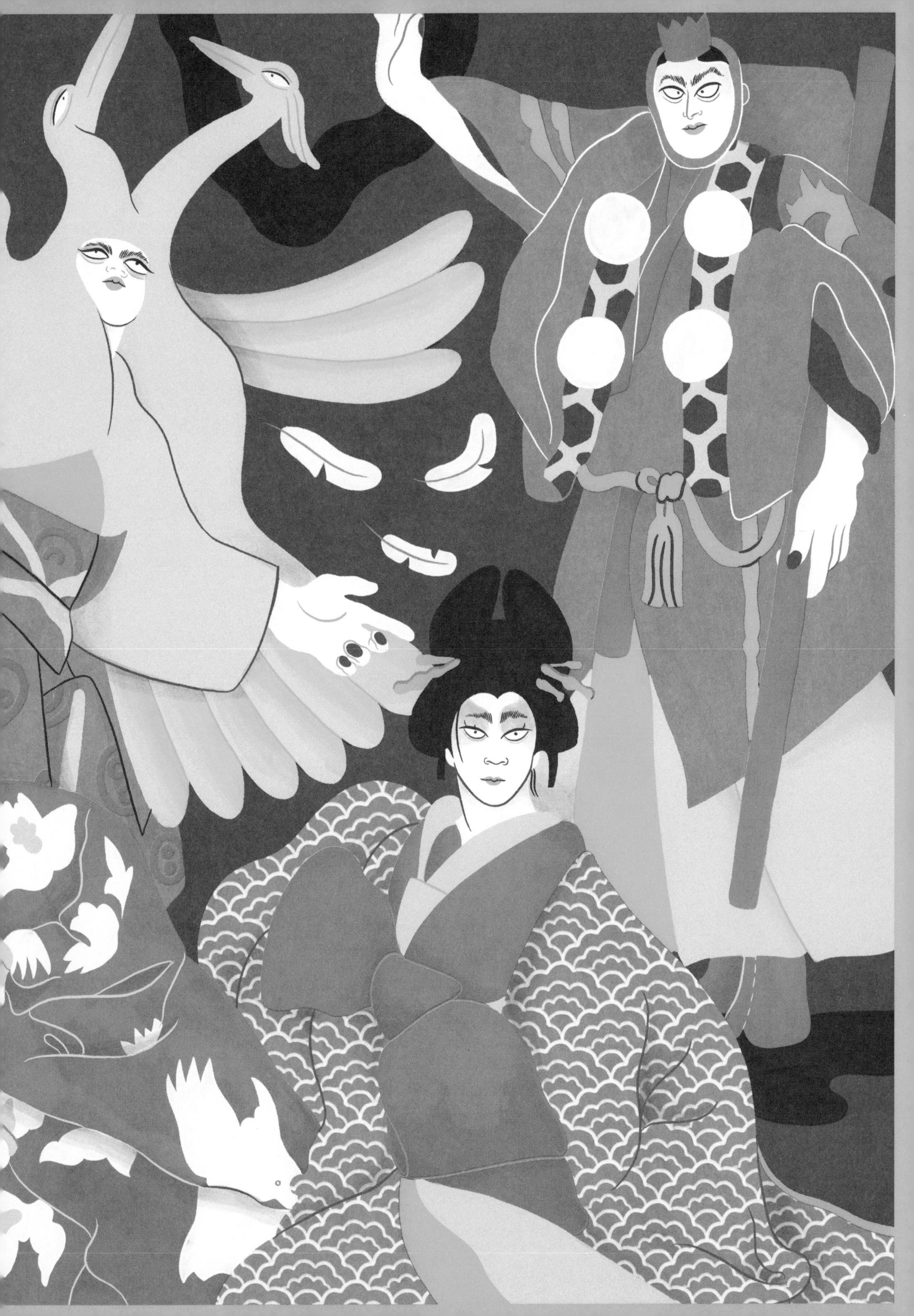

KATHAKALI

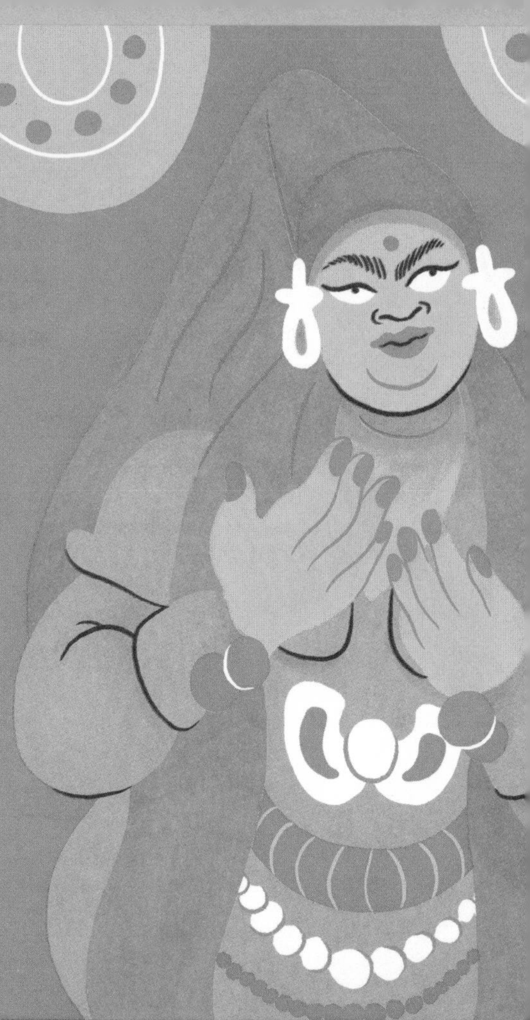

Traditionally based on Hindu folklore, Kathakali is a dance performed by men, which tells stories through music, singing, choreography and ornate costumes. Experts can't agree on the exact origins of Kathakali, but most agree that it originated in the 1700s in southern India.

The costumes are usually accompanied by enormous, heavily embellished headpieces. The make-up is equally elaborate, created using brightly coloured face paint to resemble gods, animals and even demons. Unsurprisingly, performers tend to take around four hours to get ready for a show.

It's not easy to become a Kathakali performer. Students train for more than a decade, and must master the distinctive art of 'eye-dancing' – using the eyes to convey an emotional narrative – to truly call themselves qualified. The beauty lies in these small, subtle details, which sets Kathakali apart from other traditional performance styles. And Kathakali is still evolving. While all-male troupes were once the norm, more and more women are now studying to become performers.

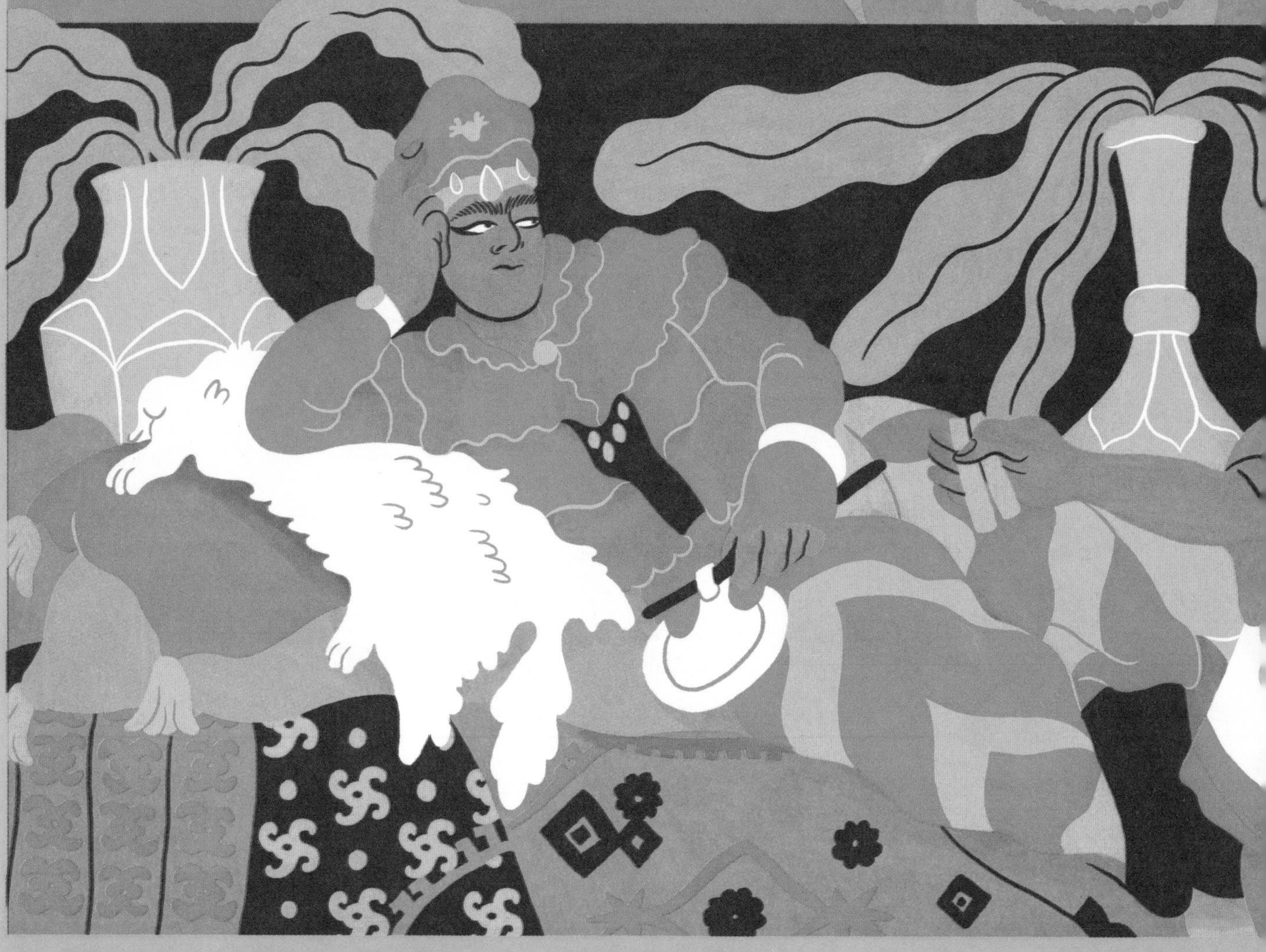

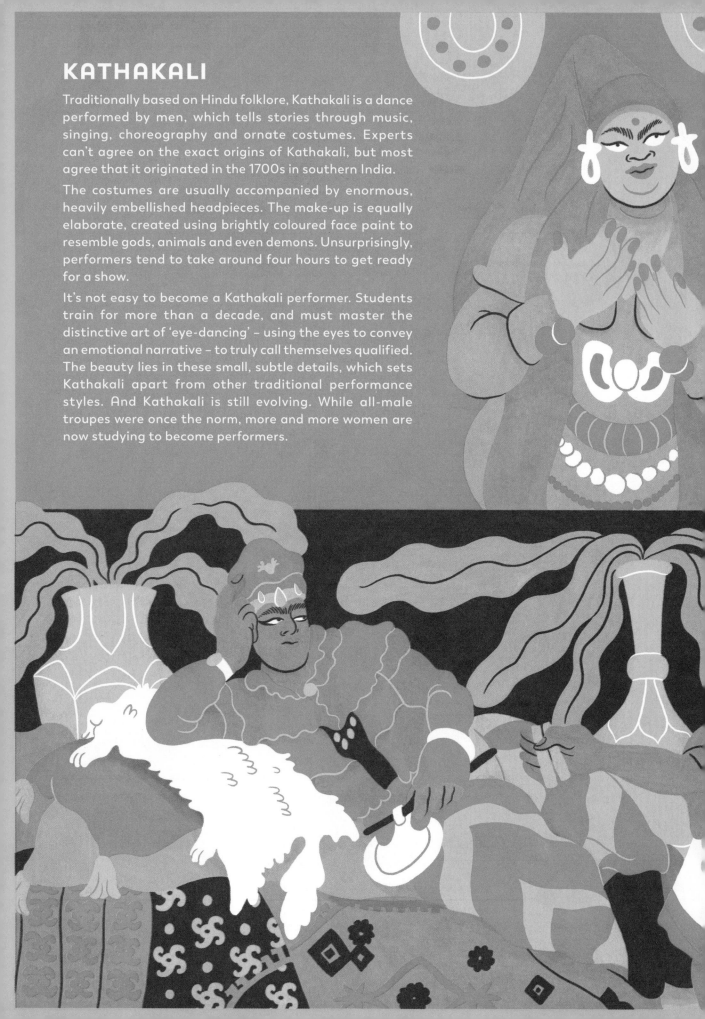

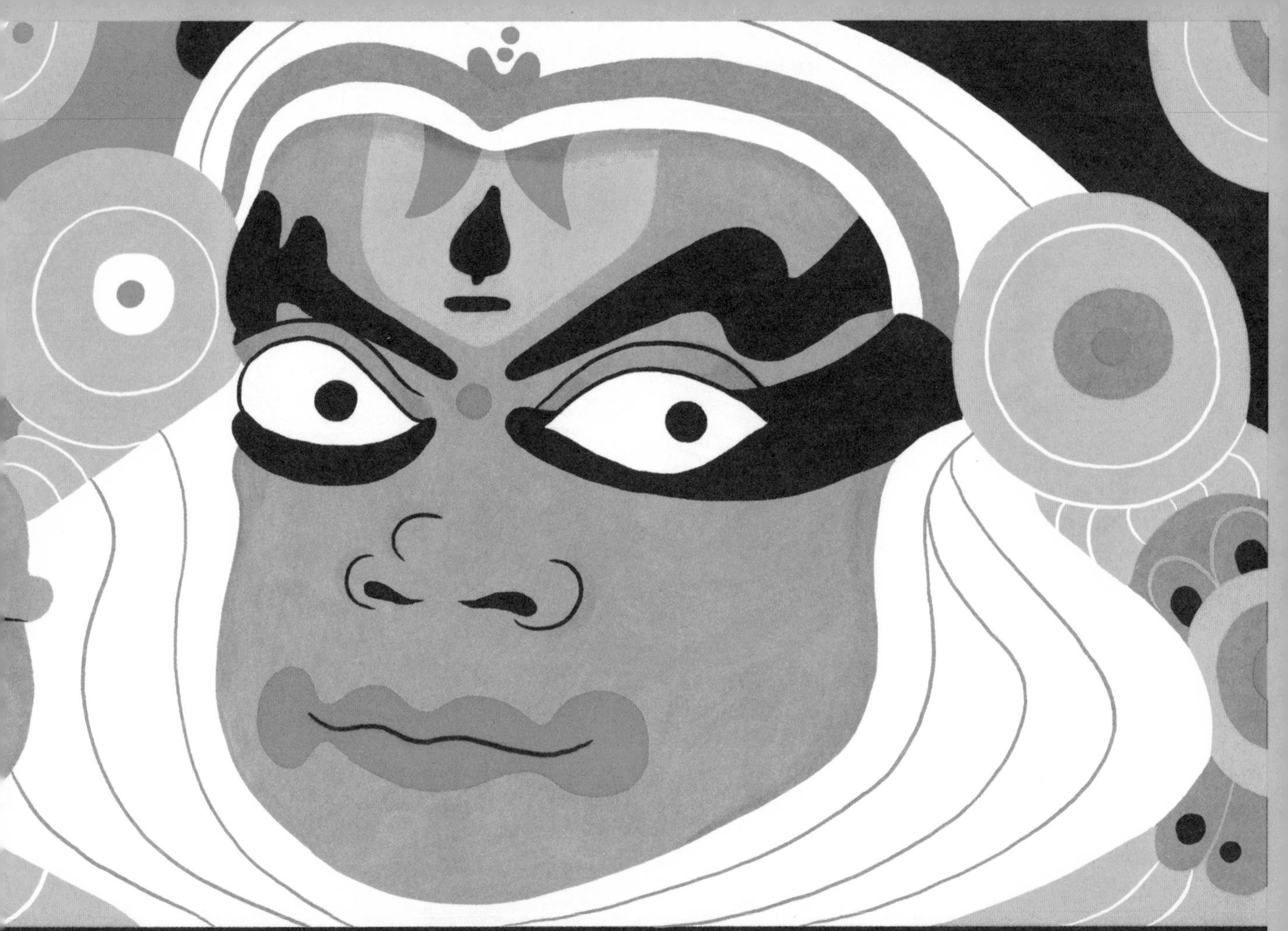

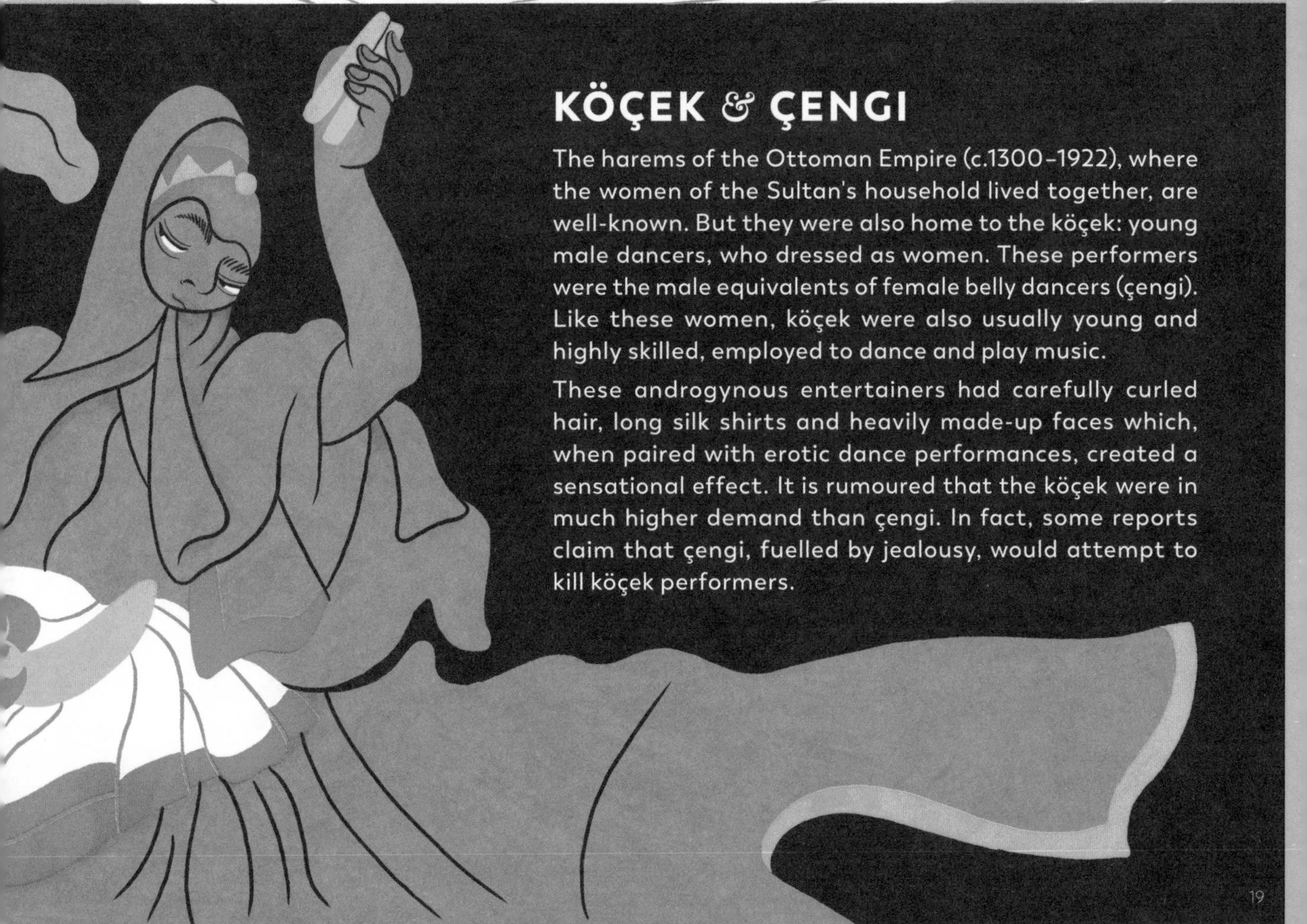

KÖÇEK & ÇENGI

The harems of the Ottoman Empire (c.1300–1922), where the women of the Sultan's household lived together, are well-known. But they were also home to the köçek: young male dancers, who dressed as women. These performers were the male equivalents of female belly dancers (çengi). Like these women, köçek were also usually young and highly skilled, employed to dance and play music.

These androgynous entertainers had carefully curled hair, long silk shirts and heavily made-up faces which, when paired with erotic dance performances, created a sensational effect. It is rumoured that the köçek were in much higher demand than çengi. In fact, some reports claim that çengi, fuelled by jealousy, would attempt to kill köçek performers.

PEKING OPERA

Chinese opera has a long and celebrated history dating back thousands of years. Arguably the best-known form is Peking Opera, which originated in the late 18th century. As expected, music and performance make up the core elements, but an emphasis on acrobatics and overblown, colourful aesthetics distinguishes Peking Opera from the styles that came before.

Performers are split into different role categories, with the most famous being the Dan – the leading female roles. Prior to 1912, the roles could only be played by men due to a longstanding ban on women in the theatre but they are now open to all genders. Whereas other roles in Peking Opera require intricate, patterned face paint, Dan make-up is comparatively demure – lashings of red eyeshadow is teamed with sharp, winged eyeliner and bold red lipstick.

After the ban on female performers was lifted, a handful of male Dan actors continued their success, becoming known as the 'Four Great Dan'. Mei Lanfang may have been the most famous of them. His bone structure, high-pitched voice and delicate manner made him a hit with audiences.

In many ways, Dan are amongst the world's original drag artists. Their patterned robes – known as *Xingtou* or *Xifu* – have grown more luxurious over time, graduating from linen to the finest silk. Their emblazoned motifs and bold, bright prints have, however, remained similar throughout the years. When combined with make-up, music and movement, these robes conjure the kind of exaggerated feminine beauty that drag queens aspire to recreate.

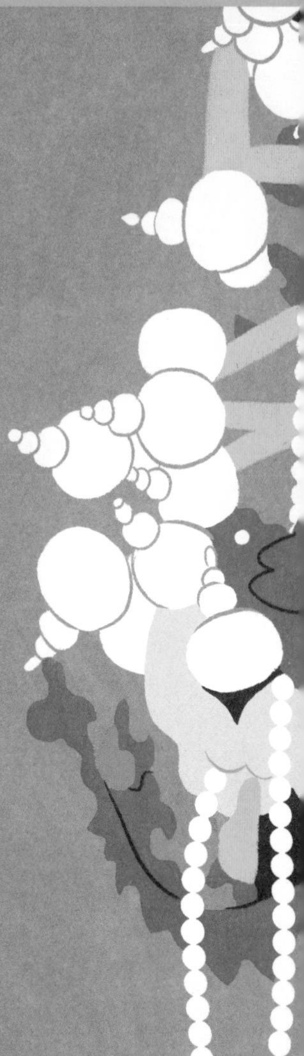

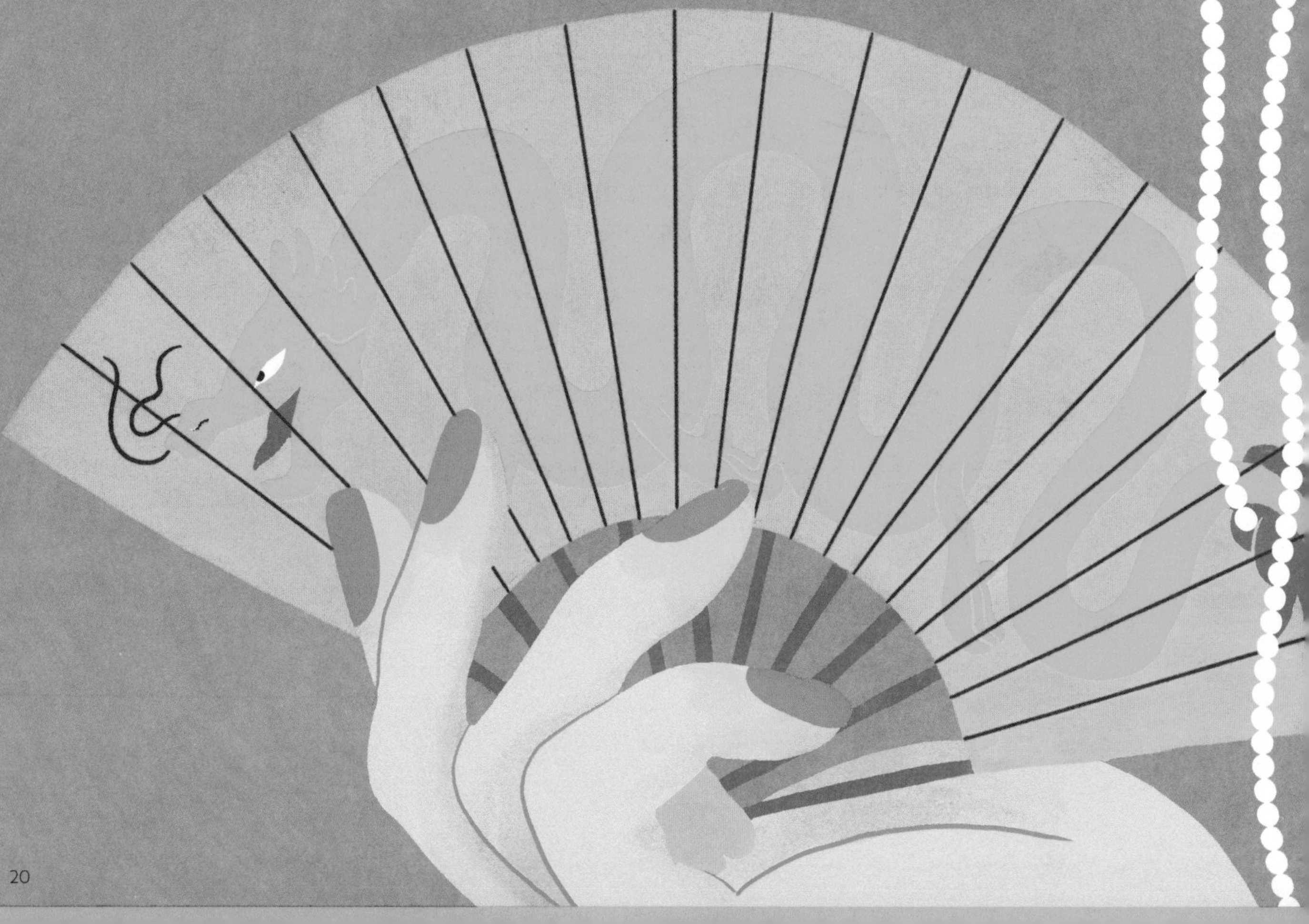

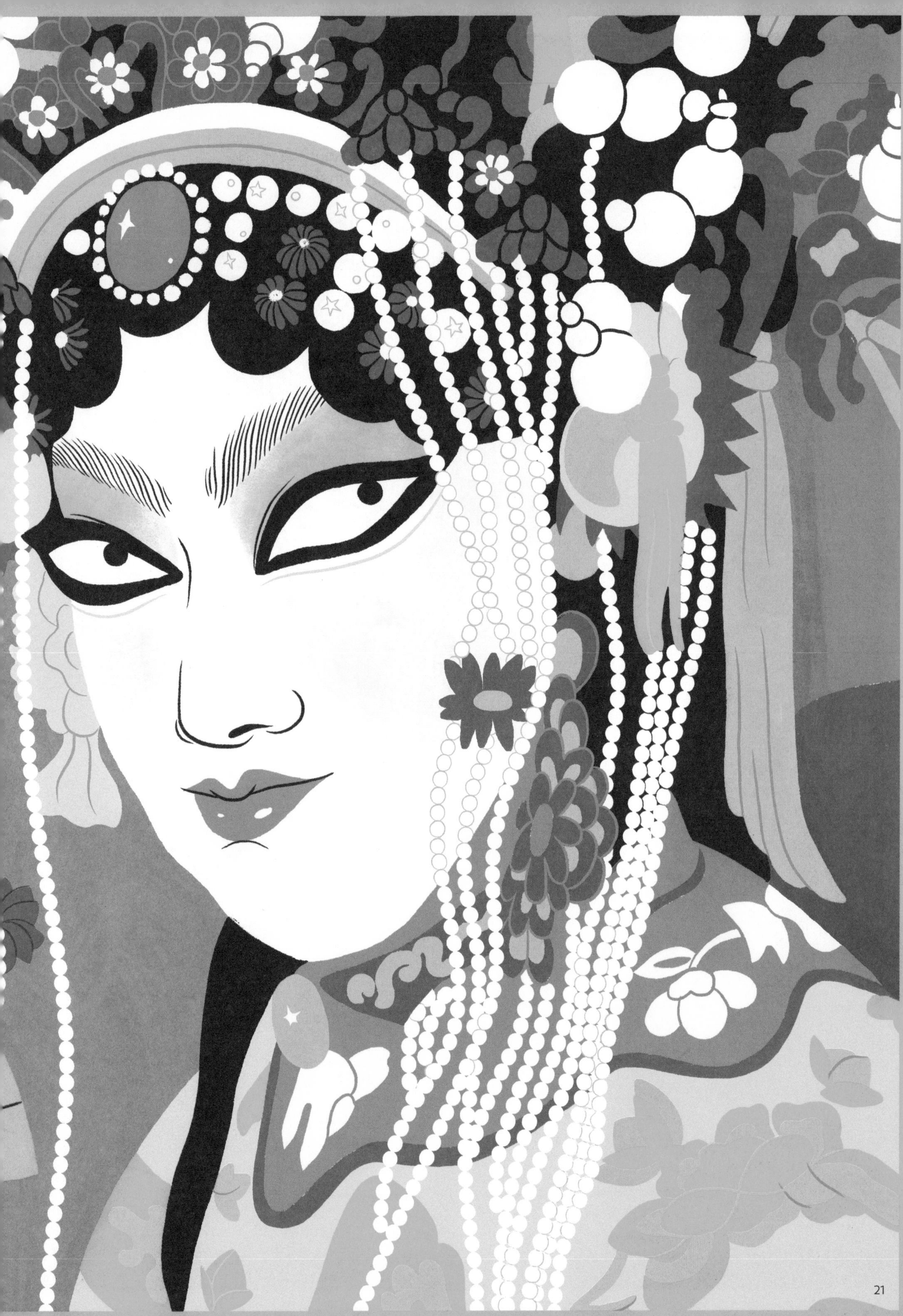

VAUDEVILLE

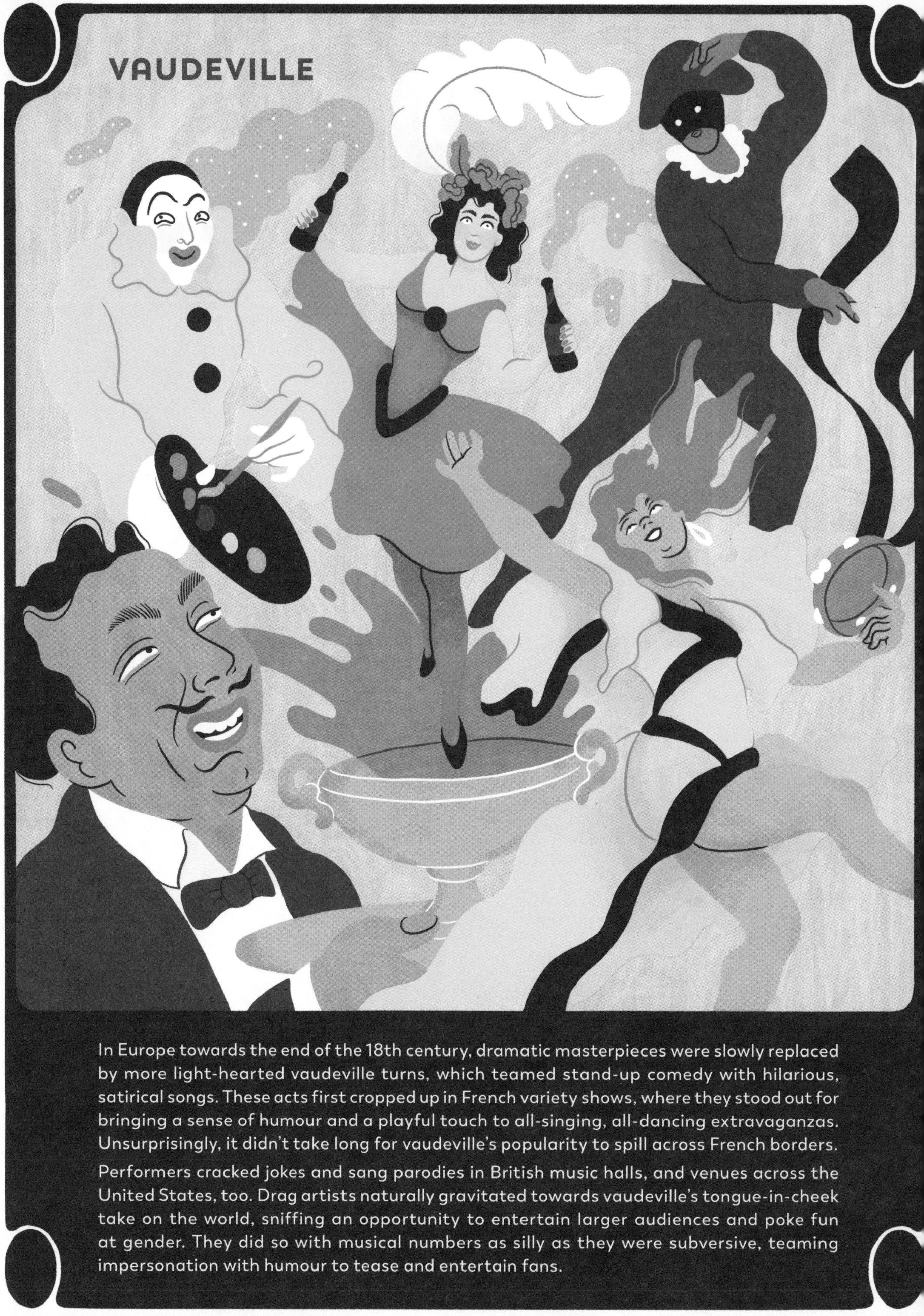

In Europe towards the end of the 18th century, dramatic masterpieces were slowly replaced by more light-hearted vaudeville turns, which teamed stand-up comedy with hilarious, satirical songs. These acts first cropped up in French variety shows, where they stood out for bringing a sense of humour and a playful touch to all-singing, all-dancing extravaganzas. Unsurprisingly, it didn't take long for vaudeville's popularity to spill across French borders.

Performers cracked jokes and sang parodies in British music halls, and venues across the United States, too. Drag artists naturally gravitated towards vaudeville's tongue-in-cheek take on the world, sniffing an opportunity to entertain larger audiences and poke fun at gender. They did so with musical numbers as silly as they were subversive, teaming impersonation with humour to tease and entertain fans.

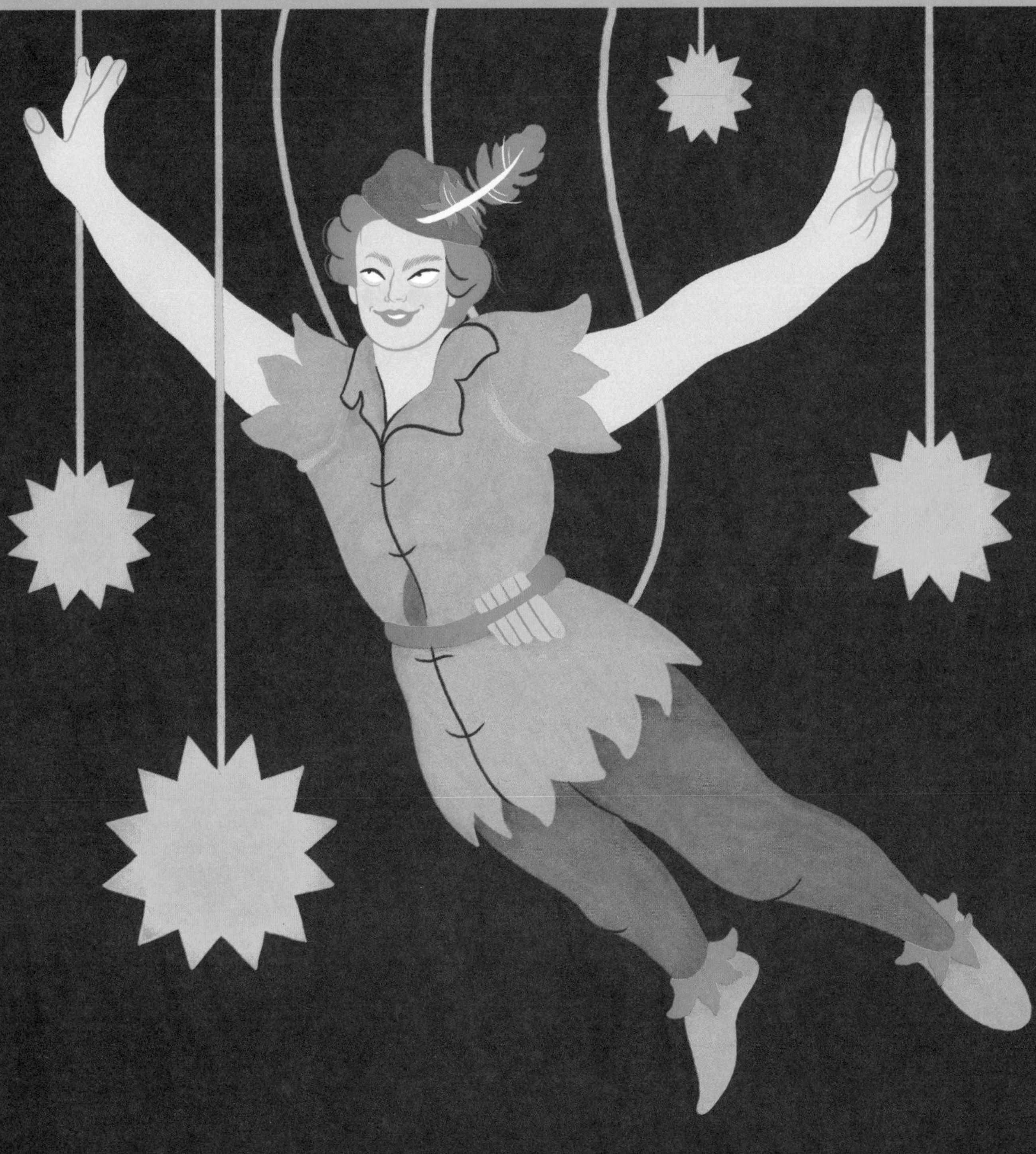

PANTOMIME

Although the ban on female performers was lifted in Britain towards the end of the 17th century, the craze for cross-gender acting continued through the very British art of pantomime, a kind of slapstick theatre whose popularity spikes at Christmas. Women began landing 'principal boy' parts where they played young men, and many drag kings started their careers in these roles. This cross-dressing became a gag in the show, where performers would joke about being free from the constriction of feminine clothes.

A handful of these 'cross-dressing' roles are still popular today: the pantomime Dame – known for crude, camp jokes – and the Peter Pan principal boy – a plucky wisecracker set to steal the hearts of the audience. These comedy stars were early examples of drag artists appealing to audiences through gags and skits. They understood that a little laughter made the subversion easier to swallow, a technique that still runs through drag today.

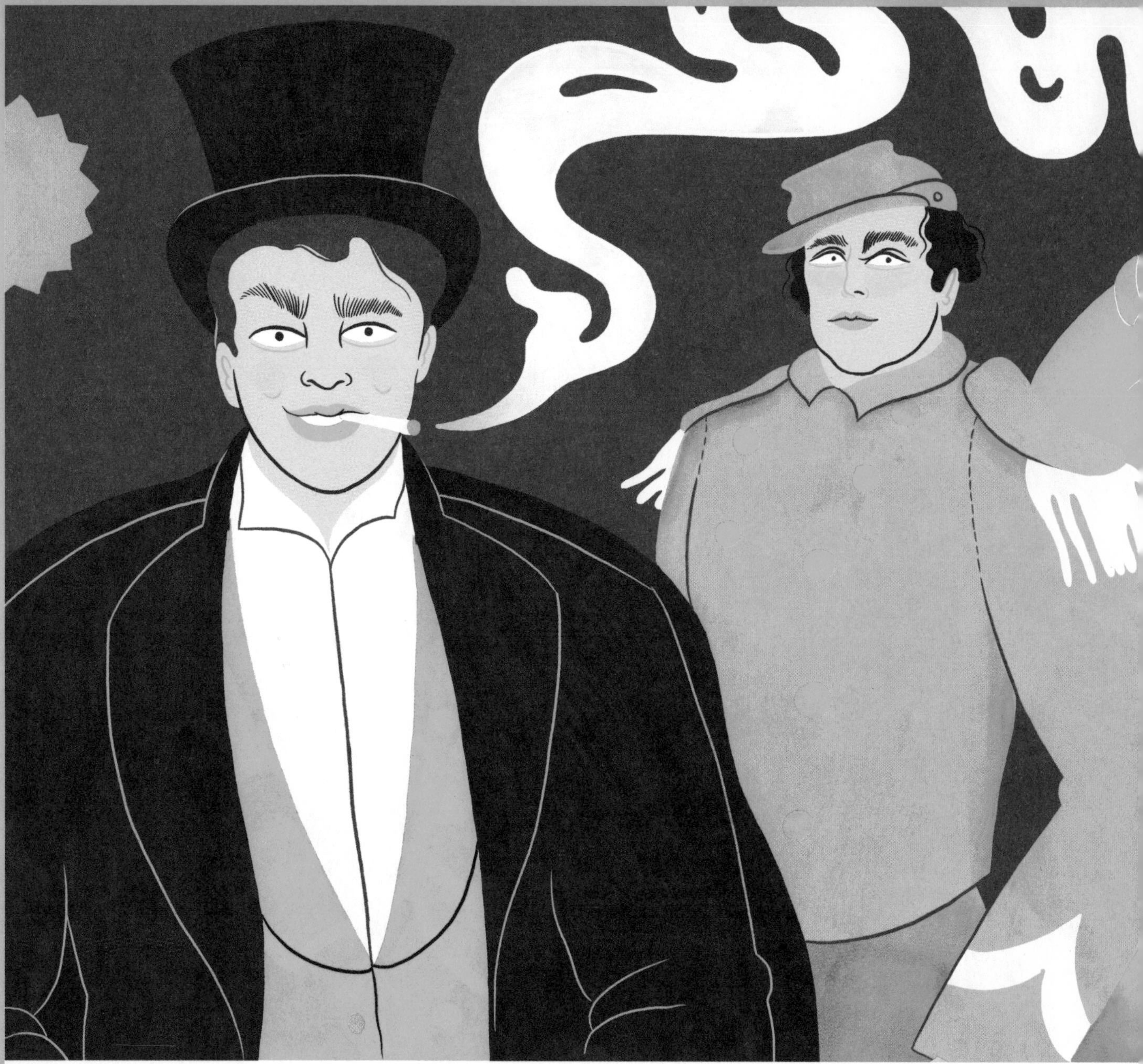

RISE OF THE DRAG KING

Victorian Britain may have been notoriously repressive, but as vaudeville began to work its way into music halls, it allowed for a surprising and dashing group of drag kings to emerge.

Like female impersonators, these male impersonators varied hugely, but their charm and tongue-in-cheek portrayals of masculinity resonated with audiences. There was Vesta Tilley, who moved from soft, sentimental songs to roaring musical numbers. With her father as her manager, she travelled the world and almost sold out her year-long farewell tour in 1919, donating the proceeds to charity. Black drag king Florence Hines began polishing her male impersonation act as part of musical revue *The Creole Show*, which deviated from racist 'minstrel shows' by portraying Black artists in a new light. Hines' trademark role was the 'dandy', a fashionable, upper-class eccentric. She reportedly earned the highest salary of any Black woman of the time.

This era of vaudeville prosperity was later dampened by the Depression, but not before it spawned a series of stars including Ella Shields and Annie Hindle, who charmed audiences in both the UK and the US. For the first time, drag was making an international impact – and it was drag kings leading the charge.

above left to right: Vesta Tilley, Annie Hindle, Florence Hines , Ella Shields

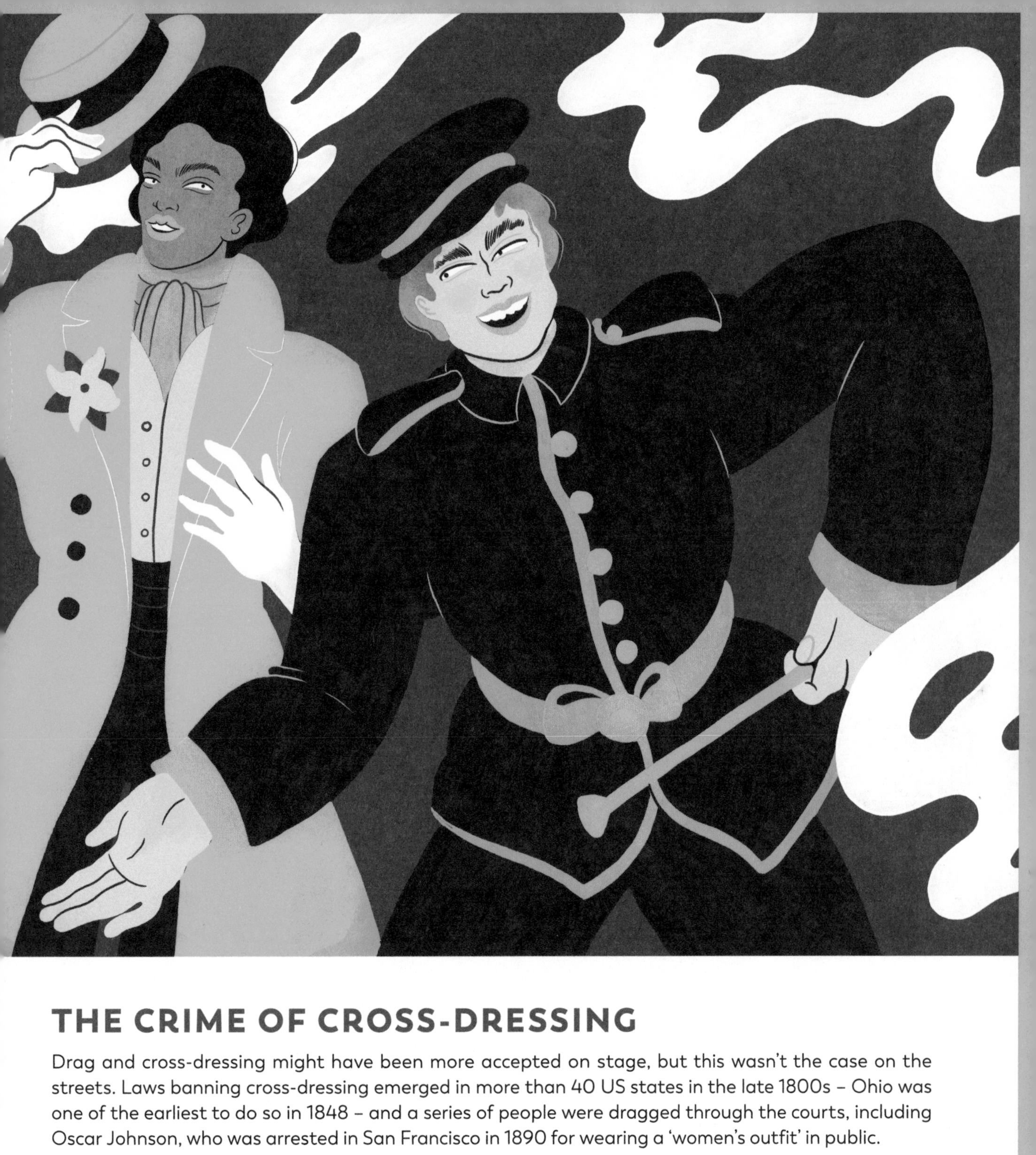

THE CRIME OF CROSS-DRESSING

Drag and cross-dressing might have been more accepted on stage, but this wasn't the case on the streets. Laws banning cross-dressing emerged in more than 40 US states in the late 1800s – Ohio was one of the earliest to do so in 1848 – and a series of people were dragged through the courts, including Oscar Johnson, who was arrested in San Francisco in 1890 for wearing a 'women's outfit' in public.

It may be that the laws were primarily passed to crack down on prostitution, as cross-dressing was seen by the law as overtly sexual. In the case of women dressing as men, the aim was to enforce an ideal femininity, resulting in butch women often being singled out. Anyone who might fit today's definition of transgender was persecuted by default and even sexually assaulted in some cases.

Early drag balls were called 'fag balls', a pointed insult, and queer people were punished for daring to step outside of society's idea of what a man or woman should be. Drag artists may have dominated the vaudeville and theatre worlds, but when cross-dressing became anything more than a stage performance, attitudes weren't so forgiving.

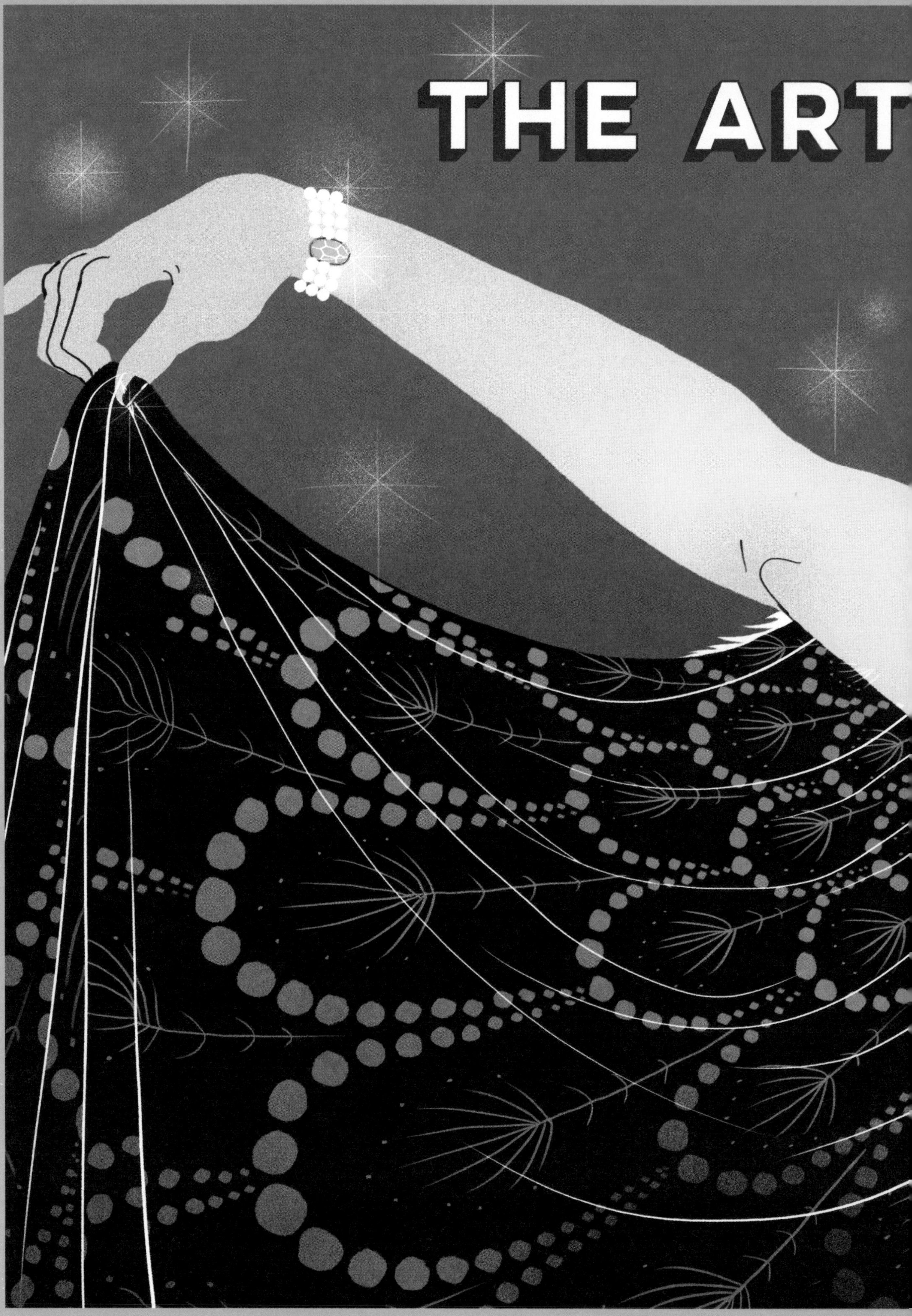
THE ART

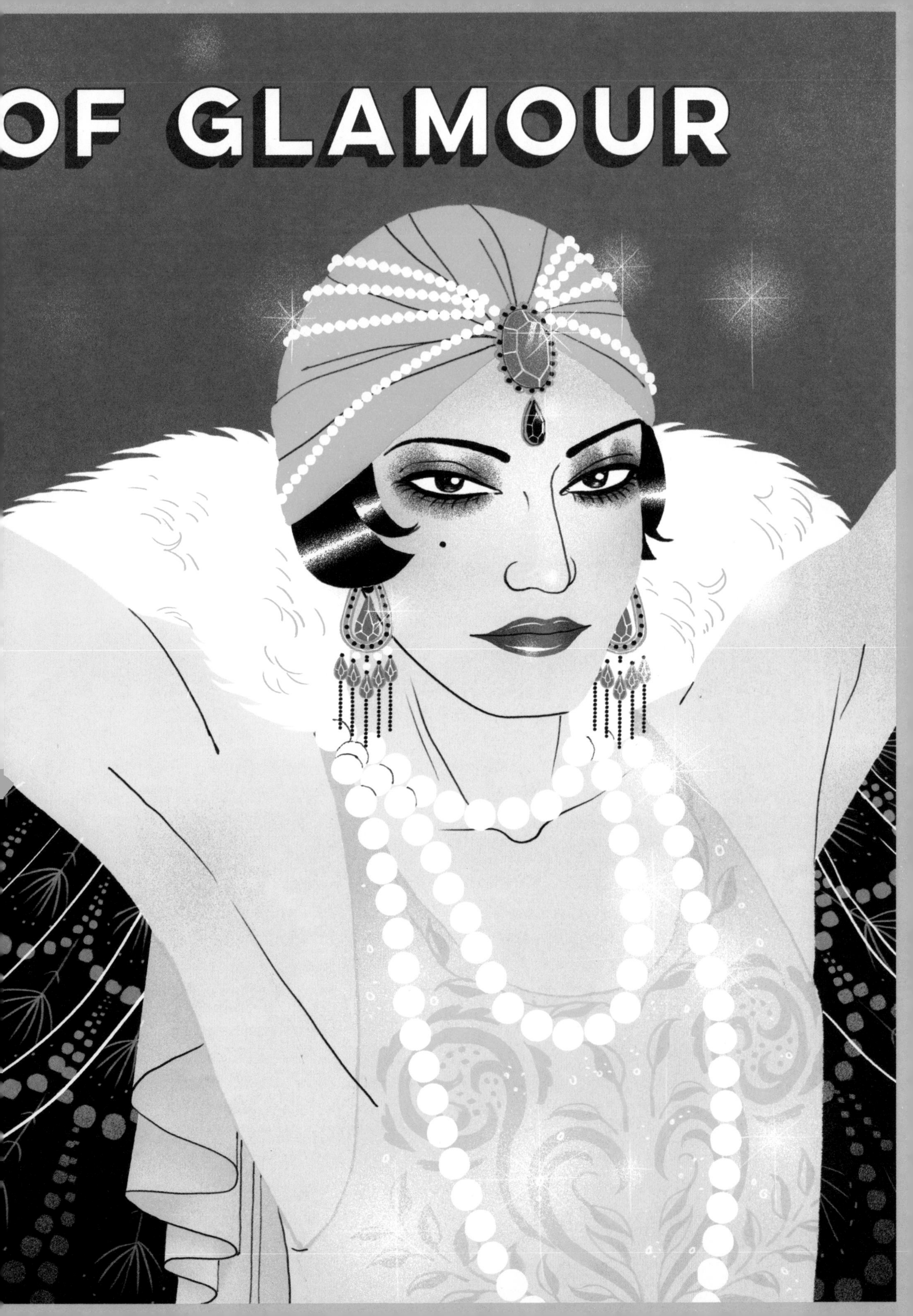
OF GLAMOUR

1900s-1950s

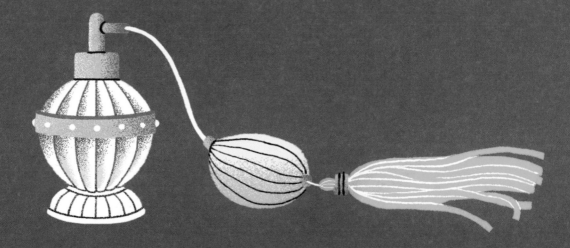

When US prohibition laws cracked down on liquor in the 1920s, criminal gangs set to work transforming underground clubs into hotbeds of hedonism and entertainment. The result was an infamous era known today as 'the Jazz Age' a period whose biggest stars were African-American jazz musicians, flapper girls and drag mavericks. For the first time, minorities were not only being accepted, they were being actively celebrated for their skills.

Drag during this period aimed to both shock and delight audiences. Vaudeville's popularity still lingered early in the 20th century but drag performers increasingly aimed for 'realness' rather than comedy in their acts. In other words, they wanted to mimic feminine and masculine beauty so flawlessly that nobody would be able to tell they were in drag. Gone were the days of campy pantomime, and in its place was an immersive fantasy.

Female impersonation began to make new fans, and the brief 'Pansy Craze' of the early 1930s saw 'femme' (feminine) drag performers more celebrated than ever. This spirit of celebration fizzled out when prohibition ended in 1933, as censorship and new laws came in to bar drag performers from screens and stages. But even during this drag drought, performers were keeping the glamour and hedonism of the Jazz Age alive. By the late 1950s, a shift towards a more progressive society seemed imminent.

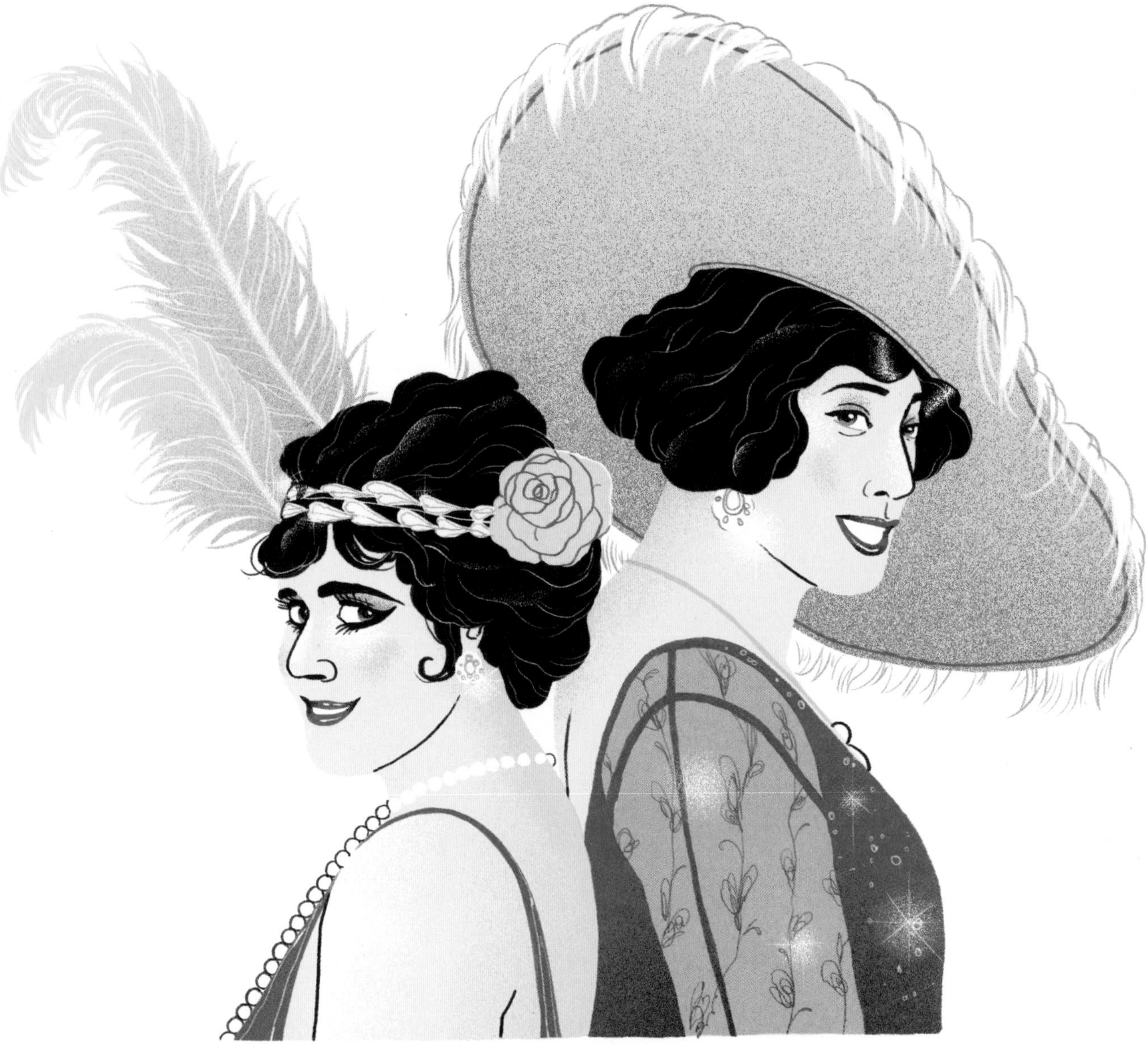

JULIAN ELTINGE & BERT SAVOY

Although the popularity of vaudeville started to wane during the 1920s and 30s, two captivating drag queens still found stardom: Julian Eltinge (above left) and Bert Savoy (above right). Both impressed audiences with a combination of comedy, music and costume, but the pair had extremely different approaches to drag. At one point, they were fierce rivals.

Eltinge's rise to fame was swift, taking him quickly from theatre stages to silent films. His drag revolved around a full feminine fantasy – teased wigs, glamorous gowns and immaculate make-up – which had audiences convinced that he was a woman. Eltinge took advantage of this false sense of security with a a dramatic wig reveal. His popularity was well-documented: not only was he one of the world's best-paid vaudeville performers, he even launched a make-up line and earned his own dedicated fan magazine.

Where Eltinge's glamour was subtle, Bert Savoy was more over-the-top, making a name for himself by coining still-used catchphrases like "You slay me!" and "You don't know the half of it!' Word has it that even Hollywood stars like Mae West were inspired by his drag mannerisms, cranking up their own campness in tribute to Savoy's charisma.

FEMME FANTASY

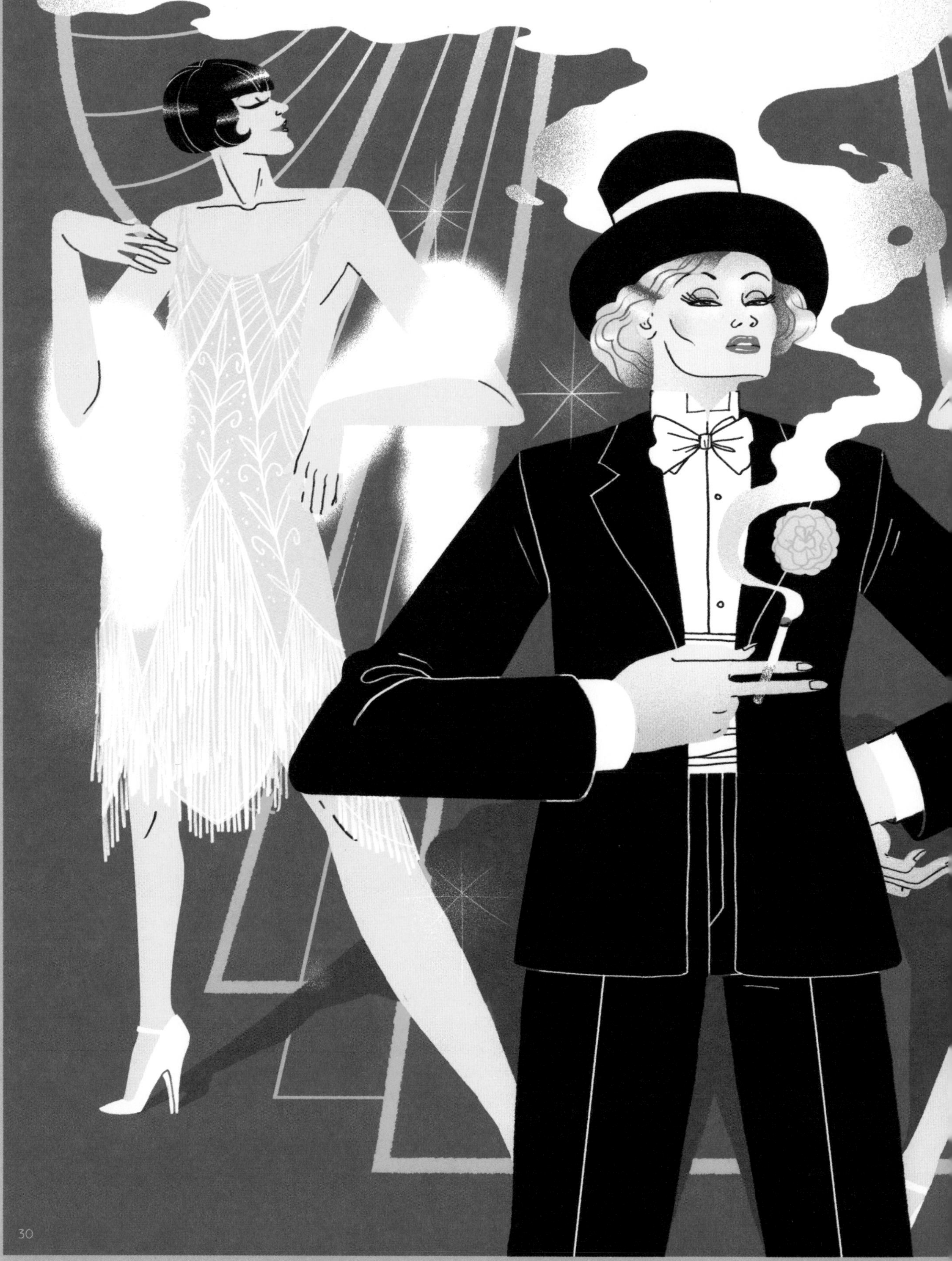

The Jazz Age saw stars fully embrace 'high-femme' aesthetics. After centuries of favouring extravagant costumes and make-up, drag performers instead dialled down their looks and began to mimic beauty trends of the time: pencil-thin brows, painted lips and smoky eyes. The aim was to create the same heightened, idealised 'femme fantasy' that Hollywood starlets were quickly mastering – but, of course, with a twist.

THE ROCKY TWINS

Norwegian brothers Leif and Paal Roschberg – better known as the Rocky Twins – mesmerised audiences first in Paris, and then worldwide, with their delicate facial features and flawless dance moves.

Glamour was their forte, and their looks were signature 1920s. As drag queens, they sported short wigs, kohl-rimmed eyes and bright lips, teamed with fringed flapper gowns and fur stoles, and then switched to sharp tuxedos, immaculately polished shoes and slicked hair, as men.

The act that found them prominence was a drag impersonation of the Dolly Sisters, vaudeville twins who had retired a few years before The Rocky Twins gained stardom. Fans marvelled at the Rockys' beauty, which was less artificial and exaggerated than other drag acts of the time, and their dazzling allure attracted lovers of all genders.

MARLENE DIETRICH

Berlin-born actress Marlene Dietrich spent her career toying with the idea of gender. She established a reputation as a chameleon, able to switch effortlessly between tuxedos and ballgowns.

When she played more masculine roles – most notably in *Morocco* (1930) – she committed fully to the part. Her attention to detail included advising costume designers to avoid using feminine fabrics like silk, which would ruin the illusion. In other films like *The Blue Angel* (1930) and *The Devil Is A Woman* (1935), she exaggerated her femininity with feathers, veils and an aura of seduction.

Whatever the part, Dietrich oozed charisma, taking on each new role as a way to break stereotypes of masculinity and femininity, making her one of the Jazz Age's most influential stars.

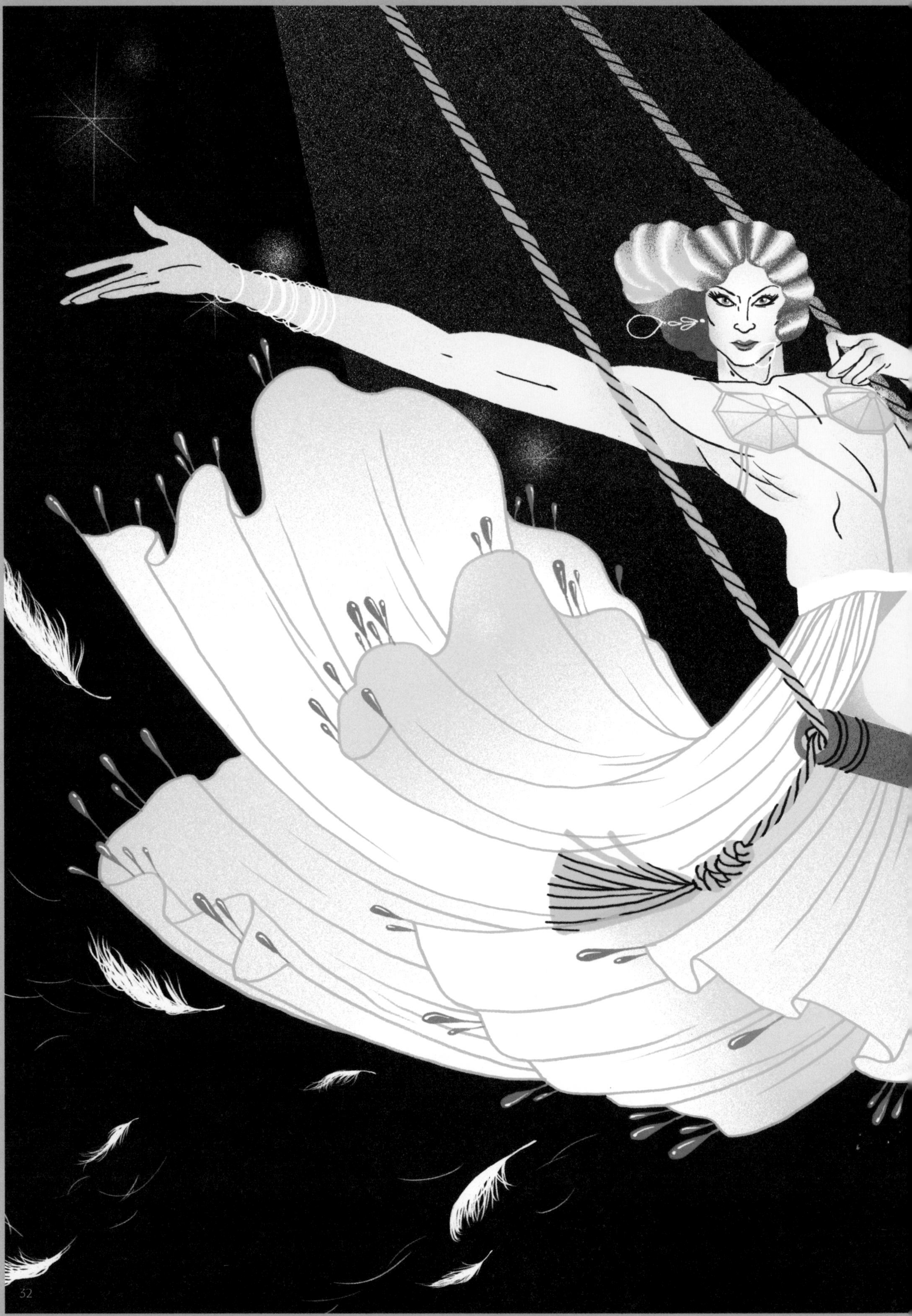

BARBETTE

When a fourteen-year-old Vander Clyde auditioned to be part of acrobatic duo The Alfaretta Sisters, the young Texan had no idea that he would be asked to drag up for the part. After a few short years of perfecting his act, he moved on to a solo career. In 1919, Barbette was born.

As his drag alter-ego, Clyde found fame as a drag circus performer, trapeze artist and high-wire act extraordinaire, travelling the world and building a celebrity fanbase in the process. As Clyde travelled, he began to notice that audiences couldn't tell he was a drag performer. His tightly curled wigs and sheer, embellished outfits were enough to convince crowds he was female. In response, he began ending his shows by striking masculine poses and ripping his wig off at the show's climax, a signature move always met with shrieks of shock and awe.

His growing popularity led to a tour in Paris, where he was praised alongside stars like Julian Eltinge and Josephine Baker. It was here that he won the acclaim of surrealist artists including Man Ray and Jean Cocteau – who was so impressed that he wrote an entire essay praising Barbette's ability to switch so effortlessly between male and female mannerisms. In Cocteau's eyes, Barbette was a genius.

Although his performance career was cut short towards the end of the 1930s by ill health, Vander Clyde continued to build a legacy as a film choreography consultant and an artistic director for numerous high-profile circuses. Rumour has it that he was even the inspiration for the 1933 film *Viktor und Viktoria* (see p.38), where the heroine rips off her wig at the end of each performance. Whether or not the film was a direct tribute, it shows that Barbette's influence was far-reaching.

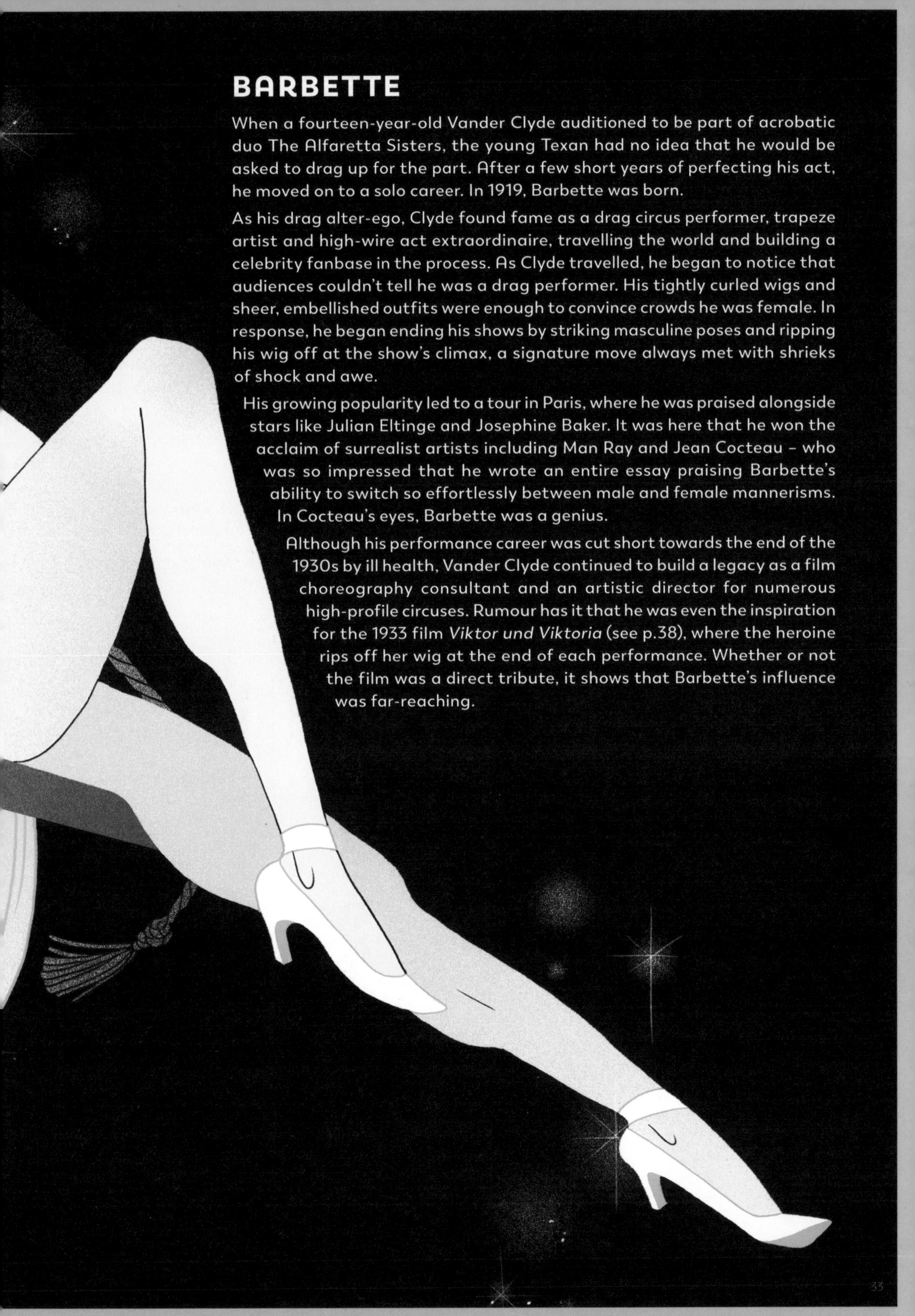

GLADYS ALBERTA BENTLEY

With her top hat, tuxedo and signature sexed-up growl, Gladys Alberta Bentley was amongst the most distinctive stars of the Harlem Renaissance. Her career began in the New York borough of Harlem when she responded to an ad for a male pianist. Bentley, who had cross-dressed in her brother's clothes as a child (and been frequently punished for doing so), dragged up and managed to land the job.

In the years that followed, Bentley became a renowned drag king and musician – and a lothario, as she famously flirted with women in the audience. Her confidence grew over time and she became even more dapper, wearing longer suit tails and larger top hats – each with a matching cane, naturally. She revelled in toying with gender, famously performing at the Lafayette Theatre alongside a troupe of six effeminate men, who referred to her as a 'gorgeous man'.

Bentley's charisma attracted other artists. Her distinctive musical performances earned her praise from writer Langston Hughes, while the novelist Carl Van Vechten wrote a character based on her in *Parties: Scenes from Contemporary New York Life*. As a Black, gender non-conforming lesbian trailblazer, she undeniably paved the way for a future cohort of drag kings to shine.

JOSEPHINE BAKER

Few performers are more synonymous with the Jazz Age than 'The Black Venus', Josephine Baker. Born in St. Louis, USA, she built a reputation as a vaudeville star in New York before moving to Paris in 1925, where she found fame as an erotic dancer, entertainer and actress. It was here that she learned to amplify and eroticise her femininity, performing it in a deliberately over-the-top way that put her on a par with the era's most forward-thinking drag queens.

Baker's sex appeal remains legendary, as does the rubber banana skirt she wore in one of her most provocative performances, *La Danse Sauvage*. Wearing little other than pearls and a bra, Baker writhed in front of the Parisian elite before crawling off the stage to enormous applause. Within months, she had earned herself a title: the Queen of Paris.

Baker performed her routines in ever more elaborate outfits, occasionally accompanied by her pet cheetah, Chiquita. She mastered the playful, camp sex appeal that cemented her status as a Jazz Age pioneer. While white reviewers expressed surprise that a young, queer Black woman could out-perform almost anyone in the city, Baker continued to shine, becoming an inspiration for other artists, in and out of drag.

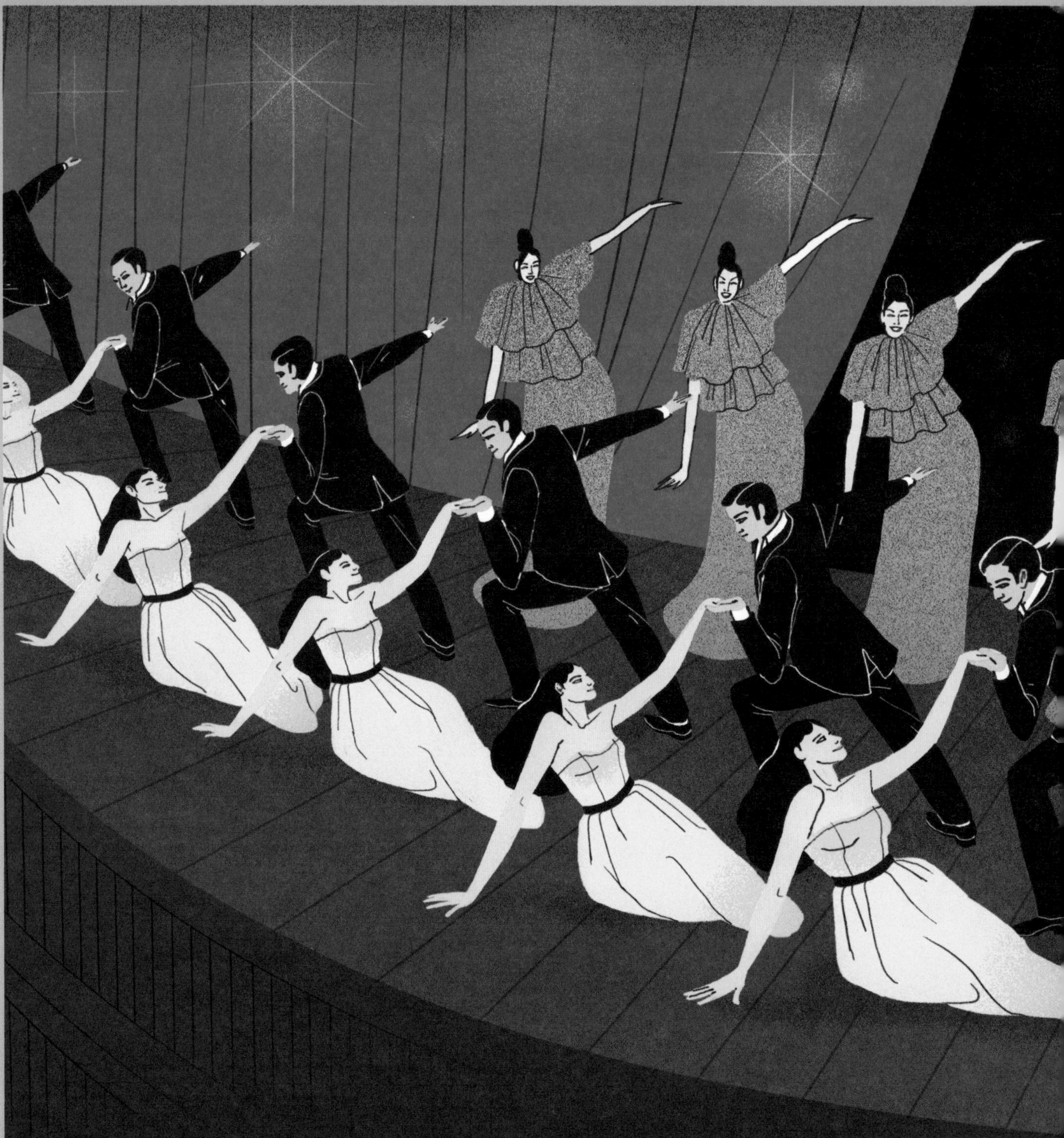

TAKARAZUKA TROUPE

When railway president Ichizo Kobayashi built a music school in 1913, his aim was simple: boost tourism and train ticket sales to the Japanese coastal resort of Takarazuka. The project would not only draw new crowds to his railway line but also tackle his long-held frustration at elitist theatre.

The president's golden idea was to train a troupe of girls and young women to perform lively, entertaining shows that had more in common with Western revues than with traditional Japanese theatre. Kobayashi wasted no time, and by 1914 he had hired and trained actors for their debut performance, *Donburako*, the story of a boy found bobbing along a stream inside of a peach. The production was successful – so successful that the troupe managed to keep performing through both World Wars.

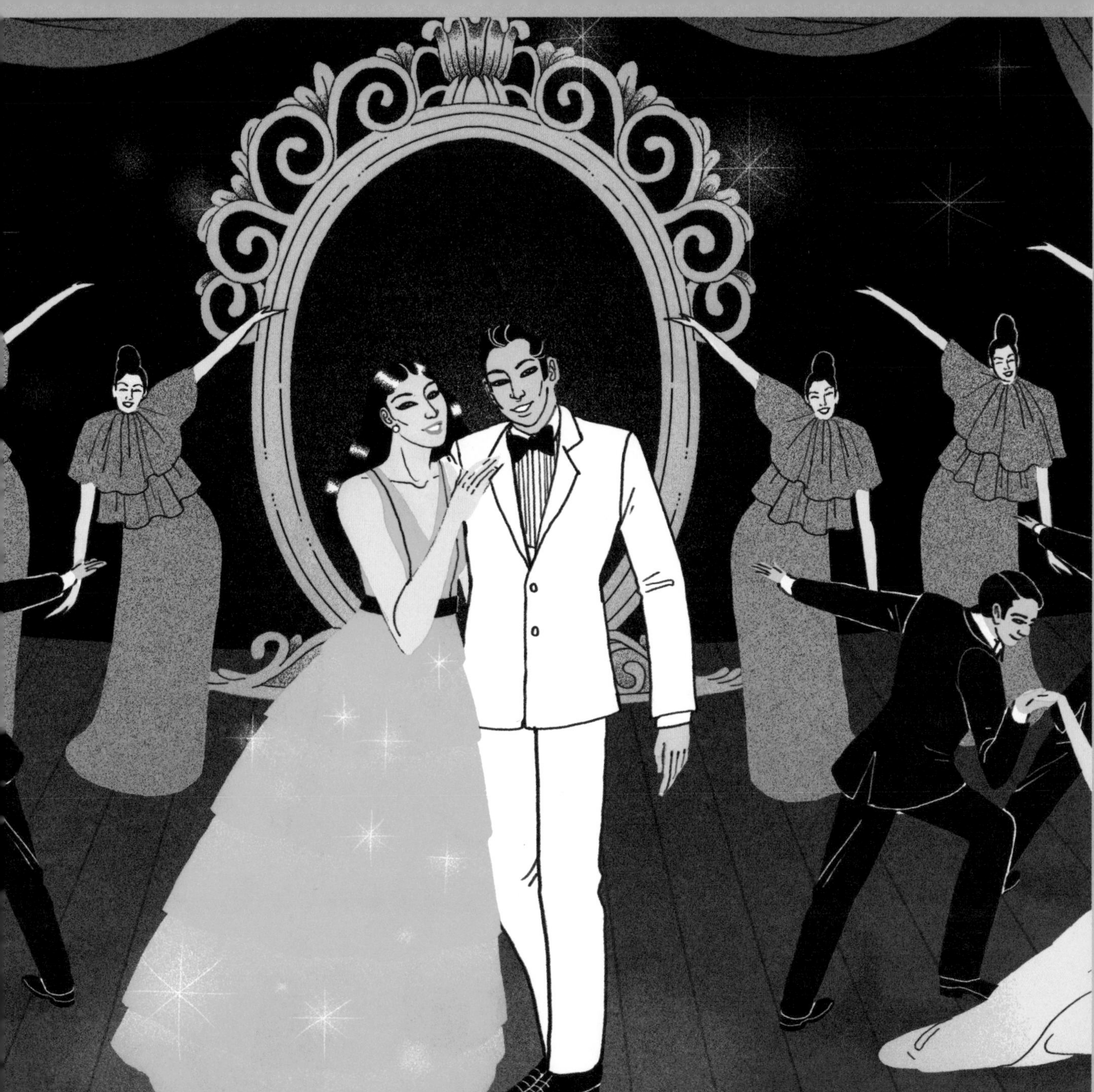

Productions became more flamboyant over time, incorporating everything from can-can dancing to burlesque. Costumes and make-up were typically extravagant and varied hugely depending on the production, but a key feature of the Takarazuka approach was that women played (and still play today) both male and female roles. In this sense it was influenced by early kabuki.

Despite this ethos, male leadership still dominated the troupe, female roles were often two-dimensional, and depictions of black characters were insensitive. Over time, more androgynous roles emerged and the troupe, which is still performing, has left behind its racist characterisations, allowing the troupe's true briliance to emerge.

DRAG ON THE SILVER SCREEN

By the early 20th century, silent film stars were starting to show drag on screen. These early depictions generally used drag as a punchline, relying on bad costumes and masculine mannerisms to tickle their audiences – an example is 'Sweedie', a gruff, Swedish maid played by Wallace Beery in around 30 short films. The Chaplin brothers, Charlie and Sydney, committed more wholly to a feminine illusion, dragging up in films like *The Masquerader* (1914) and *Charley's Aunt* (1925).

VIKTOR UND VIKTORIA

Arguably, the best-known snapshot of the Jazz Age drag scene came in the 1933 German-language release, *Viktor und Viktoria*. The film depicts the life of a struggling young actress, who follows a manager's advice to become a female impersonator. Entirely convincing, she becomes an overnight sensation, but this fame leads admirers to question her gender identity.

The drag itself is signature 1920s glamour but what truly set the film apart was its inadvertently radical stance on drag, which showed what audiences now know: women can be great drag queens, too. The film also brought the art form to a more mainstream audience (even more so when it was remade as *Victor/Victoria* in 1982, starring Julie Andrews) while immortalising the shimmer-heavy aesthetics of the Jazz Age.

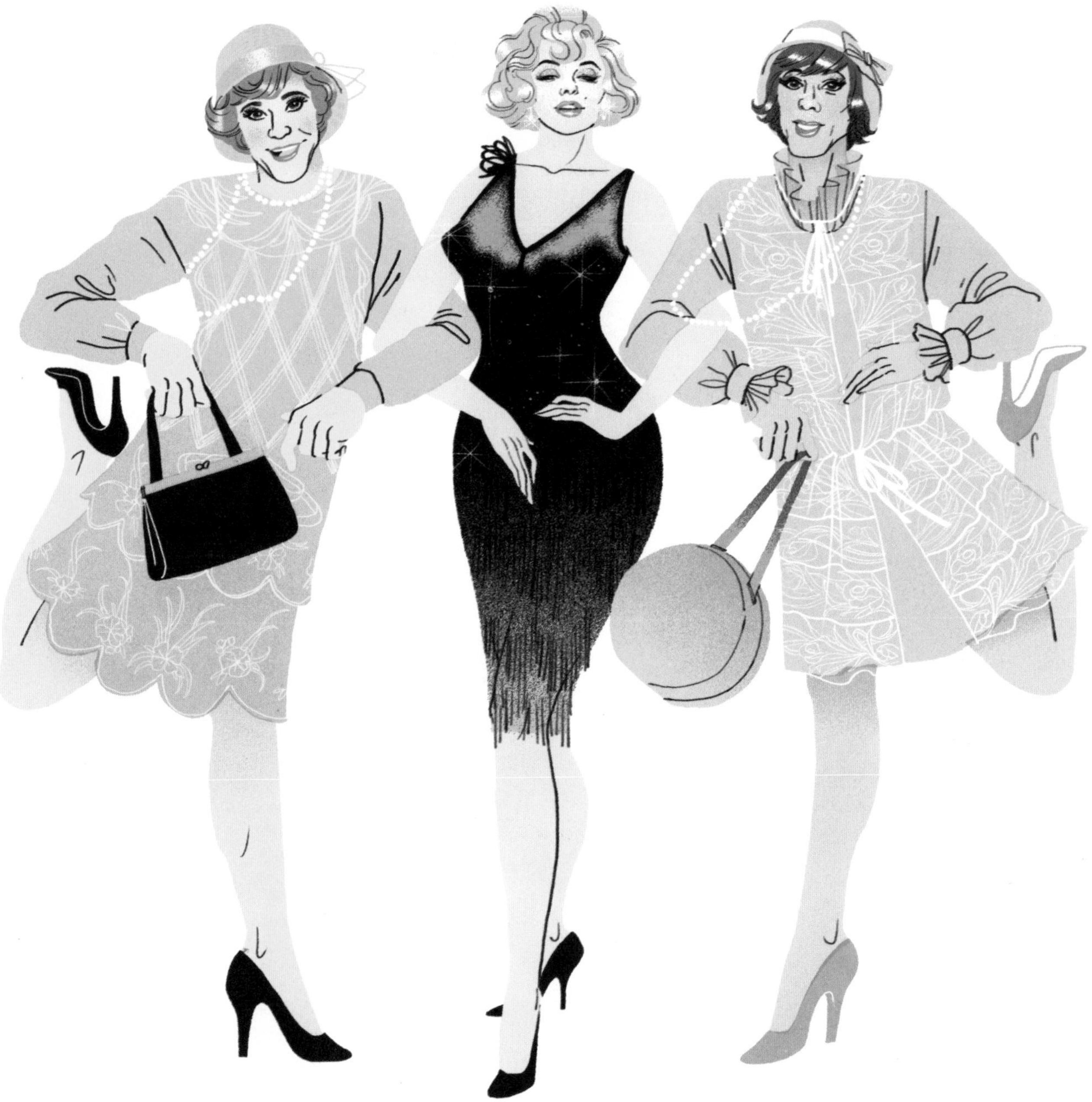

SOME LIKE IT HOT

Some Like It Hot (1959) was another film to blow things wide open. Still, the plot relies on cliché. Two men, played by Jack Lemmon and Tony Curtis, initially drag up to escape the mafia, and one soon falls in love with the impossibly glamorous Marilyn Monroe. But as the film progresses, they end up viewing drag as more than a mere goofy disguise.

Not only do the men sharpen their skills and learn to create alluring female illusions, they start to enjoy dressing up and even embrace it as an art form. Then there's Marilyn, who gives a masterclass in exaggerated femininity still mimicked by drag queens worldwide. She took the 'dumb blonde' archetype and crafted the kind of coy, playful femininity that does what drag does best: poke fun at gender. Perhaps more impressively, the film managed to slip through the net of the infamous Hays Code, introduced in 1930 to ban 'degrading content' – which often seemed synonymous with 'queer content'. *Some Like It Hot* was both a joyous celebration of, and a daring statement on, drag.

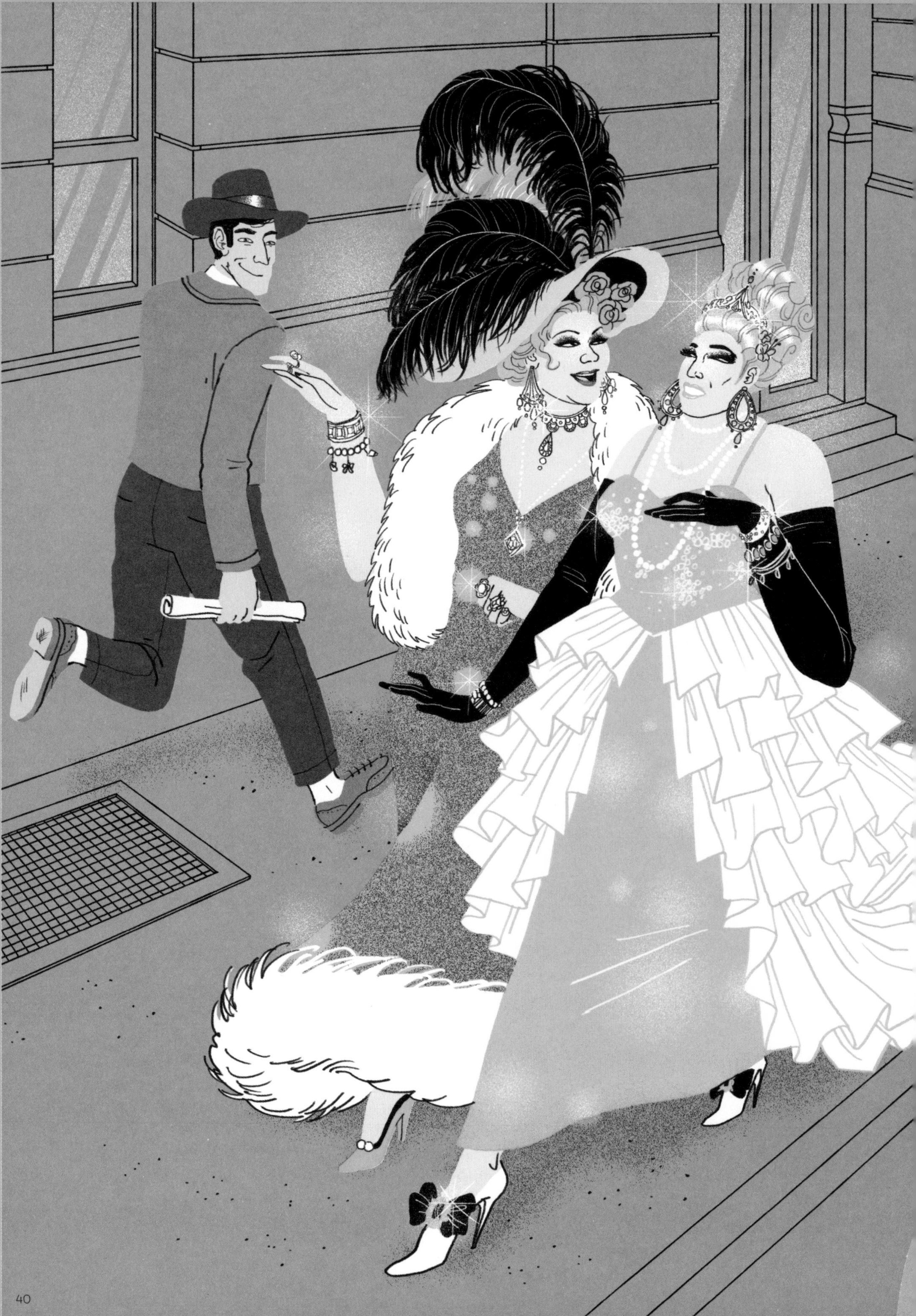

THE PANSY CRAZE

Throughout the late 19th and early 20th centuries, drag's popularity grew steadily through vaudeville, cabaret and the extravagant queer ball culture spreading throughout New York City. This fascination accelerated sharply around 1930, sparking a period known as 'The Pansy Craze' – a few short years when gay clubs and performers experienced a surge in popularity before the repeal of prohibition laws in 1933.

Pansies weren't always gay, nor were they always drag acts: generally speaking, they were men who performed femininity to the delight of an audience. But the craze did coincide with a rise in the number of queer artists in New York, drawn in by the promise of cheap rents and a few openly gay-friendly bars. Barely into the 1930s, prestigious magazines like *Variety* were praising the pansies not just in the Big Apple, but in Paris and Berlin, too.

LIVE IN NEW YORK

Drag acts were the most popular at the time. Famous 1930s and '40s drag artist Rae Bourbon (centre right) teamed female impersonation with filthy jokes, a combination that landed him a nationwide tour and even a stint modelling womenswear in a California department store. Gene Malin (centre left), a young drag queen known for his club performances, experienced similar success, but his big break came when he shed the drag for a flamboyant, risqué comedy routine, which he performed in a tuxedo. This new camp comedy didn't go down too well with some critics, but Malin was reportedly New York's highest-paid nightclub act at the time.

THE EUROPEAN SCENE

The success of performers including Barbette and Josephine Baker drew queer artists to Paris, where a lesbian salon scene was thriving. These exclusive gatherings gave influential queer women a space to meet one another and discuss culture, but far from being serious, rumours suggest salons were filled with laughter, theatrics and entertainment, as well as having guestlists stuffed with high-profile, creative power couples. Then there were Berlin's drag balls, which were slowly gaining a reputation in their own right. The Pansy Craze may have been short-lived, but the mainstream success it brought to queer and drag artists really did briefly change perceptions. For those few years, LGBTQ+ performers were rightfully seen as true bohemian artists, not deviants.

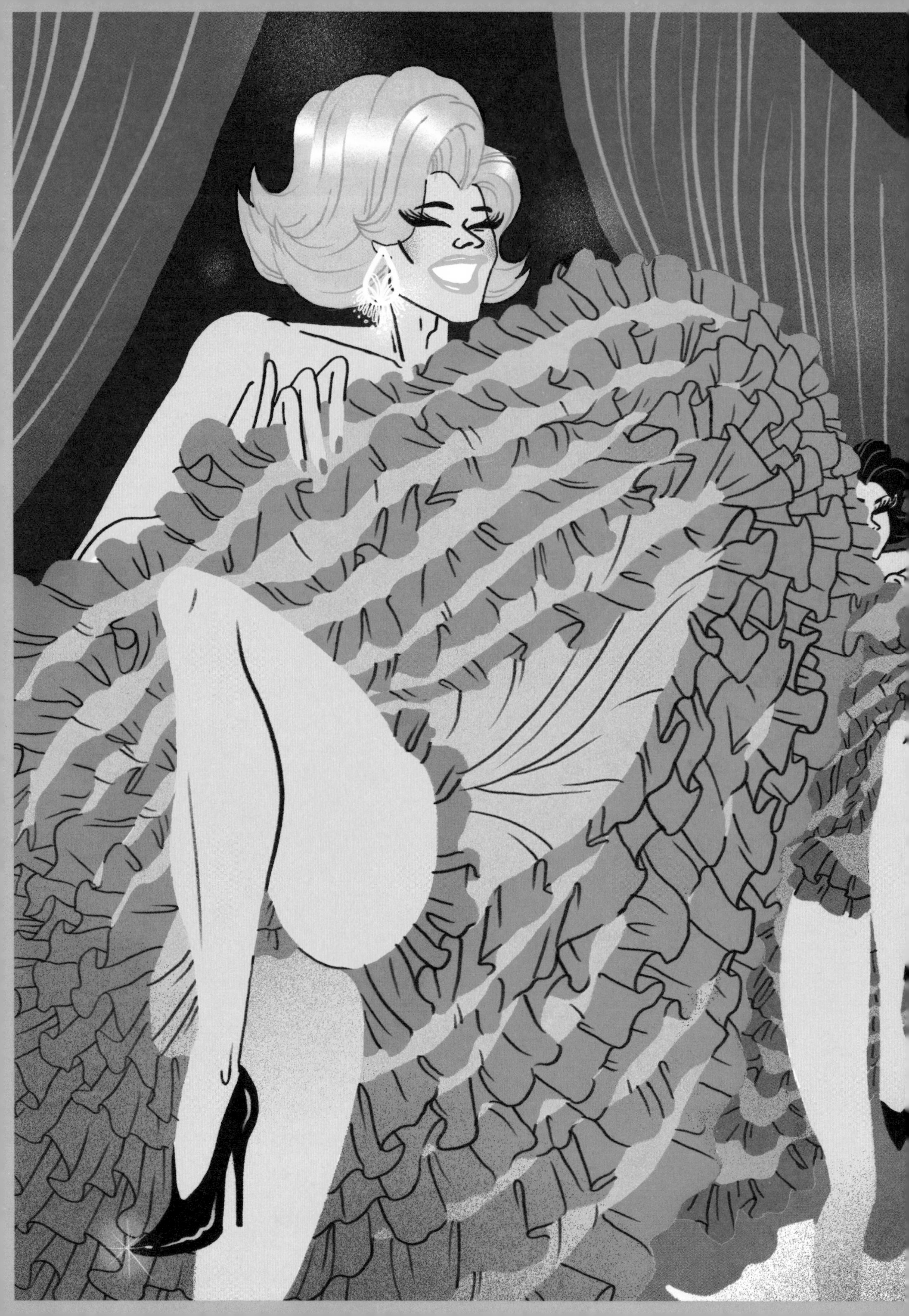

THE JEWEL BOX REVUE

The years following the Pansy Craze saw a strict crackdown on drag and queer communities in general, but there were a handful of success stories, including the Jewel Box Revue: an all-drag performance troupe founded in 1939 and the first of its kind.

Billed as an unorthodox variety show, the Revue became a nationwide success in the USA and racked up an impressive shelf life of more than two decades. Their most acclaimed performers became legendary. Before becoming a solo cabaret star in his own right, Lynne Carter was well-known for his accurate celebrity impersonations – in fact, his take on Josephine Baker impressed the real Baker so much that she sent him three taxis filled with Dior and Balenciaga gowns.

Then there was Lavern Cummings, known primarily for his ability to switch between extreme high and low notes at the drop of a hat – or in some cases, the removal of a wig. His drag was immaculate, with carefully teased blonde wigs, feather boas and figure-hugging ballgowns – and his charismatic personality later made him one of the most popular performers at Finocchio's, a San Francisco club known for its drag shows, spotlighting live vocalists as opposed to lip-sync artists.

The Revue also nurtured the talents of Stormé DeLarverie, an activist who later became one of the most important names in the international fight for gay rights. She joined the troupe in the mid-1950s, becoming the MC (master of ceremonies) for the Revue and the first ever drag king to tour with them. Various queens joined and left the troupe over the decades, but the focus always remained on the Revue's signature blend of elegance and witty entertainment.

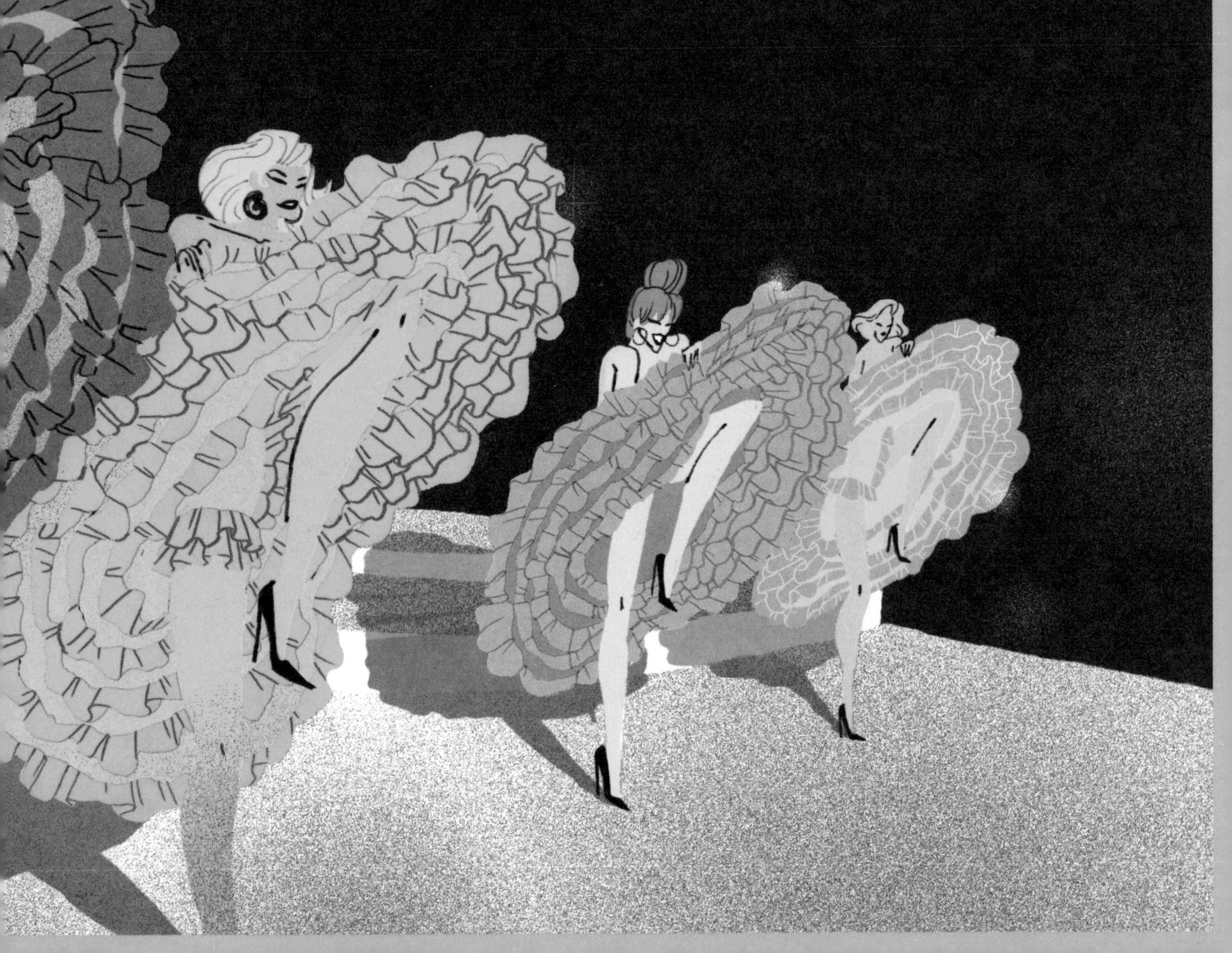

THE ART

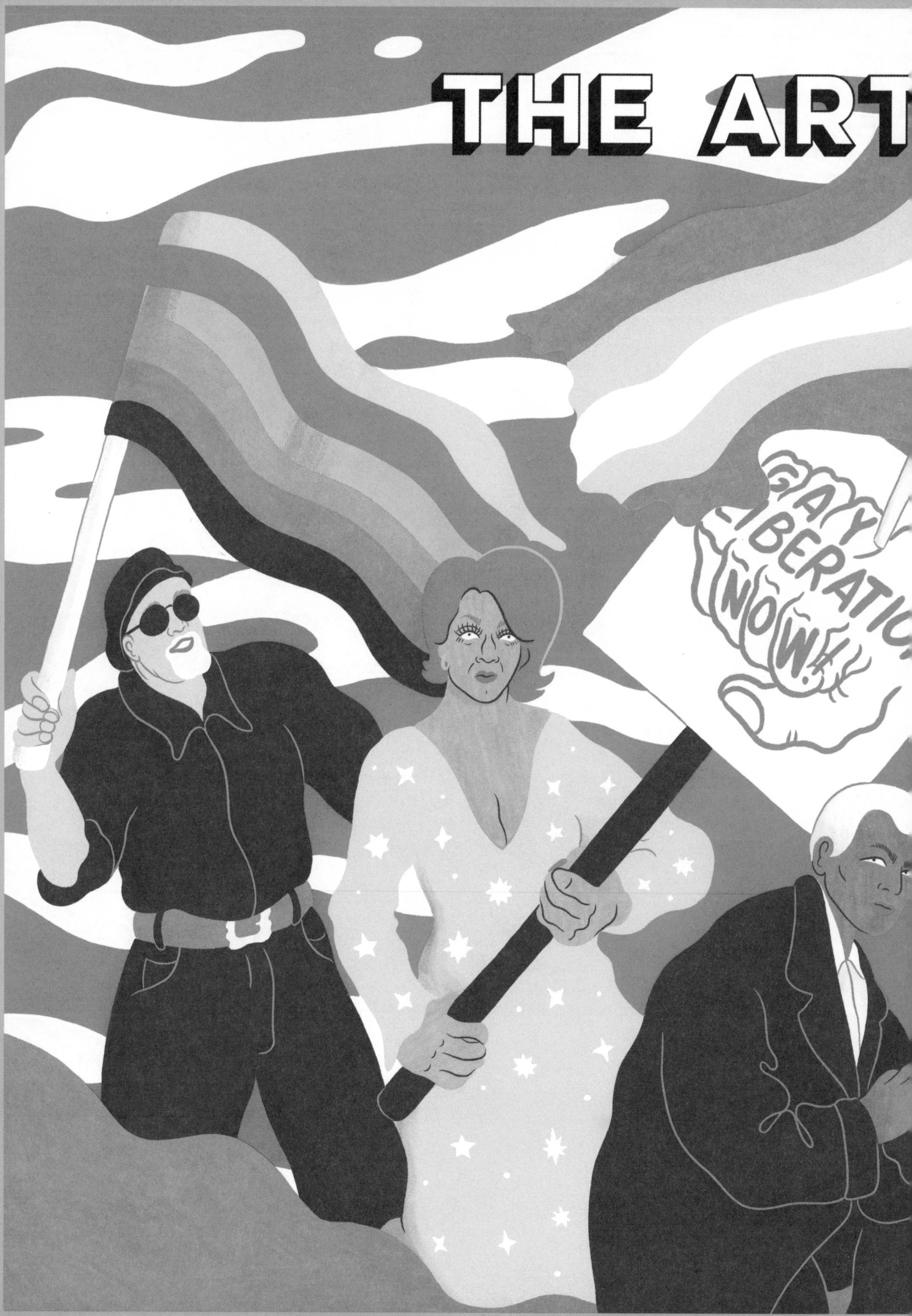
GAY
IBERATIO
NOW!!

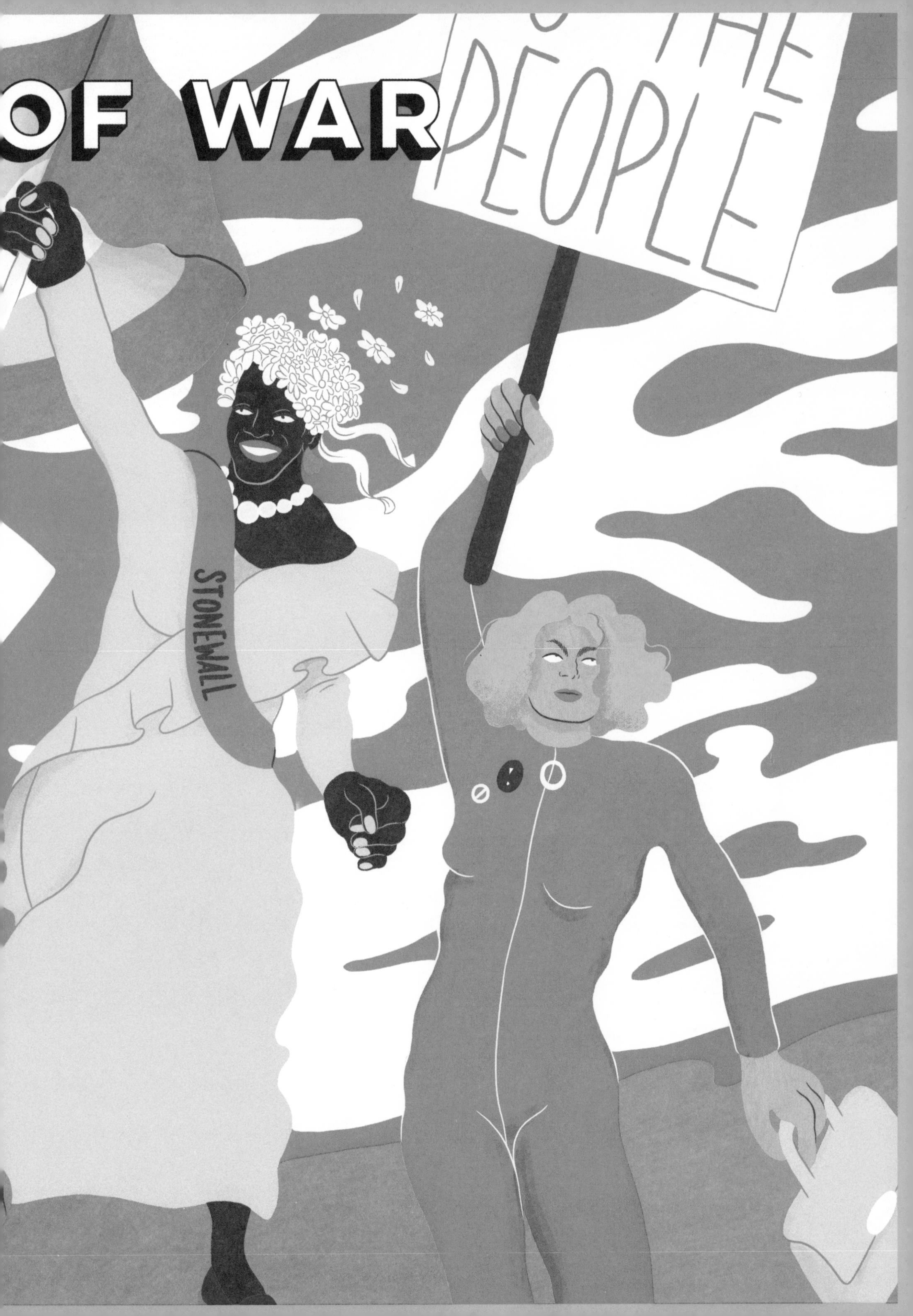

OF WAR
PEOPLE
STONEWALL

1950s-1970s

For centuries, queer people around the world have been subject to violence and ridicule, for simply daring to exist. While they've always fought back in a range of ways, it wasn't until the beginning of the 1960s, after a series of uprisings led by drag queens and the trans community, that wider society began to understand that queer people weren't just comedy entertainment, they were real people, who were tired of being mistreated.

Activist groups existed before the 1960s – the Mattachine Society and The Daughters of Bilitis were both founded in the 1950s – but it wasn't until the infamous Stonewall Riots that the campaign for mere tolerance turned to more radical tactics. This major turning point paved the way for the Gay Liberation Front, a political advocacy group responsible for a lot of the hard-won victories in the fight for queer liberation.

The spirit of defiance was upheld in the drag world, which remained unapologetic and proud. Drag artists like Marsha P. Johnson and Stormé DeLarverie led the charge at Stonewall, while iconic drag queen Crystal LaBeija rebelled against the white-dominated drag pageant scene.

A message was being sent loud and clear: *queers bash back.*

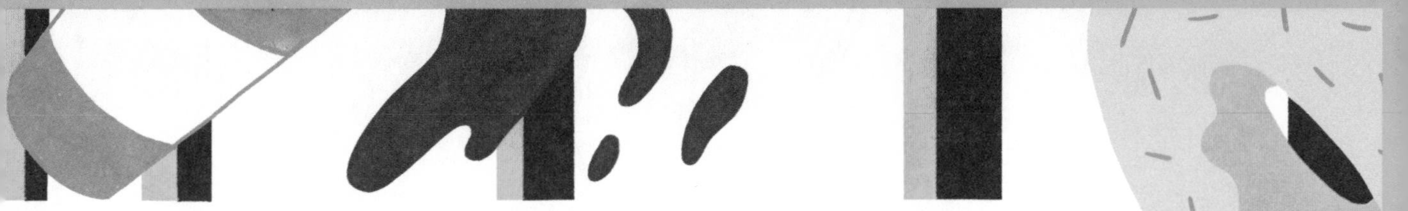

THE COOPER'S DO-NUTS RIOT

In 1963, novelist John Rechy published his semi-autobiographical debut *City of Night* about a gay sex worker living in Los Angeles. His charismatic cast of hustlers, trans folk and drag queens became famous, but one chapter in particular stood out: the story of the 1959 Cooper's Do-nuts Riot, thought to be America's first queer uprising.

The 24-hour donut shop was tucked away in the so-called "gay ghetto" of Los Angeles, where police officers routinely harassed patrons for congregating while cross-dressing. But on one fateful night in May 1959, they were met with violent resistance after trying to arrest five patrons. Soon the police were being pelted with coffee cups, litter and anything else that onlookers could get their hands on. Reinforcements soon arrived to blockade the entire street, but nevertheless, this small-scale riot set the tone for the next decade.

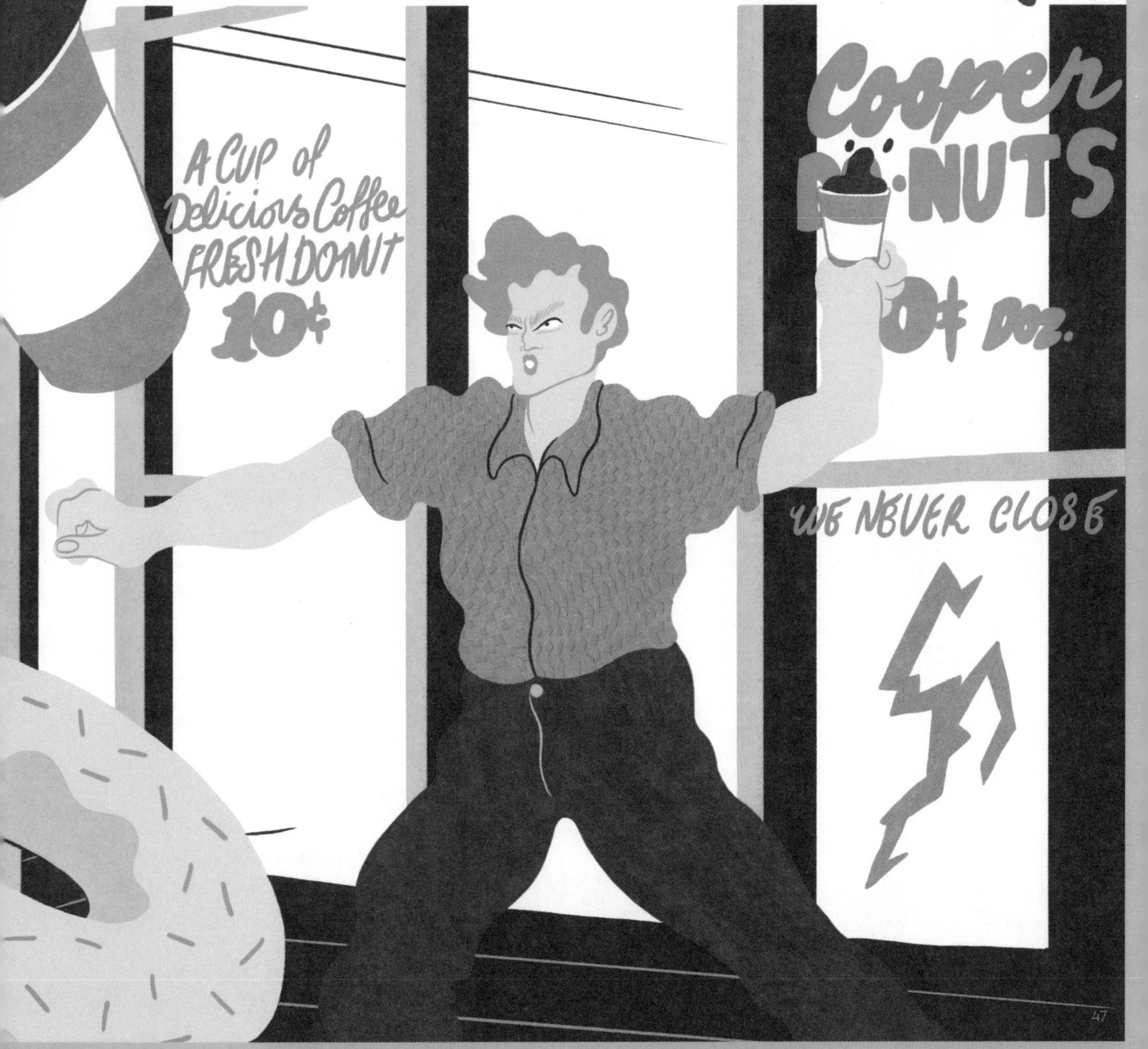
A CUP of
Delicious Coffee
FRESH DONUT
10¢
Cooper
DO-NUTS
0¢ Doz.
WE NEVER CLOSE

STONEWALL RIOTS

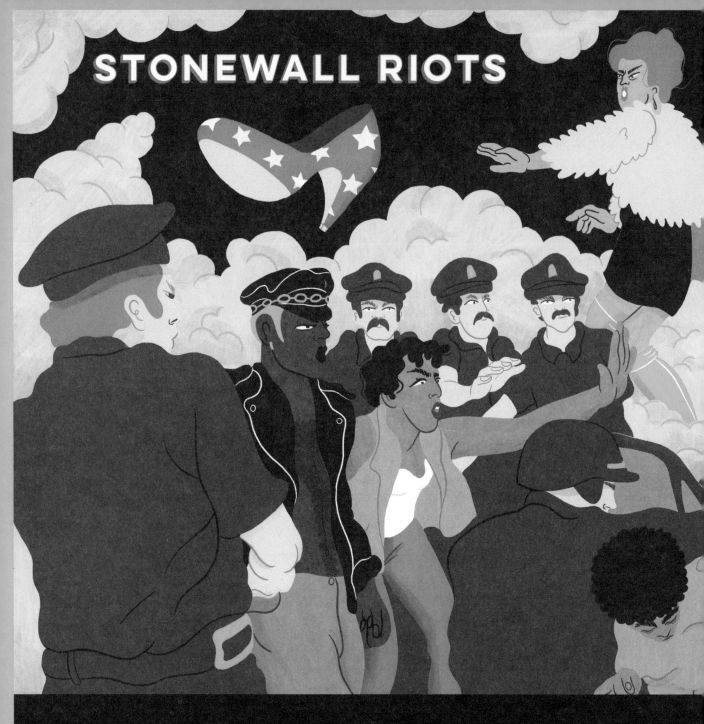

Police raids on queer hangouts in the USA continued throughout the 1960s, but communities were increasingly resisting persecution. In 1966, a crackdown on Compton's Cafeteria in San Francisco's Tenderloin District became a riot when a trans woman threw her coffee in a policeman's face. Her friends – also trans women – followed suit, beating officers with their bags and heels.

Three years later, a raid at New York's Stonewall Inn sparked almost a week of continuous riots and the first ever Pride parade. At the time, the venue was a run-down bar stocked with overpriced, watered-down drinks. New York City authorities were known to refuse liquor licenses to gay venues, so local mafioso Fat Tony stepped in to manage the venue and sidestep the license issue by claiming the bar was a 'bottle club' – a private venue where members could bring liquor, but only for themselves. Raids were commonplace, but usually resolved through tip-offs and bribes. On the night of June 28th, however, things were about to change.

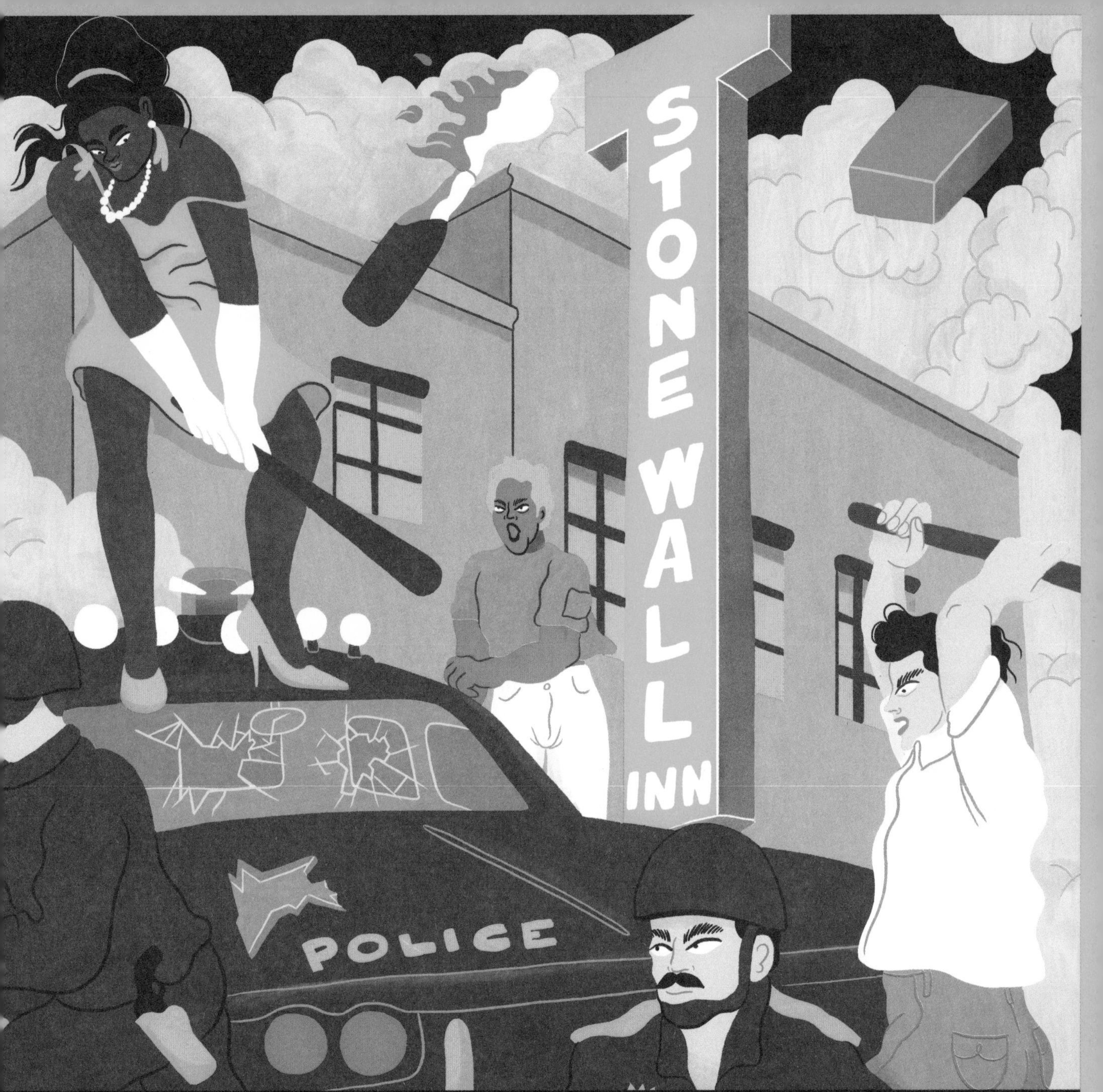
STONE WALL INN
POLICE

Plainclothes policemen stormed the venue and quickly lined up patrons, checking IDs and performing intrusive toilet checks to see if any cross-dressing laws had been broken. The raid quickly unravelled as patrons refused to cooperate with the violent police. Those kicked out of the venue taunted officers with camp salutes as the growing crowd outside applauded. As a patrol wagon arrived to pick up the arrested victims, tensions bubbled over and chaos ensued. The crowd began to throw whatever they could find and arrestees escaped.

Accounts vary from this point onwards. Police were pelted with a variety of makeshift missiles, reported to include bricks, heels and even Molotov cocktails. Some credit an unnamed drag queen with being the first to hit an officer (with her shoe); others say Stormé DeLarverie sparked the chaos by punching a cop and asking the crowd "why don't you guys do something?" Whoever the instigator was, the standoff's impact is legendary: it sparked demonstrations that lasted for six nights and kickstarted a global gay activist movement. Stonewall may not have been the *first* queer uprising, but it was the rallying cry heard across the world.

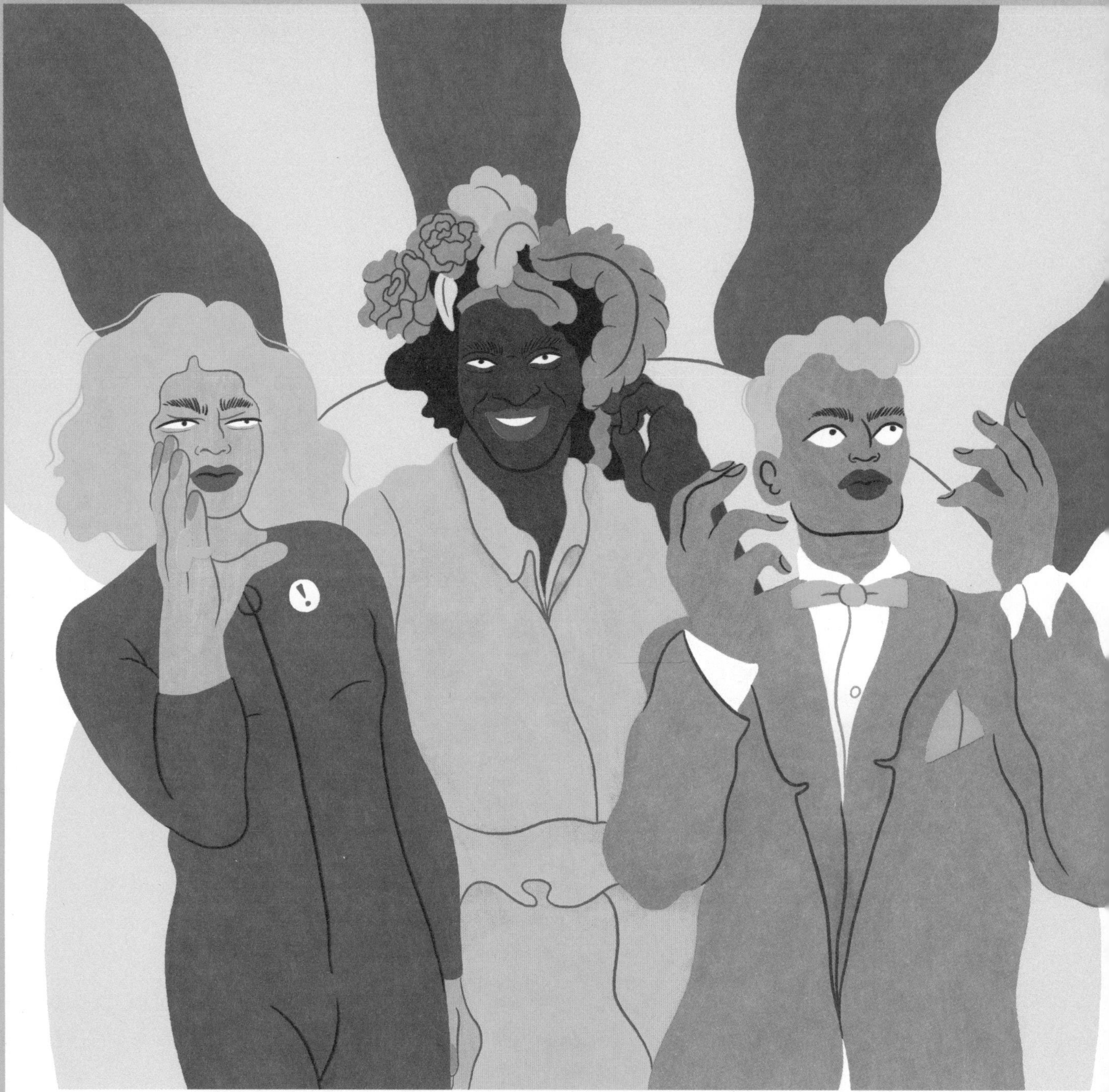

STONEWALL'S SHEROES

It's likely we'll never know *exactly* what happened during the first raid of Stonewall, but all stories tell of three daring sheroes (l-r): Sylvia Rivera (a trans woman), Marsha P. Johnson (often referred to as both a drag queen and a trans woman) and Stormé DeLarverie (a butch lesbian). All were gender non-conforming people of colour with histories of queer advocacy that continued long after the riots had died out.

Stormé was already well-known as the first drag king of the Jewel Box Revue, a charismatic performer who later used her talents to raise money for victims of abuse and domestic violence. As for Sylvia and Marsha, they co-founded the trans advocacy organisation STAR (Street Transvestite Action Revolutionaries) and led with passion, conviction and the same radical protest methods that would lead the Gay Liberation Front to make real political change. Without elders such as them in the queer community, such progress would have taken much longer to achieve.

THE MARVELOUS MOFFIES

The second half of the 20th century saw queer nightlife thrive outside of North America too. In Cape Town, South Africa, a 1959 photo-series of drag queens was published in *Drum* magazine, famed at the time for its reports on life under apartheid. Taken by Ian Berry at Madam Costello's Ball – a Cape Town drag ball akin to the ones pioneered in Harlem, New York – the arresting photos came with a headline: "*Oh, so this is what they call a Cape Moffie Drag*".

'Moffie' is an umbrella slang term: it describes a spectrum of men who don't fit society's idea of masculinity, ranging from effeminate gay men to out-and-proud drag queens. After the photos were published, their glossed lips, painted faces and beautiful ballgowns became a sensation, and similar parties soon cropped up in Johannesburg. Sadly, it didn't take long for raids on public and private queer spaces to increase in frequency. In 1967, the Immorality Act marked a fully-fledged crackdown on drag and same-sex relationships.

Despite the new legislation, moffie culture continued to thrive until the 1970s, when violence under apartheid displaced entire queer communities. Photographs of these vibrant scenes were largely lost or destroyed; a notable exception is the extensive archive of Kewpie, a gender-fluid hairdresser and queer nightlife regular. Publicly revived in a 2019 exhibition, the joyous images depict the glamour of the hidden ballroom scene, as well as the love and community spirit that bred so many years of resilience and resistance.

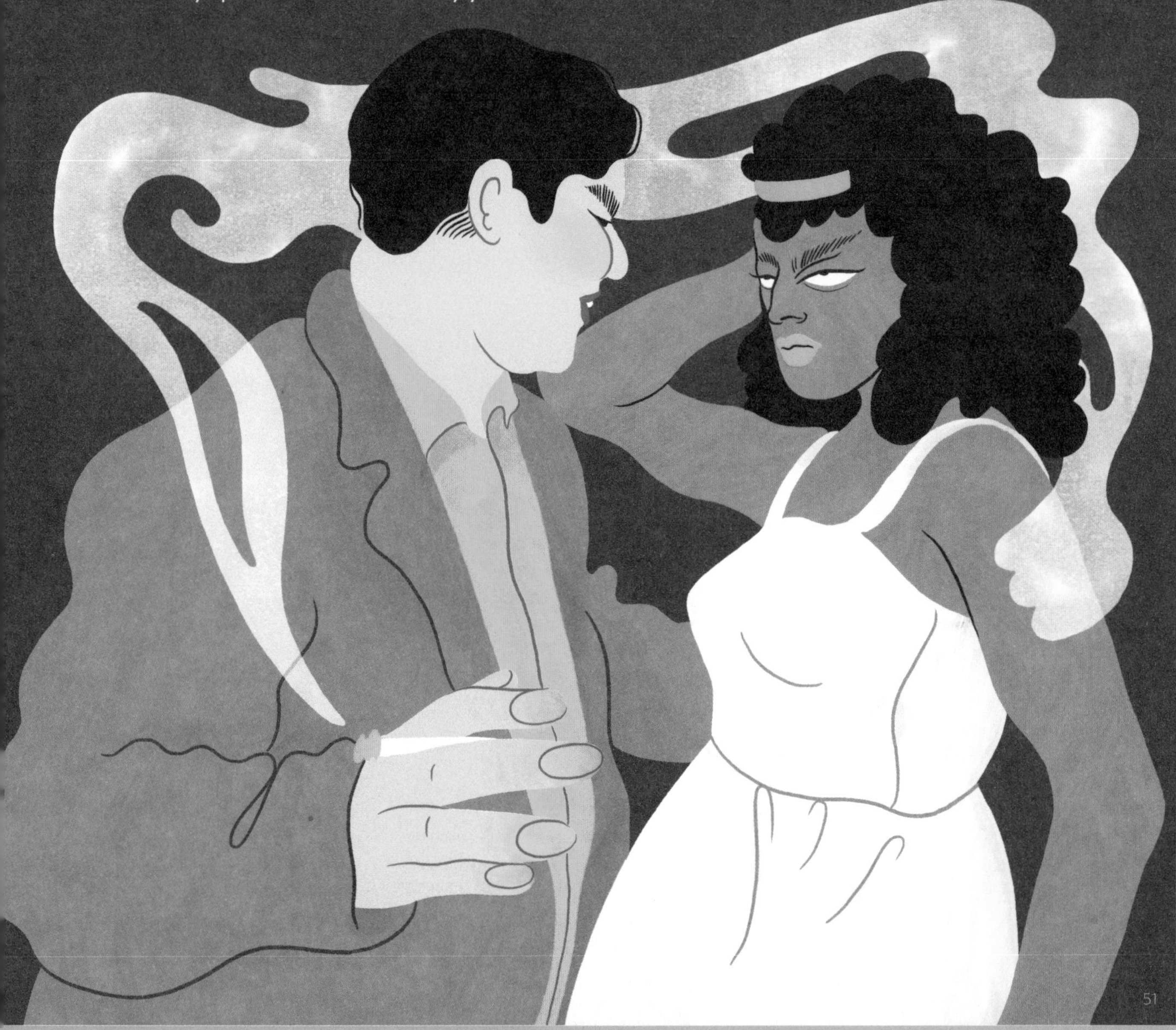

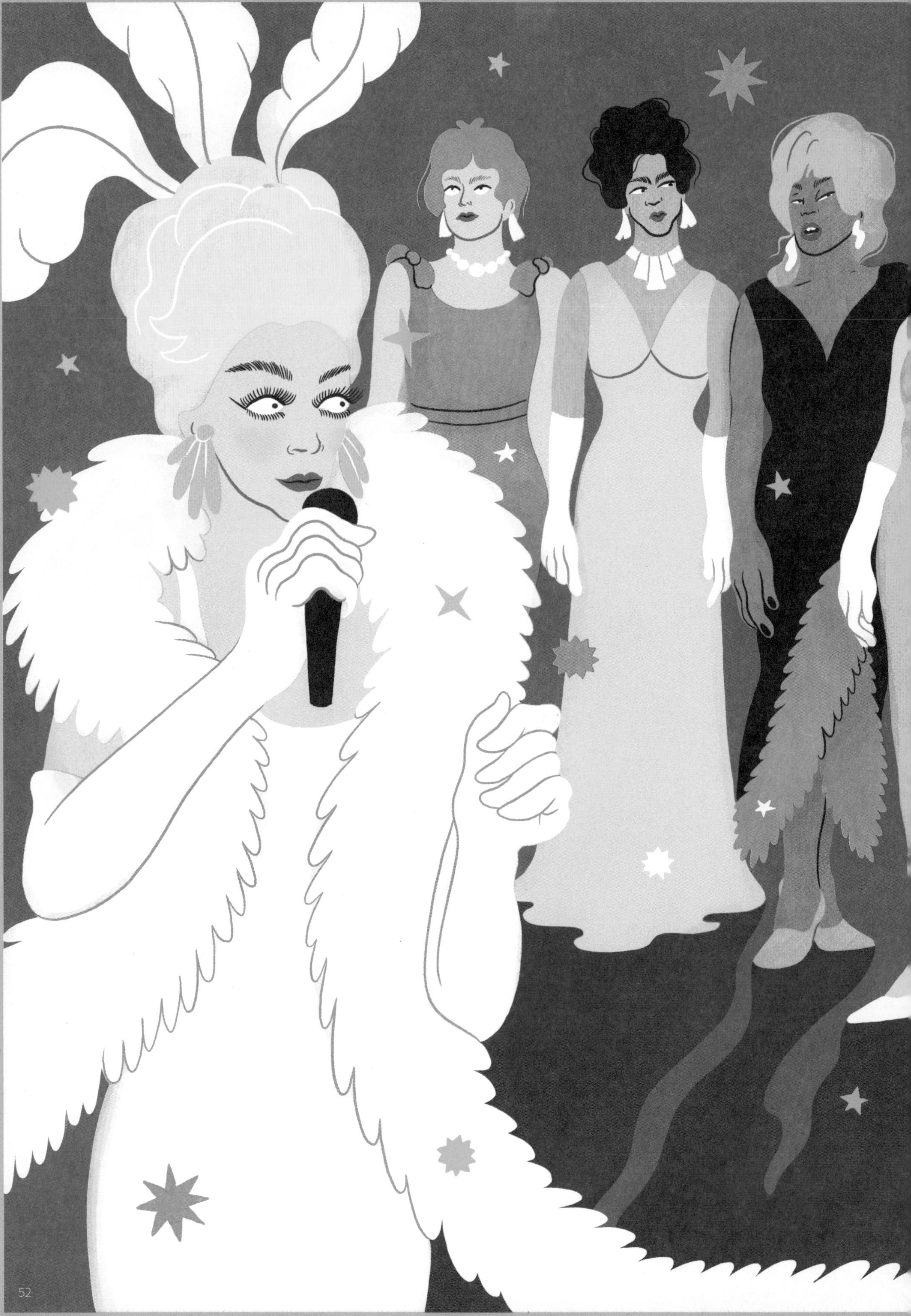

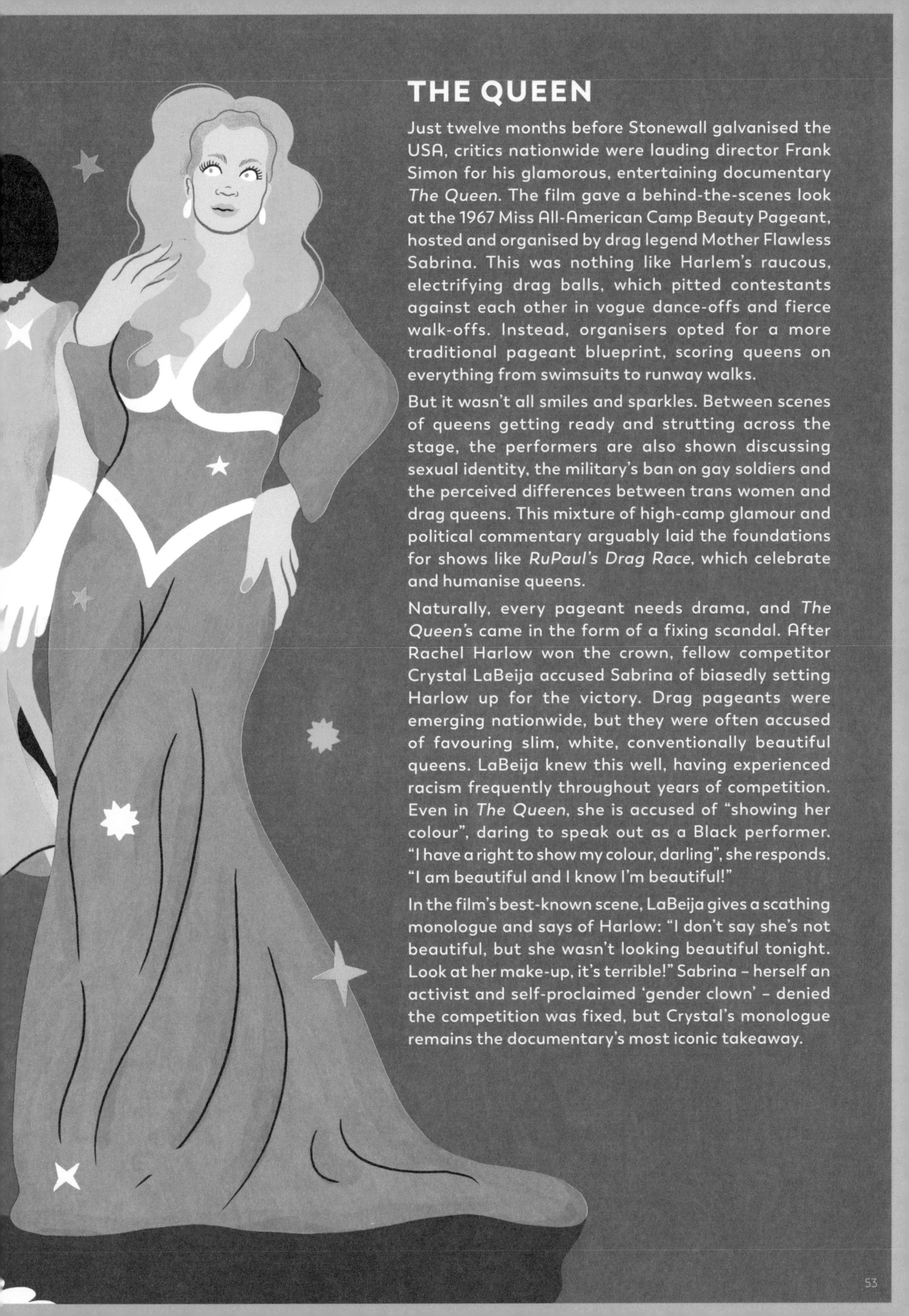

THE QUEEN

Just twelve months before Stonewall galvanised the USA, critics nationwide were lauding director Frank Simon for his glamorous, entertaining documentary *The Queen*. The film gave a behind-the-scenes look at the 1967 Miss All-American Camp Beauty Pageant, hosted and organised by drag legend Mother Flawless Sabrina. This was nothing like Harlem's raucous, electrifying drag balls, which pitted contestants against each other in vogue dance-offs and fierce walk-offs. Instead, organisers opted for a more traditional pageant blueprint, scoring queens on everything from swimsuits to runway walks.

But it wasn't all smiles and sparkles. Between scenes of queens getting ready and strutting across the stage, the performers are also shown discussing sexual identity, the military's ban on gay soldiers and the perceived differences between trans women and drag queens. This mixture of high-camp glamour and political commentary arguably laid the foundations for shows like *RuPaul's Drag Race*, which celebrate and humanise queens.

Naturally, every pageant needs drama, and *The Queen*'s came in the form of a fixing scandal. After Rachel Harlow won the crown, fellow competitor Crystal LaBeija accused Sabrina of biasedly setting Harlow up for the victory. Drag pageants were emerging nationwide, but they were often accused of favouring slim, white, conventionally beautiful queens. LaBeija knew this well, having experienced racism frequently throughout years of competition. Even in *The Queen*, she is accused of "showing her colour", daring to speak out as a Black performer. "I have a right to show my colour, darling", she responds. "I am beautiful and I know I'm beautiful!"

In the film's best-known scene, LaBeija gives a scathing monologue and says of Harlow: "I don't say she's not beautiful, but she wasn't looking beautiful tonight. Look at her make-up, it's terrible!" Sabrina – herself an activist and self-proclaimed 'gender clown' – denied the competition was fixed, but Crystal's monologue remains the documentary's most iconic takeaway.

HOUSE OF LABEIJA

The history of drag balls dates back to late 19th-century Harlem, but it wasn't until the 1970s that the first official 'house' was founded: the House of LaBeija. Crystal LaBeija pioneered the shift after her scene-stealing turn in *The Queen*, when a friend encouraged her to launch her own ball. LaBeija agreed, but on one condition: that she could be the star. With that, she declared herself House Mother and set about building an empire.

More houses emerged as a response to the disproportionately large LGBTQ+ youth homeless population. With a 'Mother' and 'Father' at the head of each house to mentor the children in the artistry of drag and provide financial and emotional support, houses became chosen families made up of queer outcasts.

Pioneered by Black and brown queer people like LaBeija, this new system gave the drag ball format a radical makeover. Before the 1970s, individuals competed; soon, entire families would compete for crowns, prizes and – most importantly – respect. It wasn't just your name on the line, it was your family's too. As it was built by artists of colour, ballroom suffered less with racism than the pageant scene. The outfits were still elaborate and extravagant, but the performances were oriented around voguing and points were awarded for oozing charisma. Inclusivity was the norm, and discrimination of any kind was met with zero tolerance.

The houses that emerged during the 70s and 80s have become legendary in drag culture: House of Xtravaganza, House of Ninja, House of St. Laurent, House of Corey, House of Dupree – to name only a few. And of course, there's the House of LaBeija. After Crystal's passing, the title of Mother was passed on to her protégé, Pepper LaBeija. Pepper remained the matriarch for more than three decades, competing in countless balls and winning more than 250 trophies. A new generation of talent has arrived to run the house: Kia LaBeija was 'Mother' from 2017–19, and Freddie LaBeija Powell serves as 'Father' as of 2020; they will likely pass on the torch again.

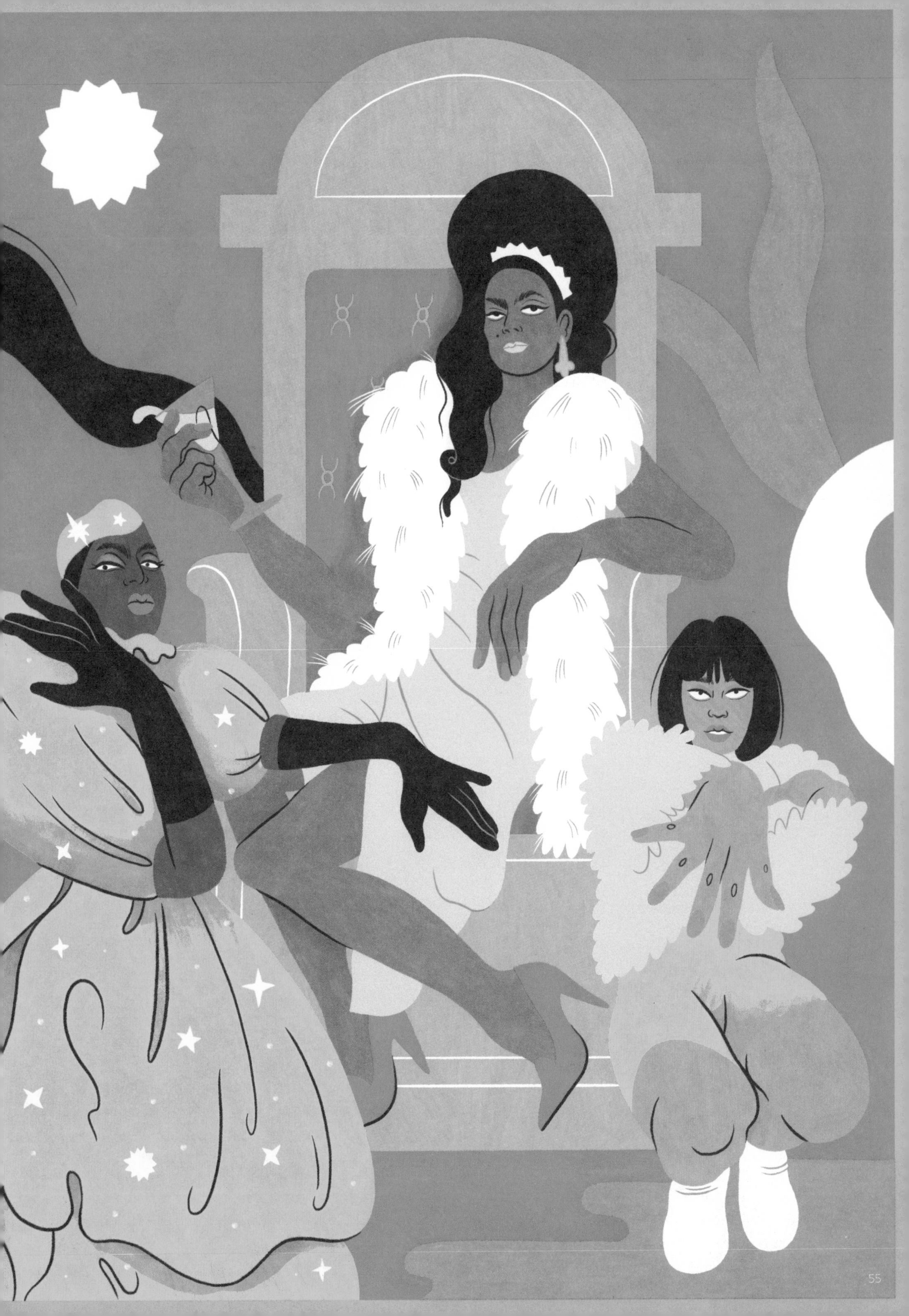

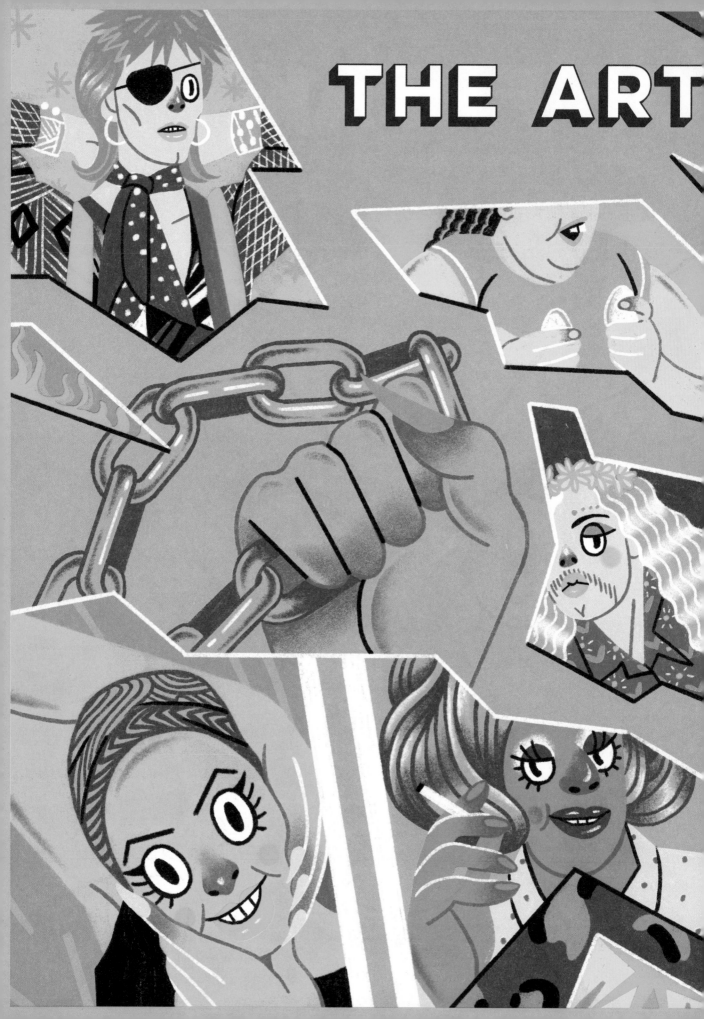

THE ART

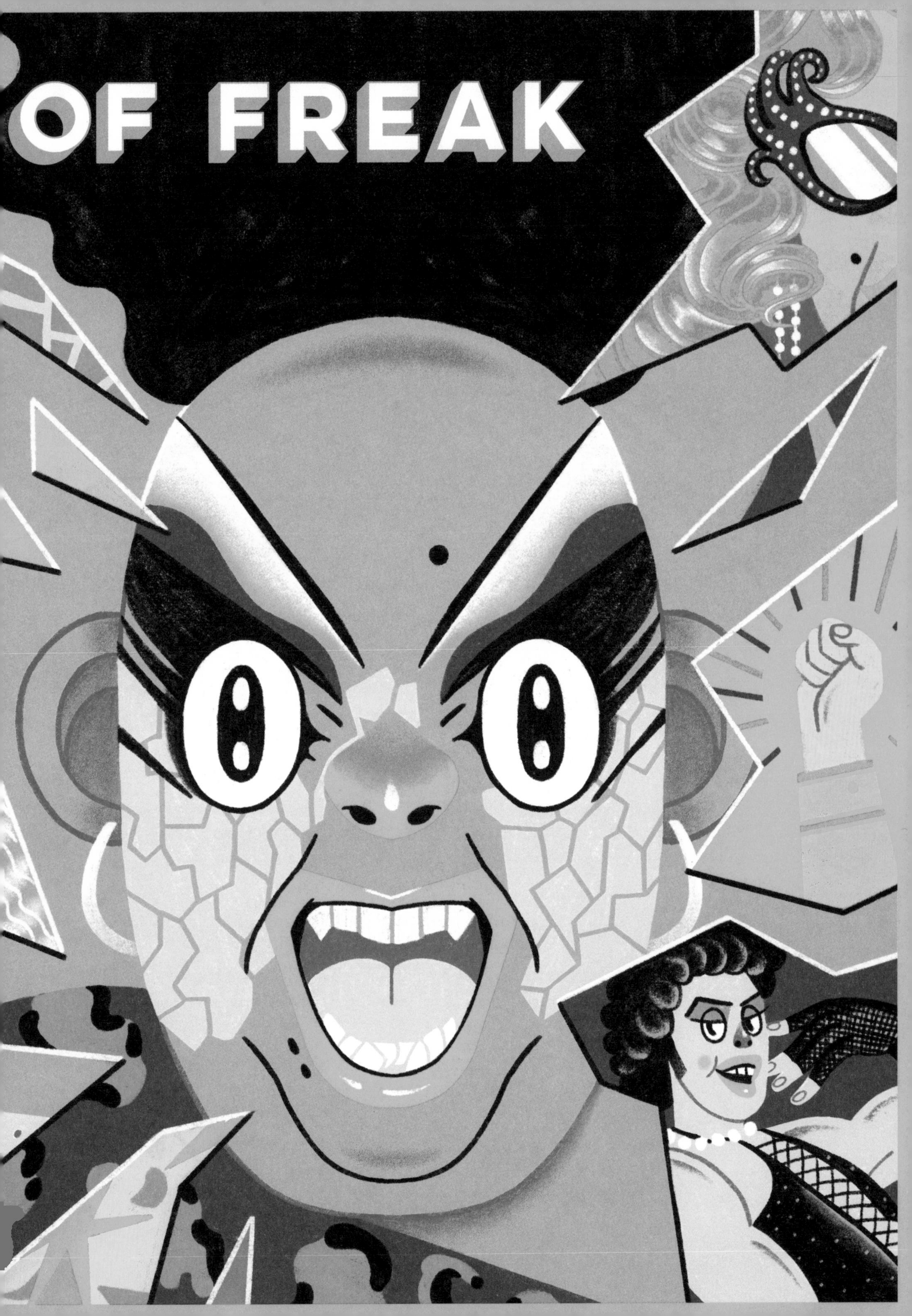
OF FREAK

1960s–1980s

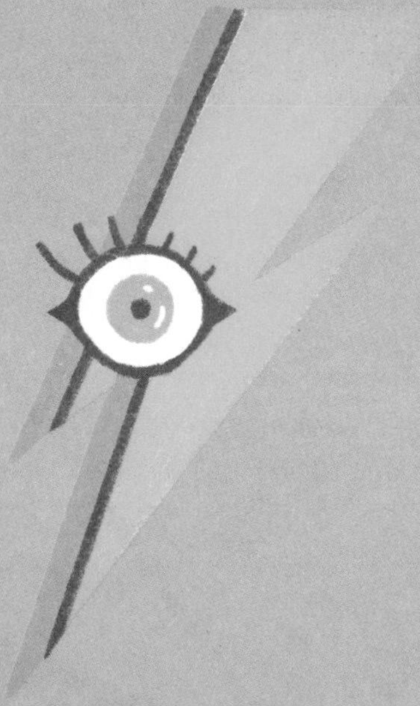

Freakiness has always played a part in drag, ever since the days of the 'half-man, half-woman' acts at the freakshow, which invited audiences to gape and marvel at the extraordinary. While the aftermath of the Stonewall Riots saw something of a drag drought in the 1970s, a wave of renewed energy was about to burst forth in the 1980s, this time with an even more intense desire to disrupt. This new era of drag leaned into filth, sex and scandal to rebel against the establishment.

Drag flooded onto screens, radios and theatre stages around the world. Andy Warhol's experimental shorts shocked the art world and ushered queer and trans superstars into the spotlight; elsewhere, drag queen Divine parlayed her cult following into a series of high-profile film roles, bringing her dirty, disruptive persona to even bigger screens.

The music industry was also embracing the rebellion. Airwaves were dominated by genres like glam rock and disco, which advocated for androgyny and made superstars of artists like Grace Jones, Prince and David Bowie. Audiences adored them and this acceptance of their non-conformity offered up hopes that weird wasn't just here to stay – it was the future.

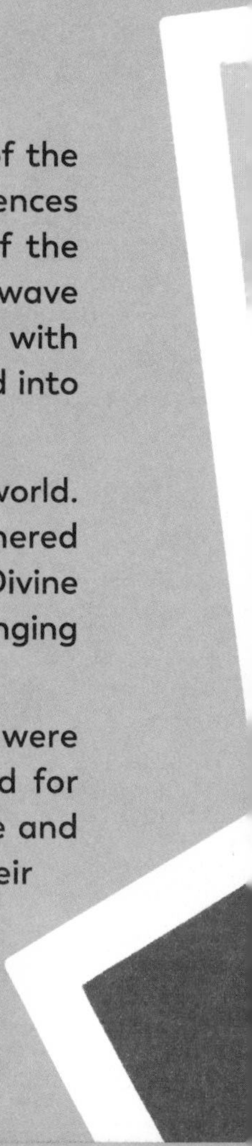

WARHOL AND THE QUEENS

Before Andy Warhol became a global icon, he was a commercial illustrator who hung out at New York nightclubs in pursuit of muses. As he developed into an experimental filmmaker, Warhol courted drag queen Mario Montez for thirteen shorts between 1964 and 1966. The films were usually simple in content – for example, *Mario Banana* features Mario, with scarlet lips and a '40s-style fur and crystal headpiece, seductively eating... a banana.

As Warhol's career grew, he remained fascinated by drag artists and gender non-conformists. He created a trio of 'superstars': Holly Woodlawn, Candy Darling and Jackie Curtis. Jackie in particular was a gender shape-shifter, known for wearing a dress and lipstick one day, jeans and stubble the next. Candy, later known as Candy Warhol, had a quick wit and glamour that left the art world in a daze, while Holly brought an unfiltered yet charming sensibility to the group.

After films like *Flesh* (1968) and *Trash* (1970), the trio of superstars finally appeared together in *Women in Revolt* (1971). Their star power was soon to be immortalised by Lou Reed in his 1972 song 'Walk on the Wild Side'.

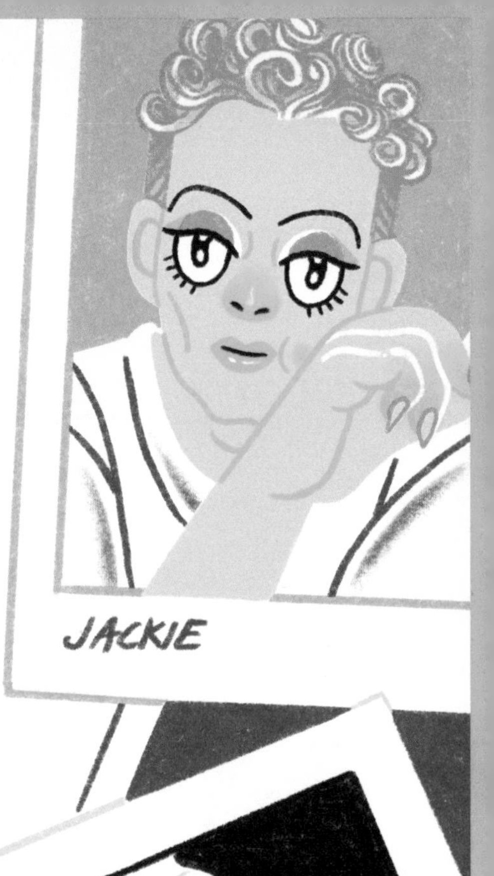
JACKIE

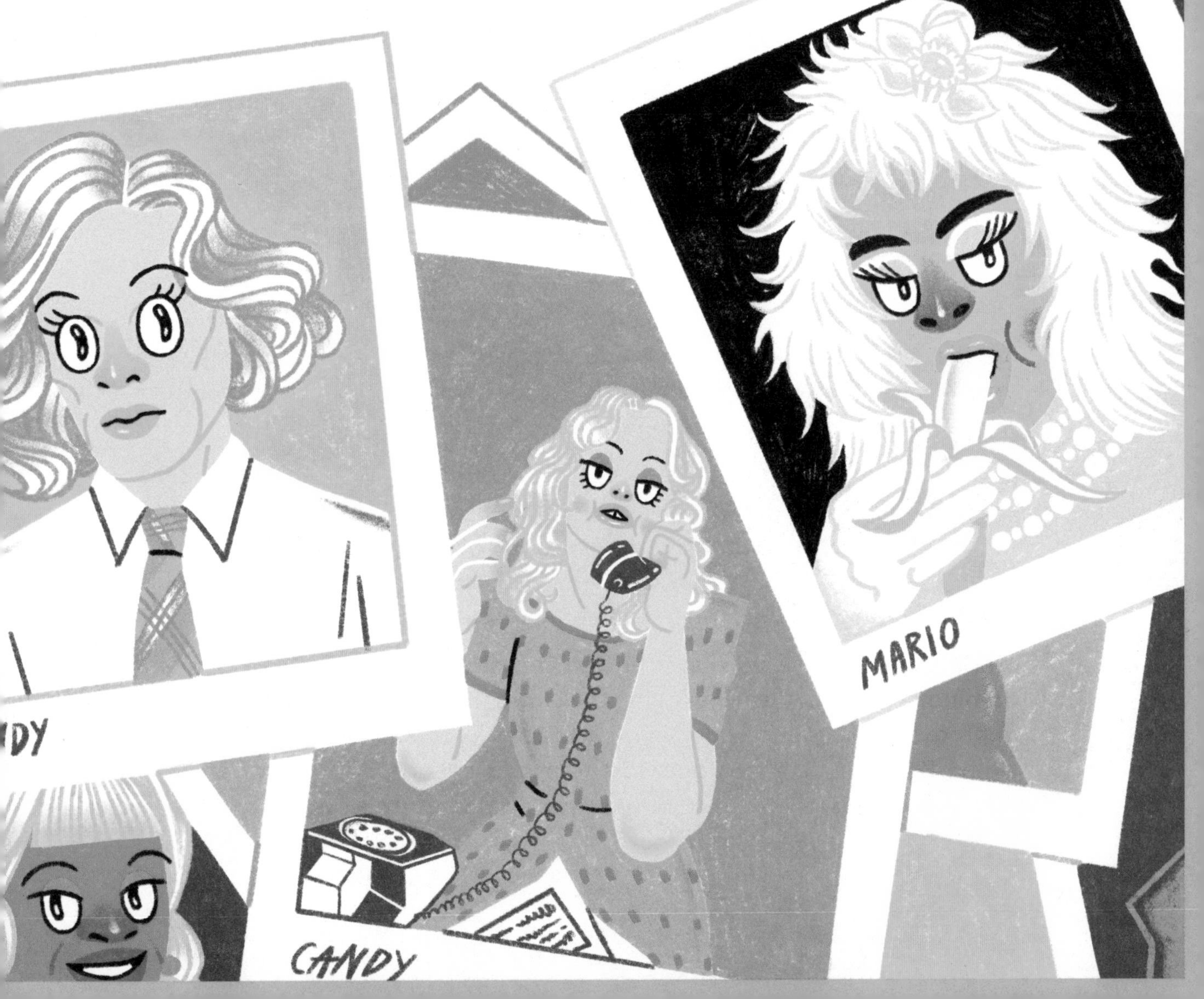
MARIO
CANDY

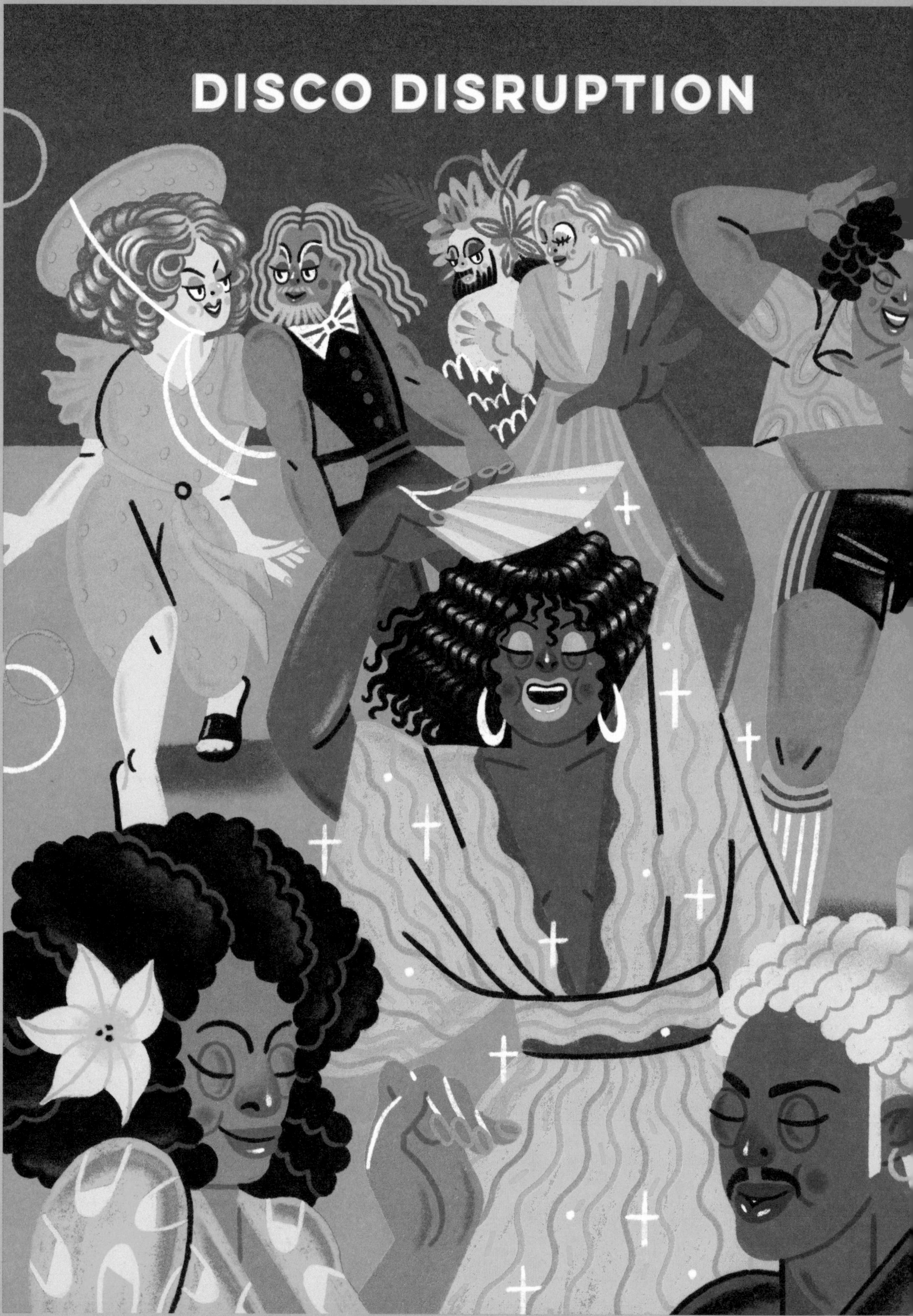
DISCO DISRUPTION

In 1970, DJ David Mancuso threw an invitation-only 'Love Saves The Day' party in his New York apartment. Frustrated by what he saw as a diluted, cleaned-up mainstream club culture, Mancuso wanted to create a dancefloor where a diverse spectrum of clubbers could be united through their love of music. The world he created was one of celebration – free of discrimination, and full of uplifting, uptempo disco.

Helmed by queer artists and people of colour, disco music was a major departure for the previously white-dominated pop music industry. By the mid-1970s, disco fever had spread worldwide. Photographs of stars and supermodels like Grace Jones and Jerry Hall at New York super-club Studio 54 gave a glimpse into a glamorous, hedonistic world where strange was in style.

SYLVESTER & THE COCKETTES

Alongside artists like Donna Summer, Diana Ross and Gloria Gaynor, disco found an eccentric poster child in Sylvester (centre). After being kicked out by his parents for cross-dressing at just thirteen years old, he began experimenting with music in the mid-1960s as part of The Disquotays, a flamboyant disco group that disbanded in the late 1960s.

In 1970, he joined The Cockettes, an experimental theatre troupe filled with fabulous, politically-charged hippies. Their costumes were androgynous and their jokes were both filthy and famously controversial. Their film *Tricia's Wedding* (1971) was a send-up of the marriage of president Richard Nixon's daughter, featuring LSD-spiked punch and a dazzling cast of drag queens. For a while, Sylvester's star quality and charisma mixed seamlessly with the collective's disruptive ethos, but chaos and unprofessionalism soon led to his departure. When he quit in 1972, he delivered a brilliantly bitchy apology to the audience calling The Cockettes a 'travesty'.

His signature falsetto had already earned him a following, so Sylvester seized the opportunity to become a solo star. Tracks like 'Do You Wanna Funk?' and '(You Make Me Feel) Mighty Real' dominated radio throughout the 1970s, and Sylvester's glamorous, androgynous look – metallic leather, sequins and rhinestones – became synonymous with disco. This combination of joy, soul and sparkle allowed queer stars and drag icons to break into the mainstream, paving the way for a brilliantly experimental new era of music.

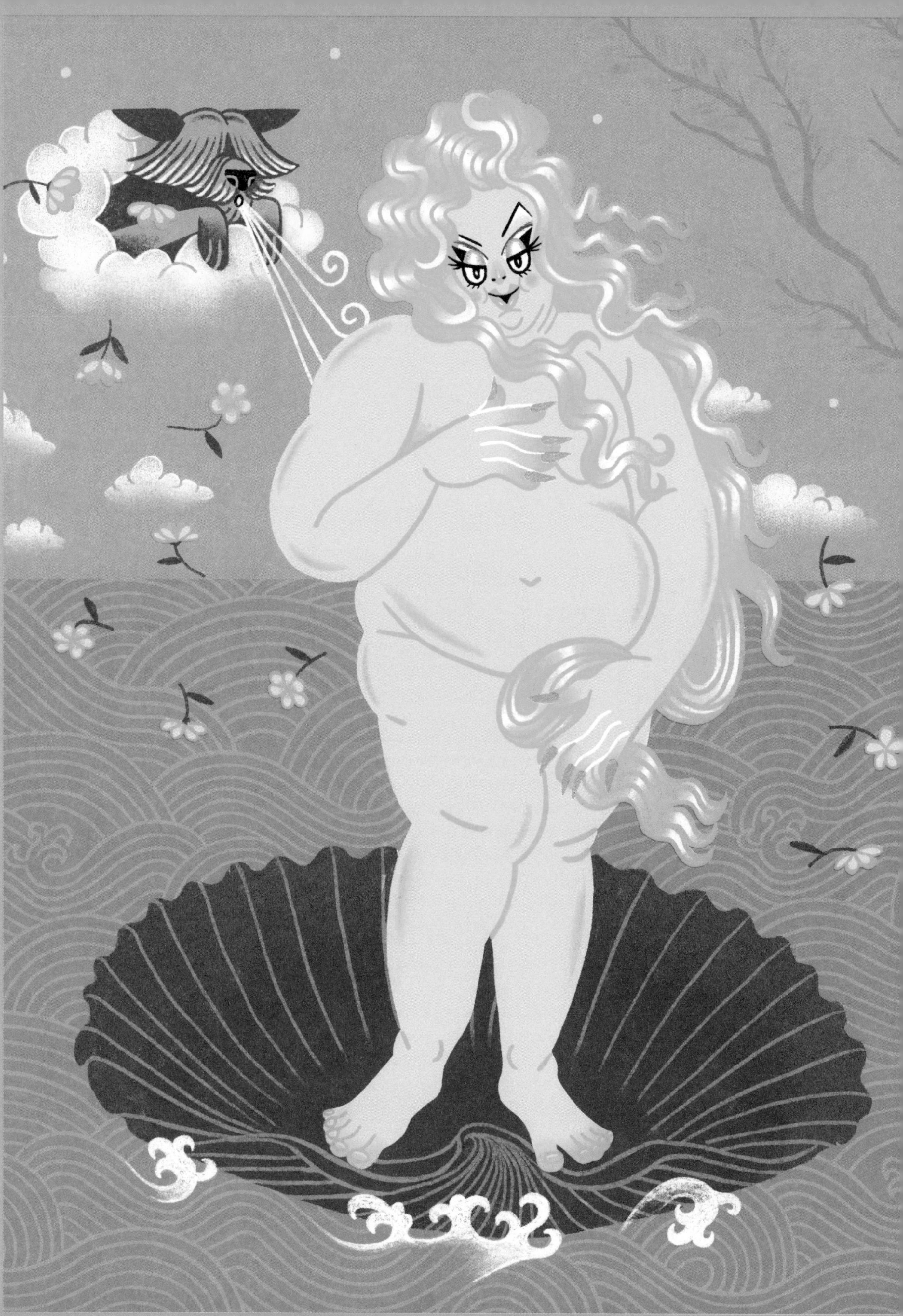

DIVINE & JOHN WATERS

"The most beautiful woman in the world... *almost*." This was how cult film director John Waters described his muse Divine, the filthy, inimitable drag persona of Baltimore-born Glenn Milstead. After meeting through mutual friends in the early 1960s, Waters and Milstead quickly bonded over a love of trashy counterculture and their shared outsider status.

The duo wasted no time in building a creative relationship, recruiting a handful of queer misfits for an art collective, The Dreamlanders. Waters had already made an experimental short film, *Hag in a Black Leather Jacket* (1964), and together they began to work on a series of trashy, low-budget shorts. The results showed that Divine could take on any role. There was the deranged, dragged-up Jackie O in *Eat Your Makeup* (1968), who kidnapped supermodels and forced them to eat their make-up kits; then there was the homicidal, bottle-blonde pin-up of *Mondo Trasho* (1969). Together, they built a reputation as the art world's most fabulous, provocative freaks.

As Divine, Milstead – who was bullied severely at school for his weight – began to embrace his body by pouring it into short, tight dresses. As the years went by, Divine's make-up developed as Waters encouraged him to go more dramatic. This led to a distinctive signature look: bright, exaggerated eyeshadow that crept up to the edge of a severely shaved-back hairline, a radical and comical commentary on beauty standards. The look was eye-catching, but it was Divine's filthy humour that marked her out as a star. When The Cockettes travelled to San Francisco, she donned a red lobster costume and joined them for a cover of their song, 'A Crab On Your Anus Means You're Loved'.

Divine was at her best when cracking dirty jokes and leaning into the freaky worlds of Waters' creation. Their shared goal was to shock audiences, which meant that nothing was off-limits: →

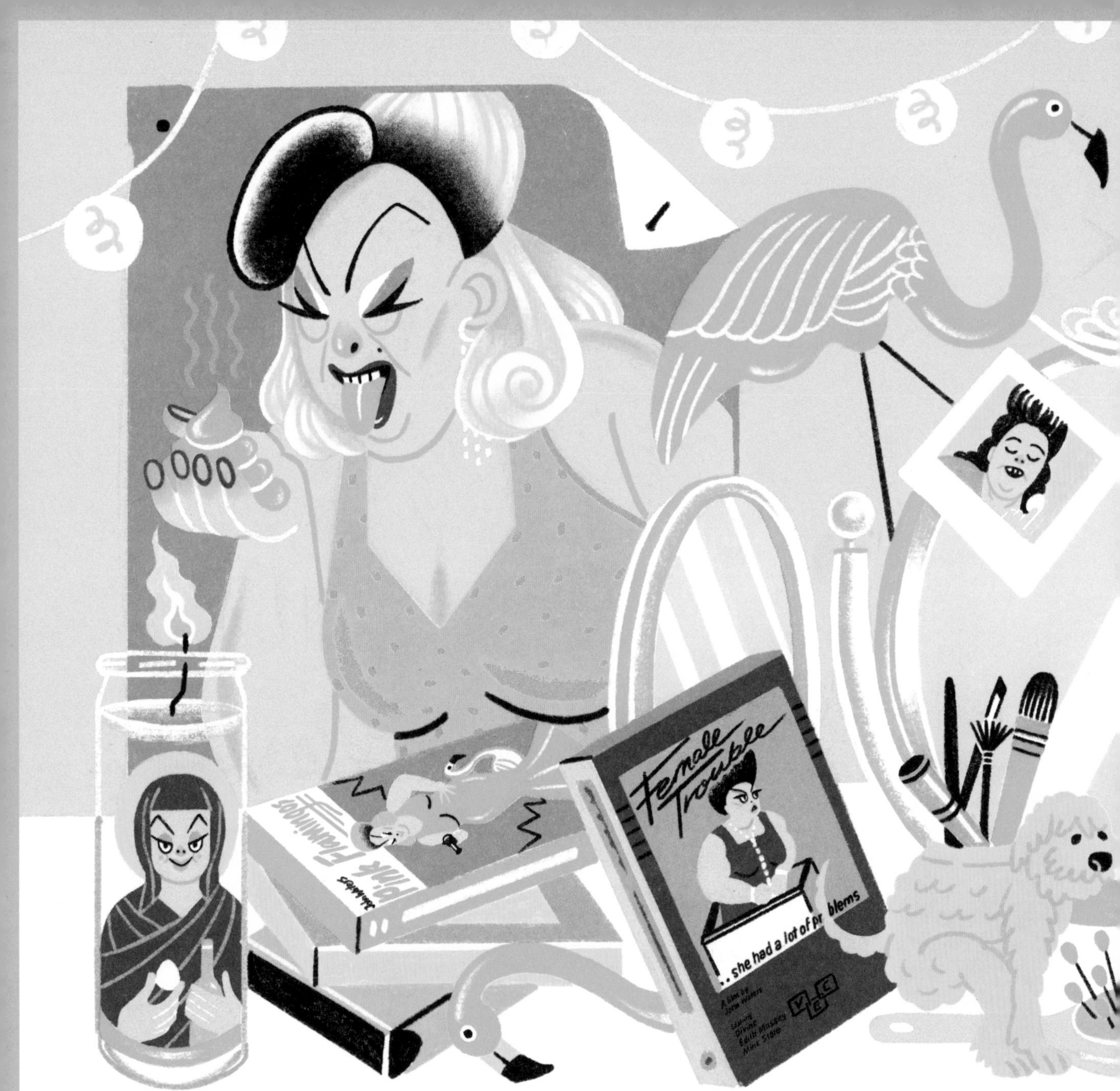
Pink Flamingos
Female Trouble

from vomit and incest to lobster fetishists and rosary-strewn sex toys. They pioneered a blueprint that intrigued fans, who were as disgusted as they were fascinated.

Divine's most infamous moment of notoriety came in 1972, when she rounded off Waters' cult classic *Pink Flamingos* with one of the most iconic scenes in cinema history. Dressed in a sparkling gold blouse and a dyed-yellow wig (roots exposed, of course), her character Babs struts down the street before stopping to scoop up, and subsequently eat, a handful of dog faeces. It's the disgusting cherry on top of a plot that also involves bestiality, cannibalism and castration – and it turned both Divine and Waters into stars.

The film was the first in a so-called 'Trash Trilogy', continuing with *Female Trouble* (1974) and *Desperate Living* (1977), which introduced their work to a wider, more bewildered audience. Divine was hailed as the filthiest person alive and Waters was her provocative partner-in-crime. Their success wasn't limited to the silver screen. In 1980, Divine's profile skyrocketed thanks to an unlikely music career, which spawned songs like 'Jungle Jezebel', 'Born To Be Cheap' and

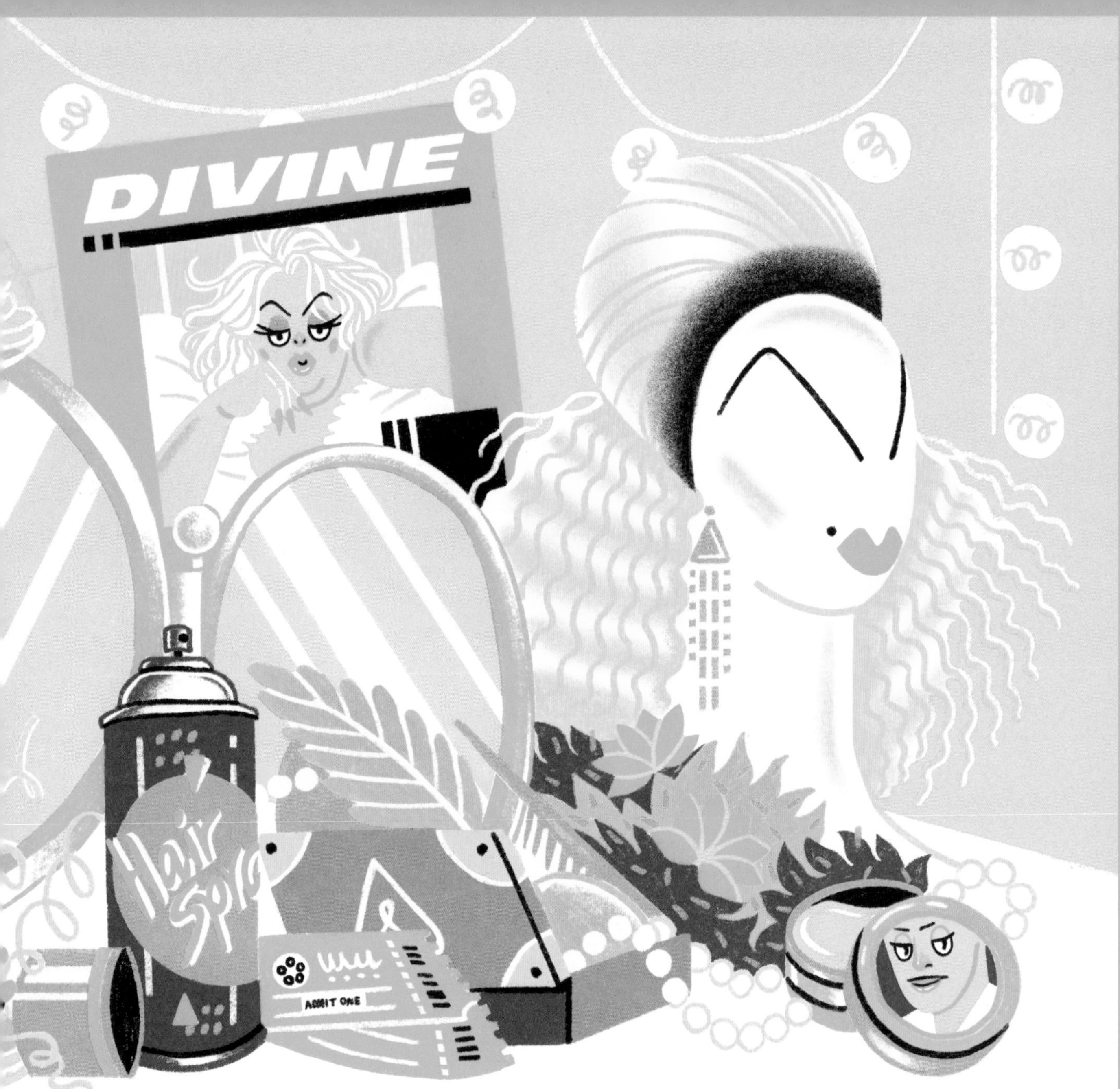
DIVINE
Hair spra
ADMIT ONE

'Psychedelic Shack'. Early single 'You Think You're A Man' even charted worldwide, leading to a series of genius primetime performances.

Divine teamed up with Waters again for a leading role in *Hairspray* (1988), starring alongside Debbie Harry and Ricki Lake. Directed by Waters, the PG-rated film was a marked departure from their previous work. Deliberately less filthy, it was designed to lure in a wider audience. The film had limited box office success, but a later home release did the trick and attracted a cult following. Viewers were buying into Waters' wacky world – the film landed a fanbase that led to a later Broadway musical and 2007 film remake.

Sadly, *Hairspray* was to be the duo's last collaboration. Divine died of a heart attack just months after *Hairspray*'s release, leaving behind such a legacy that *People* magazine named her 'The Drag Queen of the Century'. Together, John Waters and Divine brought filth, wicked humour and an embrace of total freakiness to a global audience. Theirs remains one of the most influential creative partnerships in drag history.

A REBEL SOUND

In 1970, after years of struggling to settle on an identity as a musician, David Bowie donned a velvet dress and reclined seductively across a satin-draped chaise longue for his *The Man Who Sold The World* album artwork. That year he also formed The Hype, a short-lived band of rock superheroes intended to add a layer of theatricality to his shows. This combination of projects launched Bowie as we know him today: a spandex-wearing, gender-bending icon.

Although Bowie wasn't the first musician to toy with drag, his timing was perfect. T-Rex frontman Marc Bolan appeared on *Top of the Pops* just months later, teaming his shaggy hair with a shimmery satin look thought to have sparked the 'glam rock' movement. Rock bands quickly followed suit, and before long the signature 'rock star' look – extreme backcombed hair, theatrical make-up and tight, shiny catsuits – had been fine-tuned.

Of course, there was backlash. Glam rock band The New York Dolls suffered numerous record label rejections before signing to Mercury Records in 1973. Even then, the label was not a fan of the band's trademark platform boots, lurex trousers and artfully smudged lipstick. The Dolls were asked to tone it down. They refused. Instead, they made a point of dressing in full drag on their self-titled debut album cover.

The late 1970s saw Grace Jones transition from modelling to music. Despite experimentation with different musical genres, her aesthetic signatures remained the same: razor-sharp cheekbones, androgynous silhouettes and an iconic buzzcut. Her masculine energy led interviewers to ask intrusive questions about her gender and sexuality, but Jones always shrugged them off. "I think it's ridiculous trying to categorise people's feelings", she said in 1985. "Do what you feel, when you feel like it – if you feel like it!"

A long list of musicians including Prince, Annie Lennox of The Eurhythmics, and Freddie Mercury kept this spirit alive, dragging up in their videos and playing with ideas of what a man or woman should look like. Fans reacted with glee and hysteria, and it seemed like the stigma around playing with gender was starting to disappear. Disruptions weren't just tolerated any more – gender-bending was becoming legitimately cool.

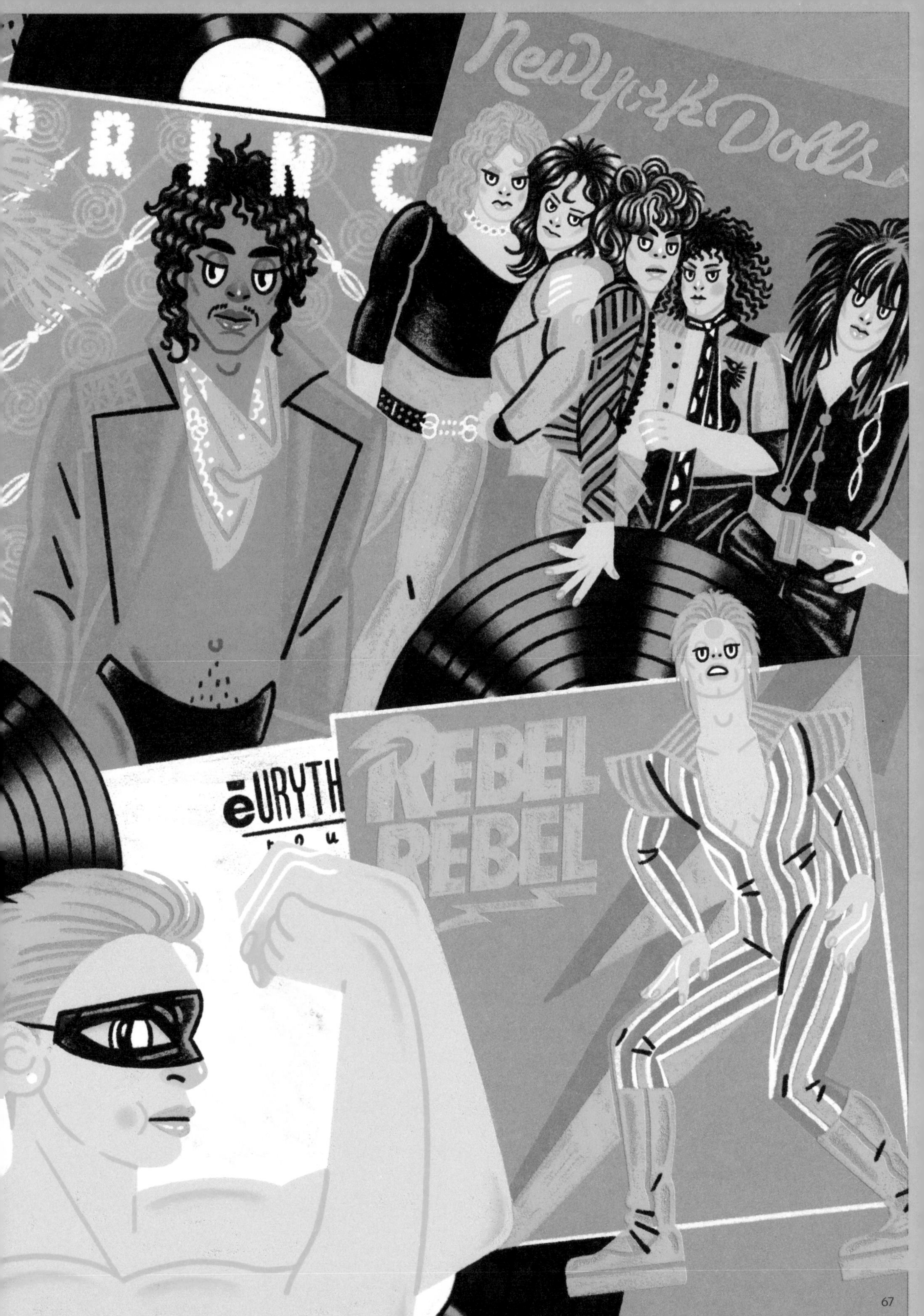
PRINC
New York Dolls
ēURYTH
REBEL
REBEL

THE ROCKY HORROR PICTURE SHOW

When Richard O'Brien dreamed up *The Rocky Horror Show* as a stage musical in 1973, he likely had no idea that his brainchild would become an international success. In 1975, a film remake was pulled together in just six weeks – and that's a key part of its charm.

The camp classic tells the story of Brad and Janet, a suburban, middle-class, white couple who inadvertently find themselves trapped in the queer lair of 'sweet transvestite' Dr Frank-N-Furter, who introduces them to his fabulous cast of drag oddities, including O'Brien himself. The film's combination of glam rock, sci-fi chaos and absurd horror is irresistible, but the undeniable draw is Frank-N-Furter, whose fishnets, black underwear and tight-laced corset made actor Tim Curry an unlikely sex symbol.

There's a ramshackle, rough-around-the-edges sensibility to the film's make-up looks, which were softer than the thick, elaborate stage make-up worn for the original musical. The man behind this transformation was Pierre La Roche – also responsible for David Bowie's

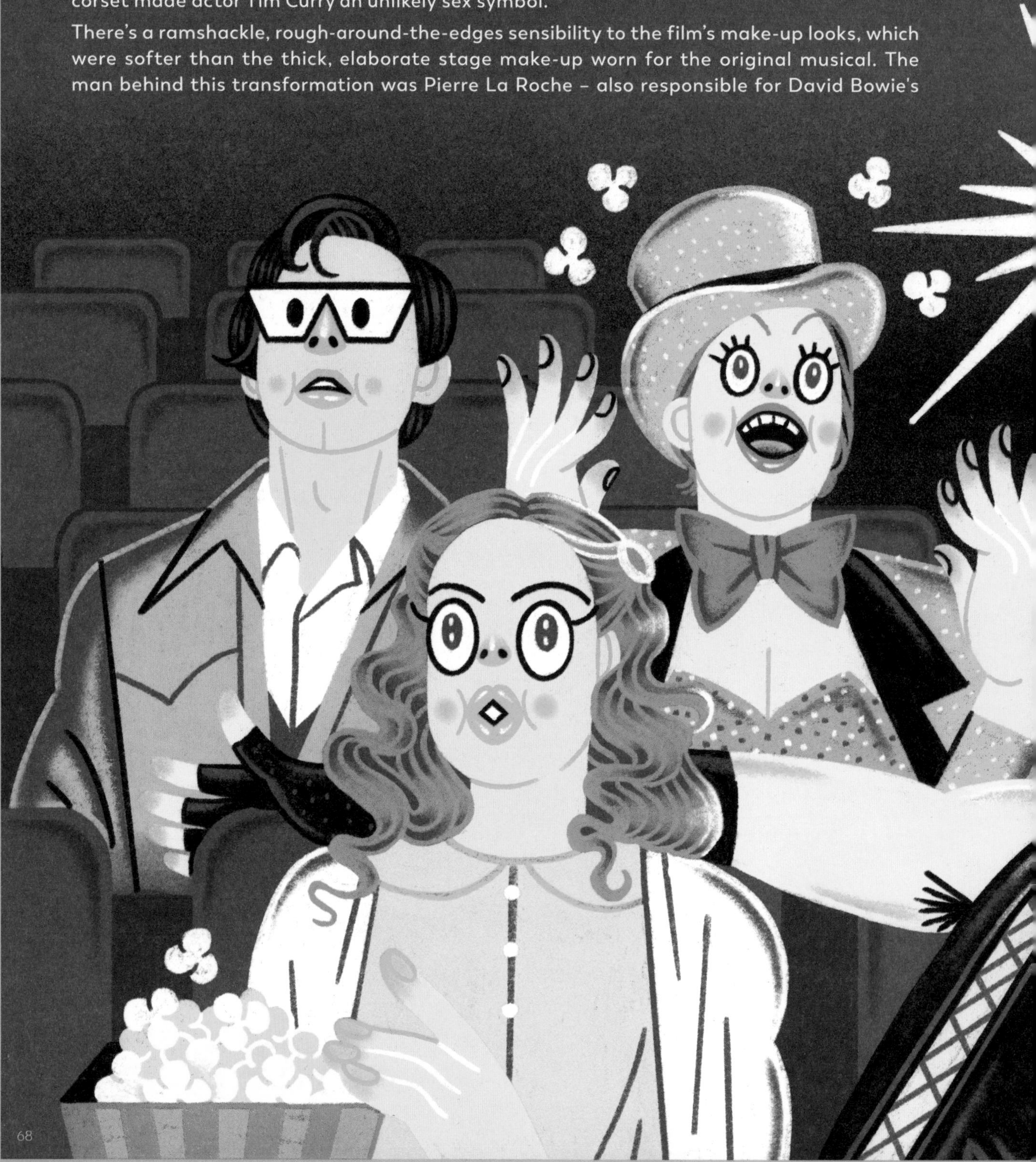

visual transformation. This more delicate approach ultimately worked, spawning a series of legendary looks destined to be recreated at Hallowe'en parties worldwide.

Critics initially ignored the film, but programmers began screening it in their midnight 'cult slot', attracting rowdy audiences who delighted in singing along, dancing through the aisles and even ad-libbing their own script additions. Screenings like these are still popular, as are *Rocky Horror* parties. Its ongoing popularity comes down to the film's mantra, "Don't dream it. Be it." The film encouraged people to cast off the shackles of normality and give in to their freakiest impulses – a sentiment that still resonates hugely with audiences worldwide.

Rocky Horror drag never feels overly serious or inaccessible. Glamour was never the aim. Instead, the cast found joy in freaking out new fans, boggling their mind with campy costumes while cracking outrageous gags designed to loosen them up and, most importantly, open their minds to the thrill of breaking the rules.

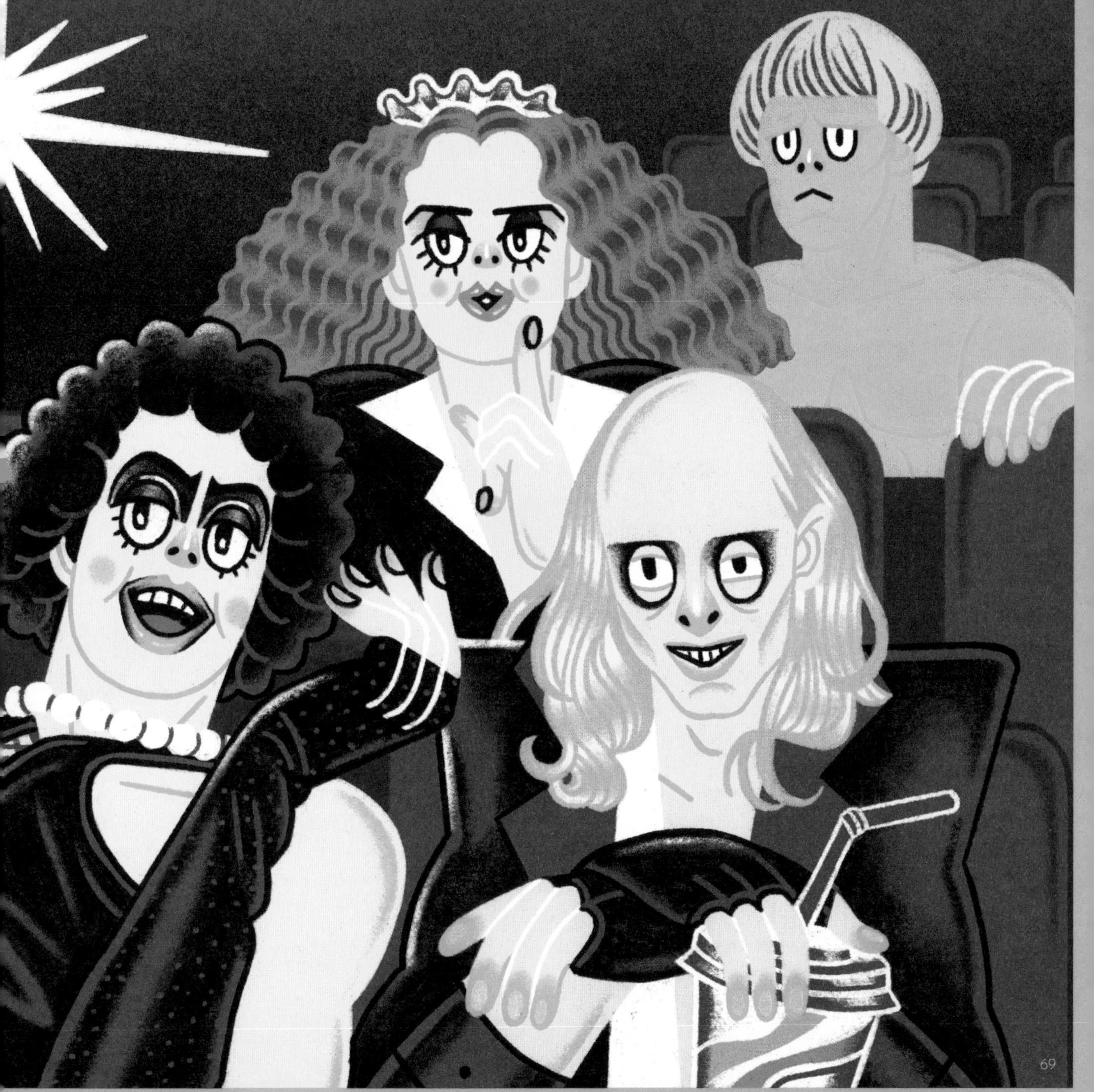

INVASION OF THE PINES

Few holiday destinations are more gay-friendly than New York's Fire Island. From before the Stonewall Riots, the picturesque holiday resort was known as a safe haven. In 1968, a boat full of plainclothes policemen headed there in search of gay men having sex outdoors. The officers tracked down and arrested 27 victims with plans to leak their details publicly, but activist group The Mattachine Society soon heard of these plans and hired lawyer Benny Vuturo to fight their corners. He succeeded spectacularly – all 27 cases were thrown out.

Fire Island's gay-friendly reputation was threatened in 1976, when drag queen Terry Warren was refused service in a restaurant at Fire Island Pines, one of the island's richest areas. Outraged, Terry's friends – who were staying at the nearby Cherry Grove – slapped on their make-up, donned their most extravagant outfits and 'invaded' the Pines, demanding service. This spontaneous protest inadvertently launched an annual tradition. Each year, on 4th July, crowds of drag-happy revellers gather at Cherry Grove to board a huge ferry to the Pines, where they're greeted by a cheering audience. It's one of many queer traditions that began as a protest and was made possible by the strength and resilience of drag queens.

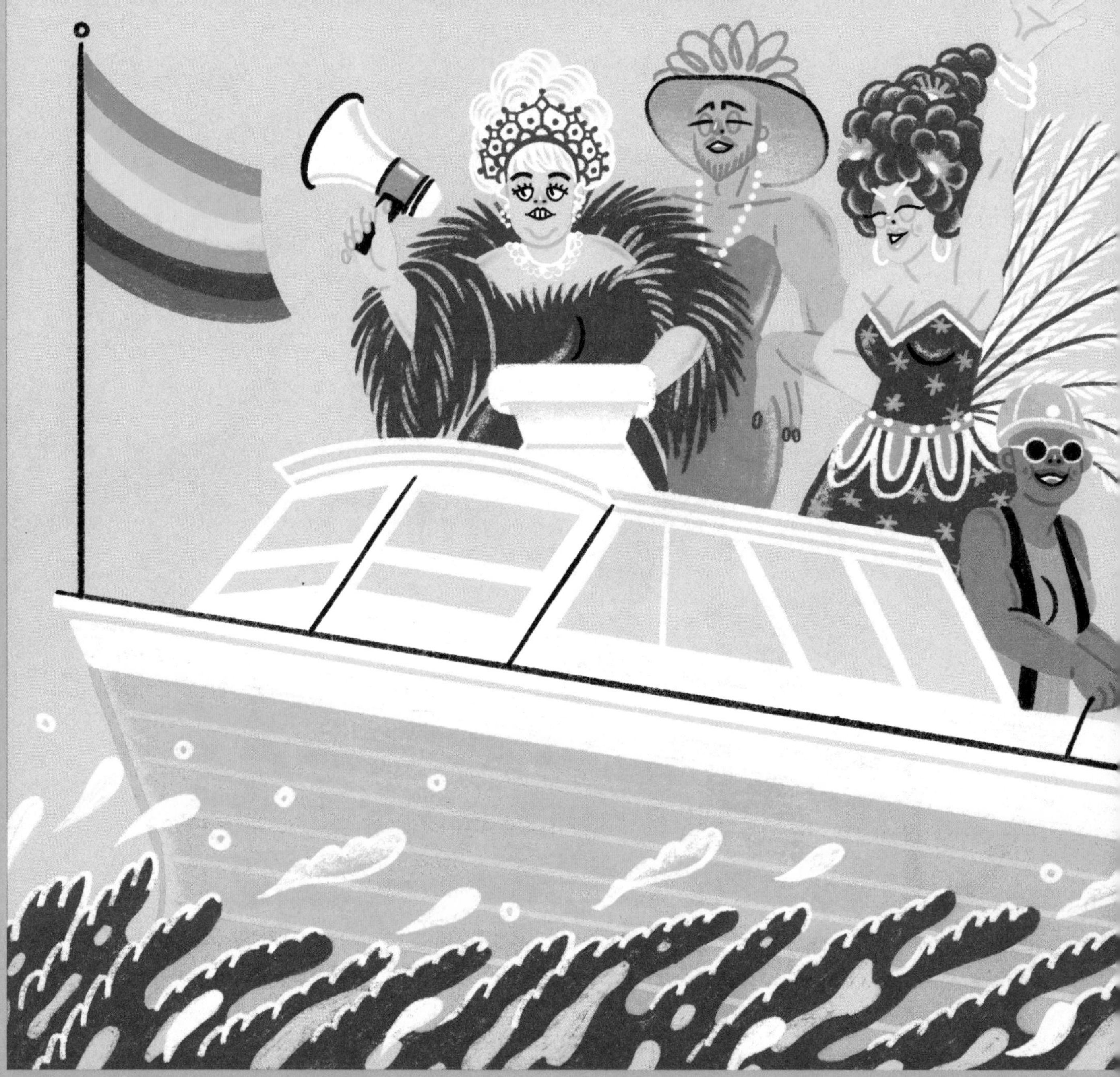

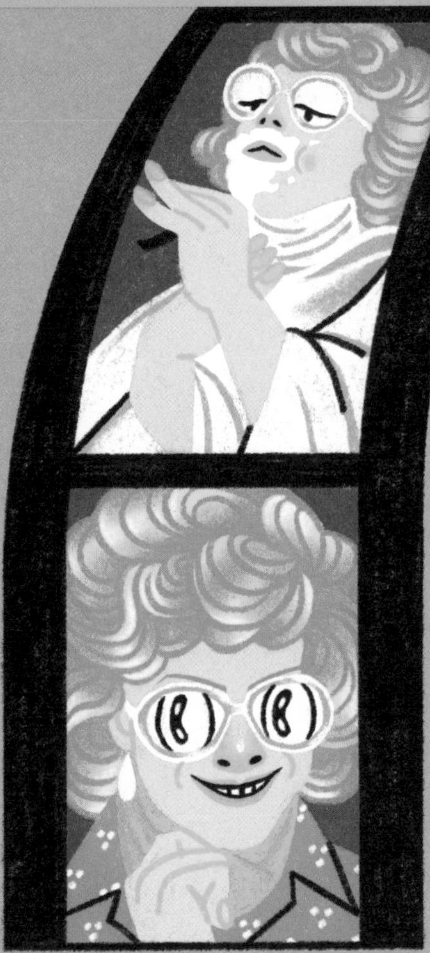

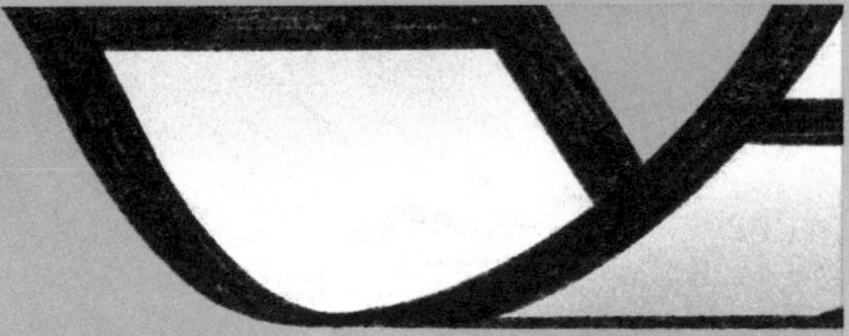

TOOTSIE

The 1980s saw a shift in the kind of drag queens depicted on screen. Two breakthrough films, *Tootsie* (1982) and *Torch Song Trilogy* (1988), portrayed drag heroines who were more tortured, neurotic and layered than others who came before them, signalling that directors were warming up to the idea of giving drag characters more in-depth stories.

Although *Tootsie*'s core plot (a straight man impersonates an actress, wins acclaim and then has to hide the truth) plays on old stereotypes, there's an unexpected tenderness that sets the film apart. It blends humour and subversion with new twists on old tropes. This formula managed to please mainstream viewers without alienating LGBTQ+ fans.

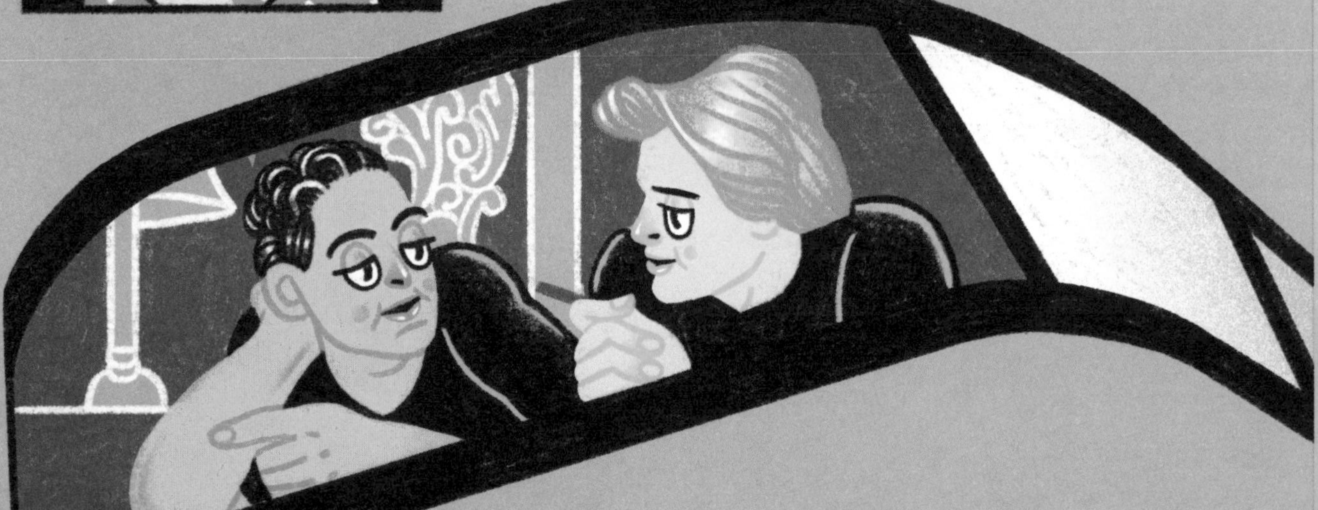

TORCH SONG TRILOGY

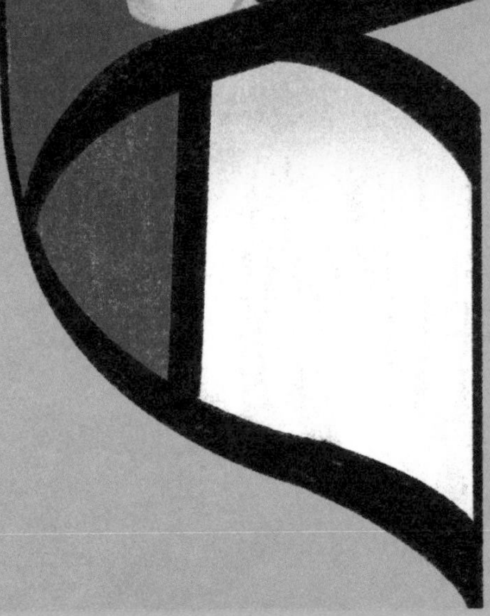

Harvey Fierstein's *Torch Song Trilogy* was adapted from his own three-act play. It sensitively depicts lead character Arnold – an emotional, Jewish, homosexual, drag queen torch singer – and deals with weighty issues including gay bashing, bisexuality, same-sex adoption and the unique complexities of queer child/parent relationships.

"I think my biggest problem is being young and beautiful," Arnold says. "It's my biggest problem because I've never been young and beautiful." These lines set the bittersweet tone for a landmark portrayal that peeled back the mask of drag to expose the human vulnerabilities beneath.

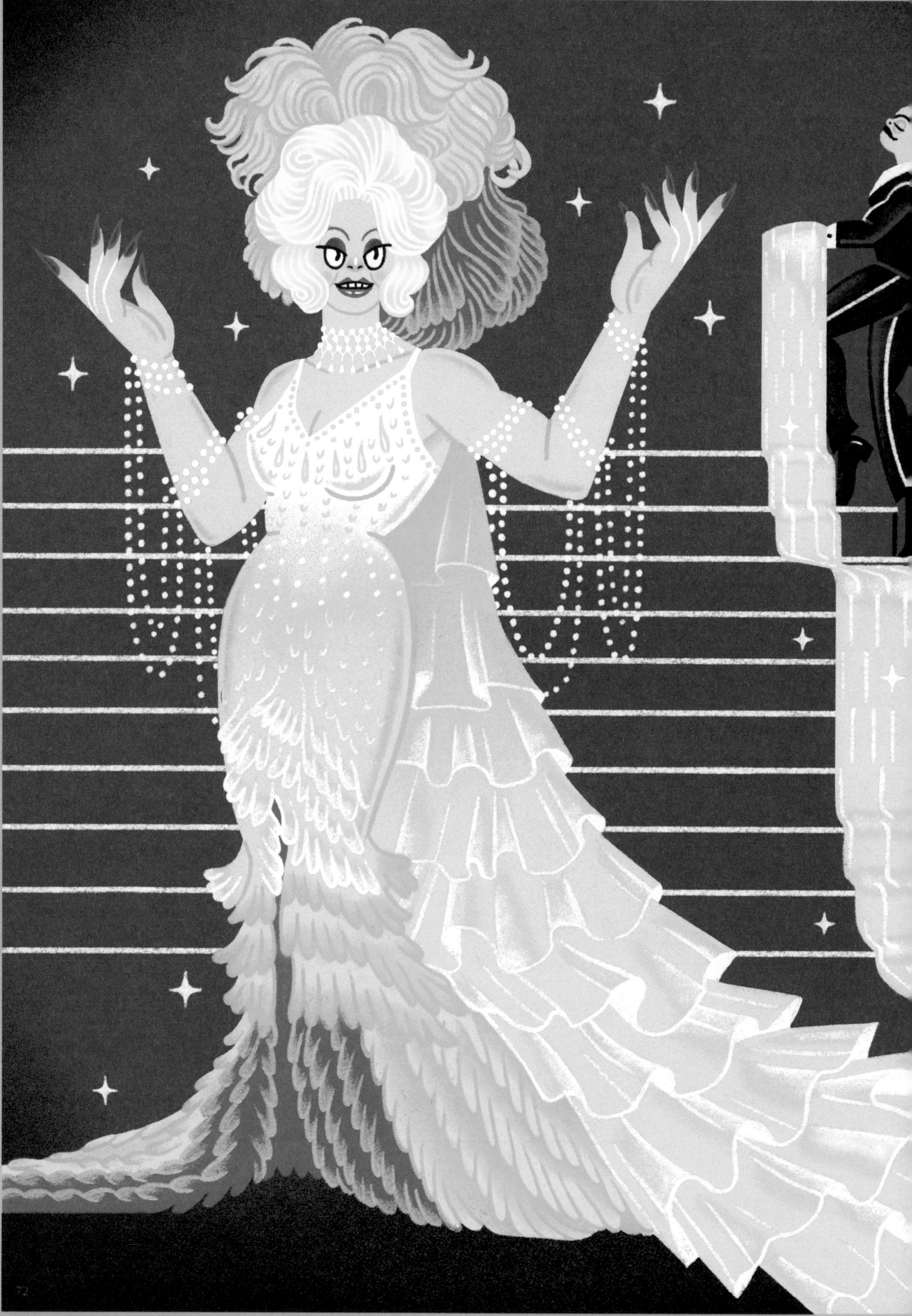

DANNY LA RUE

In 1970, a bewildered *New York Times* reviewer went to see Anglo-Irish female impersonator Danny La Rue at London's Palace Theatre. His glowing article – titled *Is It a Male or Female?* – praised the show, but also argued that drag has "no homosexual connotation". Instead he insisted that it was merely a comedy device.

This was La Rue's brand of drag – a nouveau pantomime dame. His piled-high wigs, campy mannerisms and feminine walk all created the exaggerated femininity of a drag queen, but La Rue preferred to be called a "comic in a frock". He was skilled in the art of switching in and out of character to shock and confuse his audience, using a low, masculine growl for one joke and a high-pitched, dainty squeal for the next.

Celebrity impersonations were another of La Rue's specialities – from Judy Garland to former British Prime Minister Margaret Thatcher, there was seemingly no woman he couldn't mimic. His unique comedy earned him an invitation to perform for Queen Elizabeth II at the 1972 Royal Variety Performance, a slew of TV and stage roles and, in 2002, an OBE – the second-highest order of chivalry in Britain.

Other drag acts of the time adopted similar tactics. Their costumes were bejewelled parodies of feminine stereotypes: England's Lily Savage played the old-school glamour girl and Australia's Dame Edna the eccentric housewife, both slipping into a lower voice to make crude jokes. This brand of self-aware drag allowed audiences to feel comfortable instead of threatened, a method which allowed a handful of drag entertainers to work their way onto television screens worldwide.

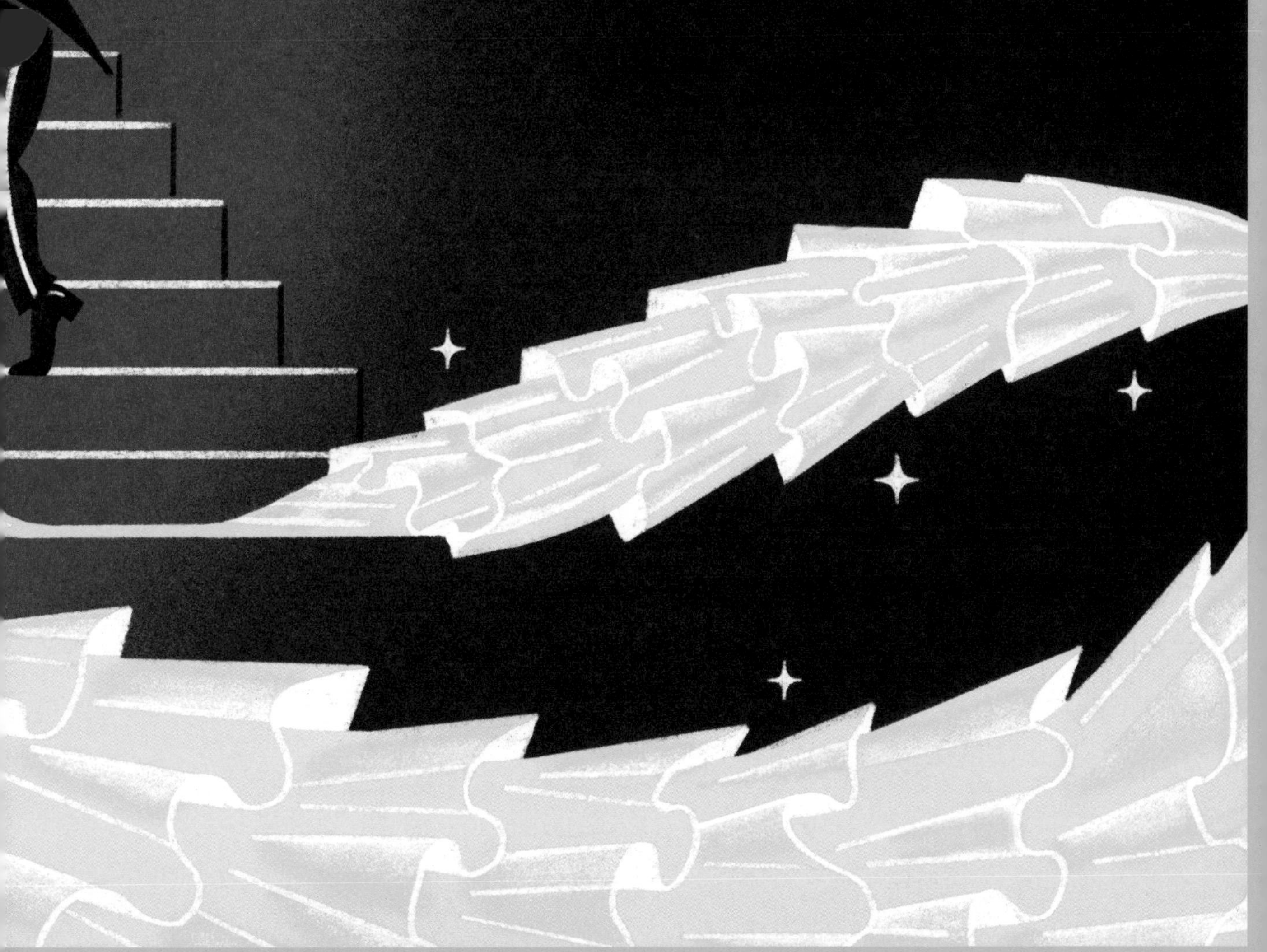

SERVING LOOKS

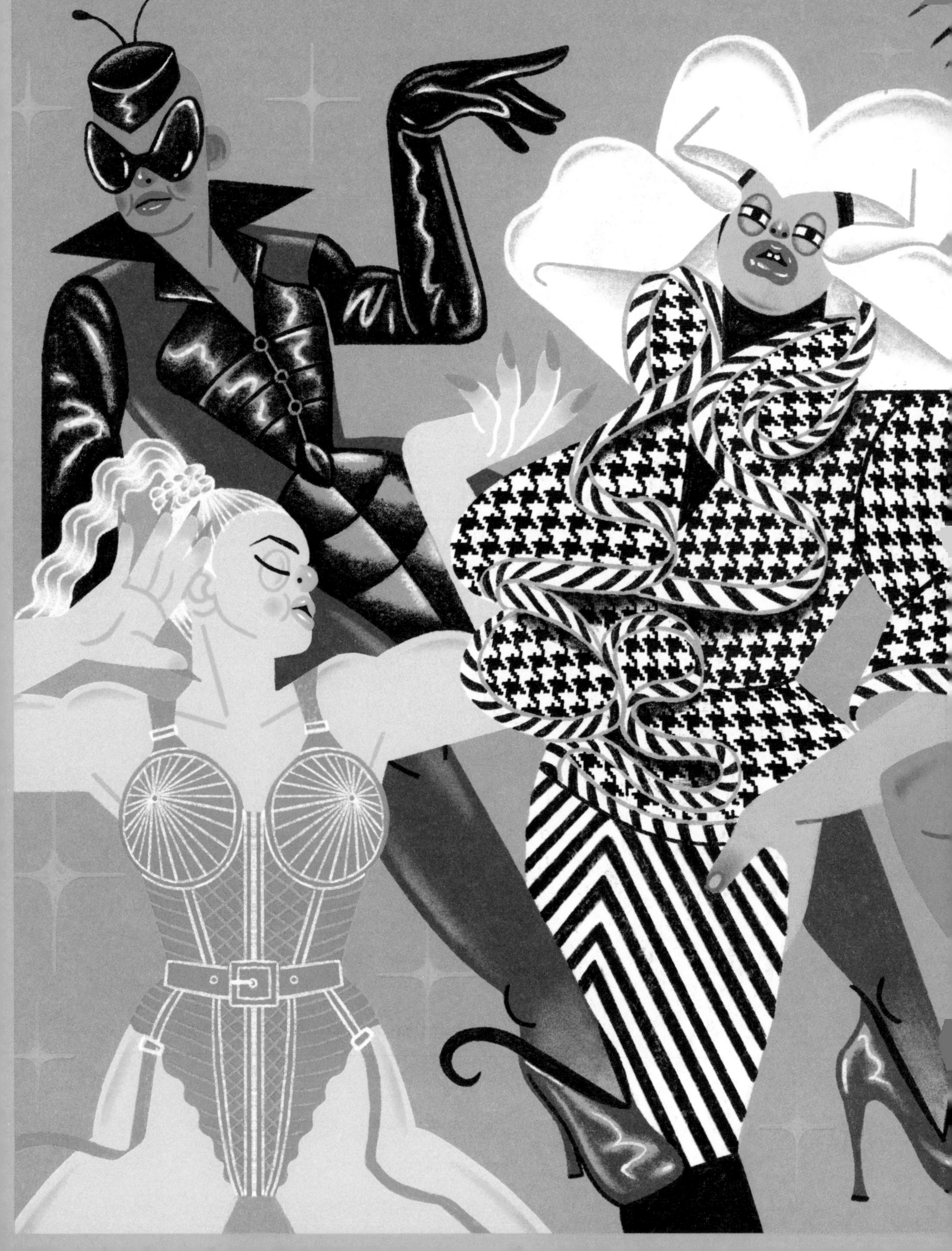

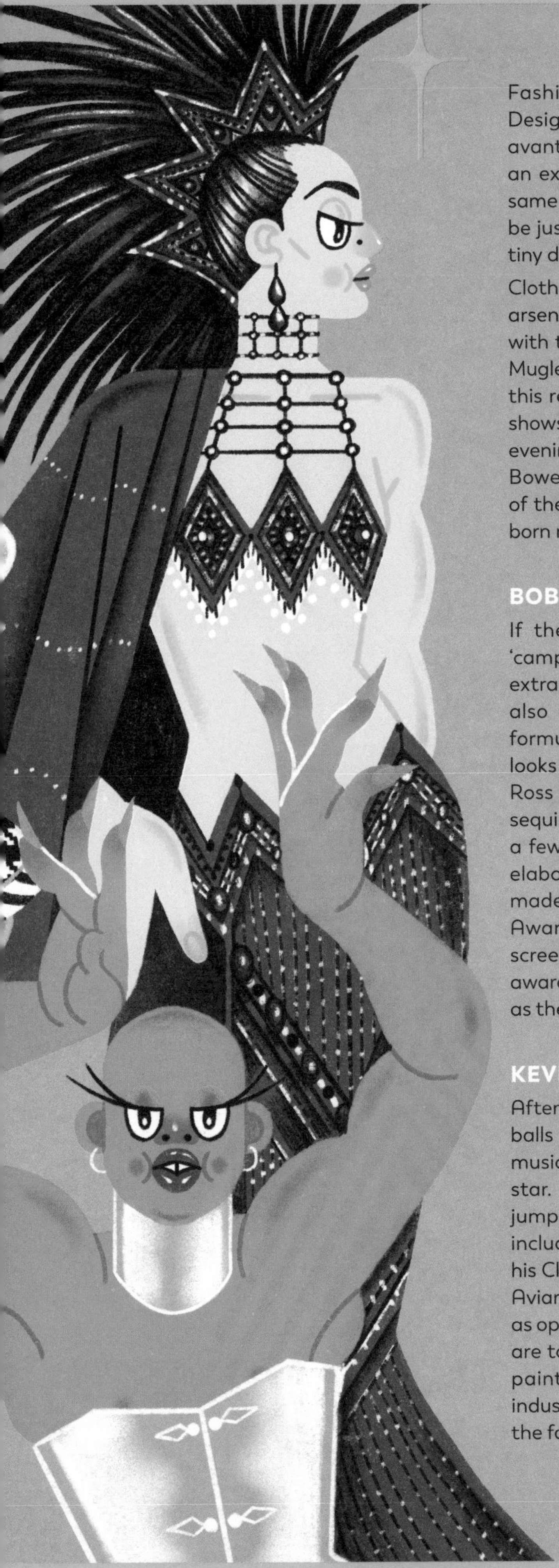

Fashion and drag go hand-in-bejewelled-hand. Designers have always sought inspiration from the avant-garde, and vice versa. Supermodels perform an extremely heightened, idealised femininity in the same way that glamorous queens do, and the looks can be just as exaggerated: think towering heels, big hair, tiny dresses and ramped-up proportions.

Clothes are also a vital tool in any drag performer's arsenal, used to build charismatic characters and toy with the visual codes of gender. Designers like Thierry Mugler and Jean Paul Gaultier have long acknowledged this relationship, casting drag queens to walk in their shows, while Alexander McQueen was known to spend evenings soaking up the energy of Club Kids like Leigh Bowery. In other words, fashion is an integral part of the illusion of drag. As RuPaul once said, "we're all born naked and the rest is drag".

BOB MACKIE

If there's one word that best sums up drag, it's 'camp'. The best costumes tend to be exaggerated, extravagant and unspeakably glamorous, but they're also intentionally playful. Few designers nail this formula better than Bob Mackie, whose outlandish looks have been worn by everyone from Cher to Diana Ross and, of course, drag legend RuPaul. Feathers, sequins and outsized, over-the-top headpieces are just a few of his visual signatures, one example being an elaborate gown designed for Cher (top right), which made an appearance in 1986 at the 60th Academy Awards. Mackie's designs have appeared on both screen and stage for over 50 years, seeing him win awards, build an enduring legacy and earn a reputation as the King of Camp Fashion.

KEVIN AVIANCE

After years of snatching trophies at New York's vogue balls in the 90s and building a reputation as a house music trailblazer, Kevin Aviance is a bonafide fashion star. His skintight lycra, rainbow jewels and metallic jumpsuits have earned him a slew of famous fans including Janet Jackson and Whitney Houston, and his Club Kid looks have made him a red carpet regular. Aviance is unlike other drag queens: he usually sings live as opposed to lip-syncing, and his conceptual creations are topped off by his signature bald head and bright, painterly make-up. His influence spans various industries, but the impact of his avant-garde looks on the fashion industry is undeniable.

THE ART OF

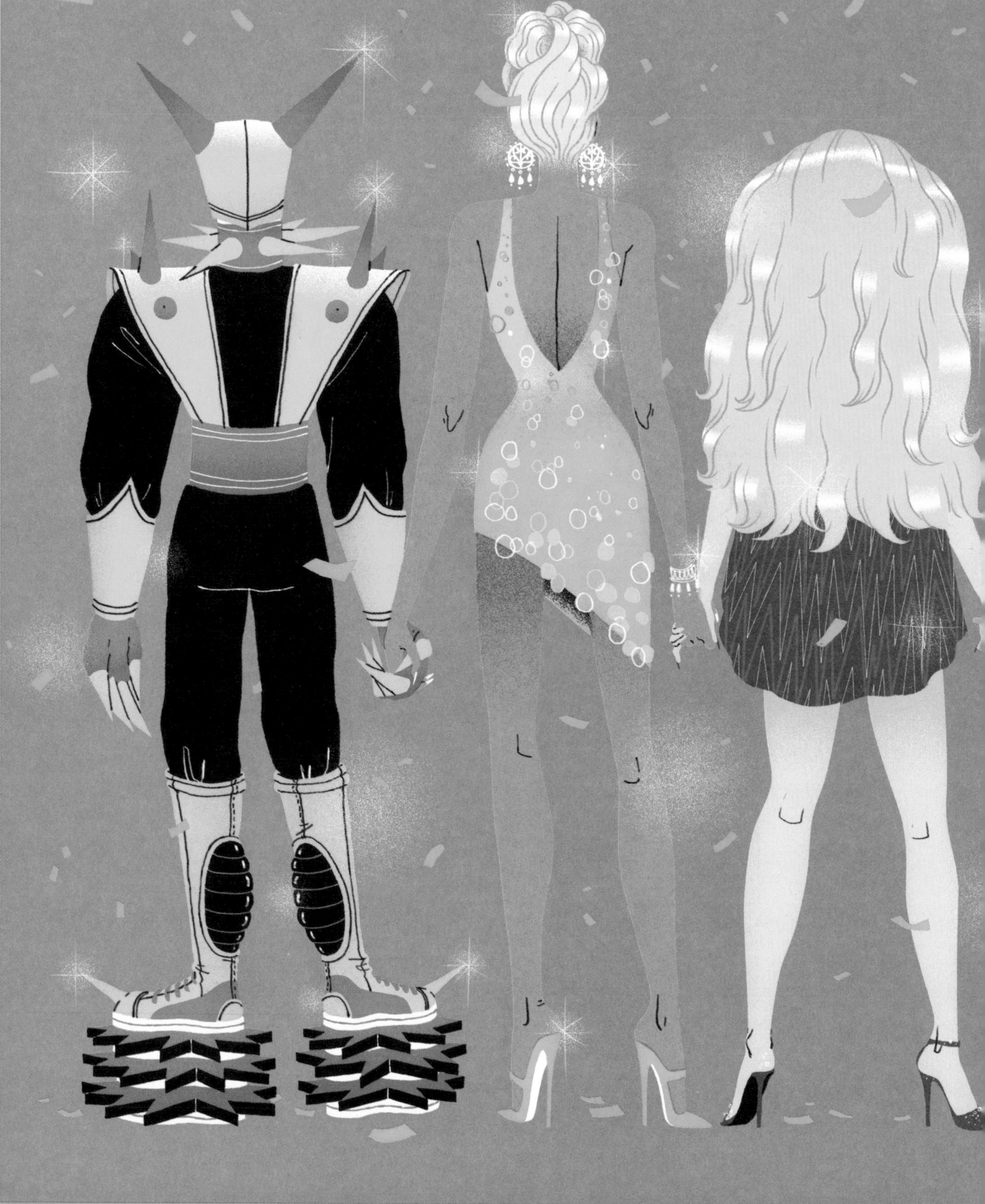

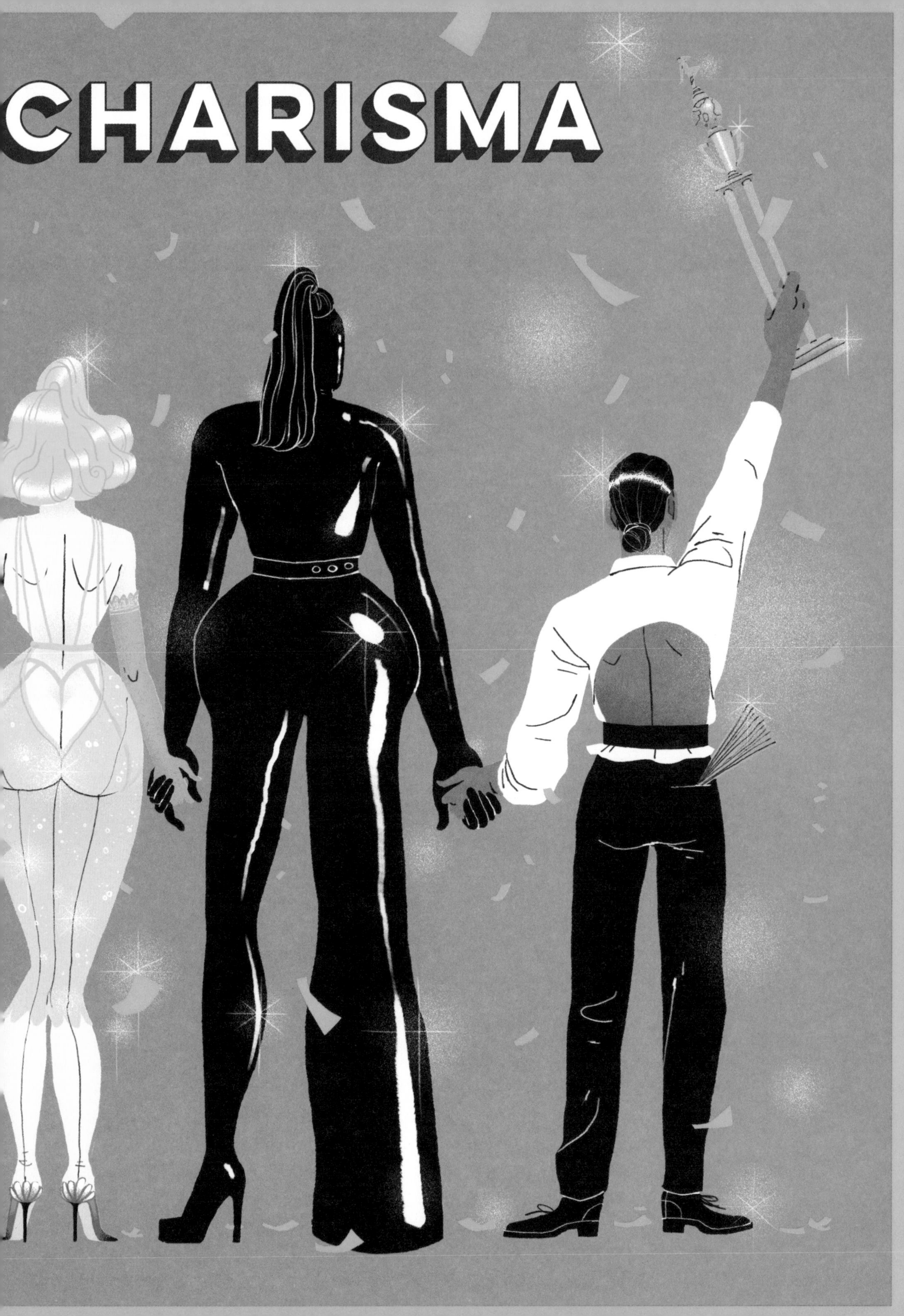
CHARISMA

1980s-2000s

The beginning of the AIDS crisis in 1981 sent shockwaves through the gay community, sparking a more radical, political era of drag. Although a handful of stars had succeeded in winning acceptance throughout the 1970s, media coverage of the crisis halted this progress. Headlines blamed the LGBTQ+ community for the virus, and fear-mongering in the press led to an increase in racism and homophobia.

Instead of backing down, drag artists amped up their outrageousness and spearheaded fundraising efforts, which led to huge medical breakthroughs. Activists reclaimed words like 'queer' for good, and drag was pushed beyond masculinity and femininity by Club Kids, whose 'genderfuck' aesthetics trickled into fashion and television.

Documentaries like *Paris Is Burning* (1990) and outdoor festivals like Wigstock celebrated queer communities, and a handful of stars like RuPaul and Amanda Lepore started to gain international recognition. As research into AIDS continued and the myths surrounding it were dispelled, the tide began to shift and make way, once again, for a drag renaissance. From theatre to cinema and beyond, queer artists began to claw their way back into the mainstream – and look damn good doing it.

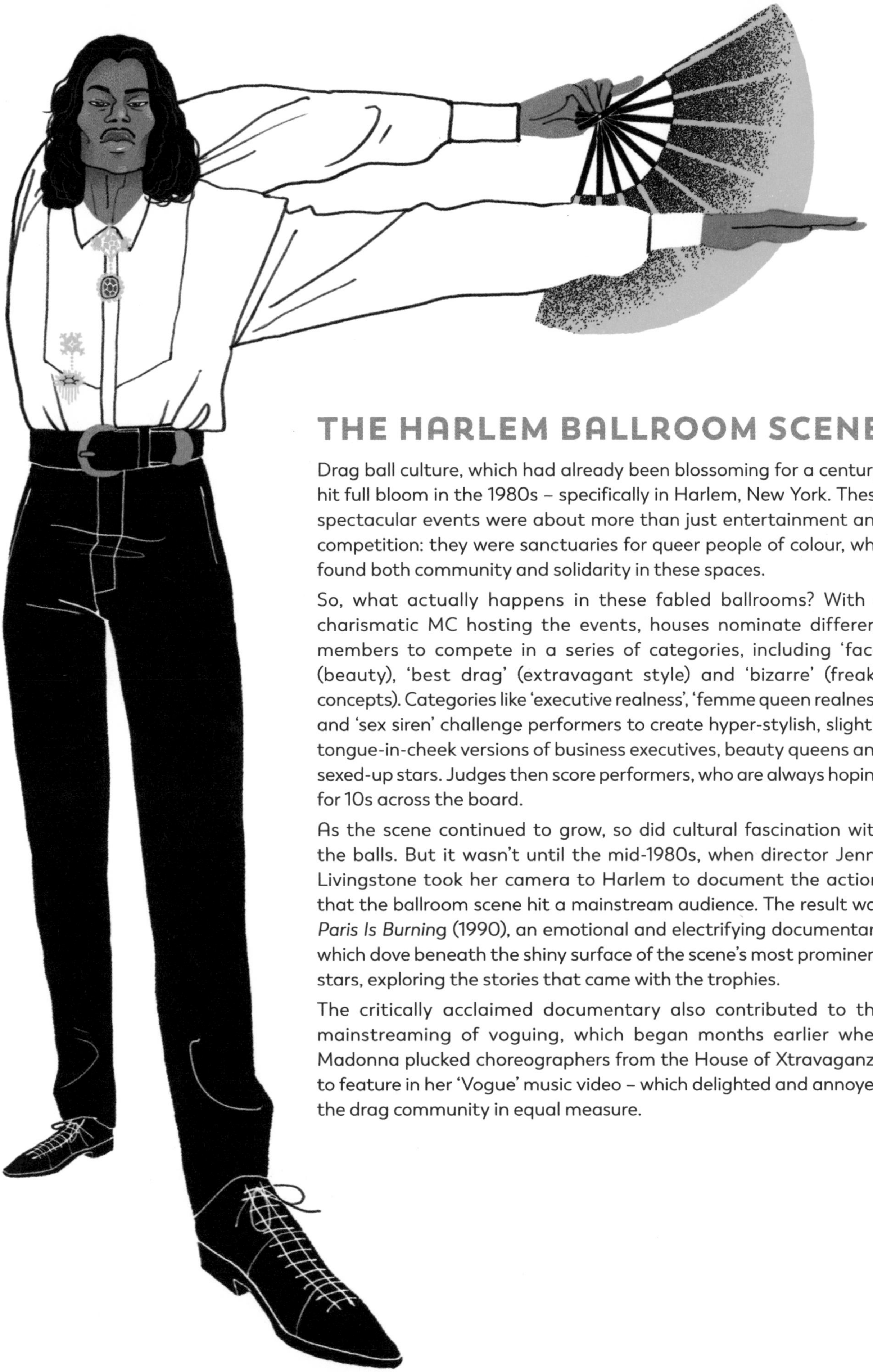

THE HARLEM BALLROOM SCENE

Drag ball culture, which had already been blossoming for a century, hit full bloom in the 1980s – specifically in Harlem, New York. These spectacular events were about more than just entertainment and competition: they were sanctuaries for queer people of colour, who found both community and solidarity in these spaces.

So, what actually happens in these fabled ballrooms? With a charismatic MC hosting the events, houses nominate different members to compete in a series of categories, including 'face' (beauty), 'best drag' (extravagant style) and 'bizarre' (freaky concepts). Categories like 'executive realness', 'femme queen realness' and 'sex siren' challenge performers to create hyper-stylish, slightly tongue-in-cheek versions of business executives, beauty queens and sexed-up stars. Judges then score performers, who are always hoping for 10s across the board.

As the scene continued to grow, so did cultural fascination with the balls. But it wasn't until the mid-1980s, when director Jenny Livingstone took her camera to Harlem to document the action, that the ballroom scene hit a mainstream audience. The result was *Paris Is Burning* (1990), an emotional and electrifying documentary which dove beneath the shiny surface of the scene's most prominent stars, exploring the stories that came with the trophies.

The critically acclaimed documentary also contributed to the mainstreaming of voguing, which began months earlier when Madonna plucked choreographers from the House of Xtravaganza to feature in her 'Vogue' music video – which delighted and annoyed the drag community in equal measure.

CATEGORY IS...

At a drag ball, not only do the the competitors stomp the runway, they also vogue. The most popular origin story of the distinctive dance style begins in an underground Manhattan club with Paris Dupree, who reportedly snatched a copy of *Vogue* magazine from her competitor's handbag and began imitating models' poses. Alternate histories trace vogue back to an unnamed Rikers Island prisoner, but whatever the truth, vogue is a reclamation: it's a uniquely Black, queer art form pioneered by ballroom regulars creating their own interpretation of out-of-reach fashion editorials. By framing their faces with their hands to resemble cameras, vogue dancers nod to this idea of creating their own beauty and imitating the angular, elegant poses of models.

Definitions differ and have changed over time, but ballroom scholars generally agree that there are three main styles of voguing: Old Way, New Way and Vogue Femme. The latter is the most recent variation, consisting of five key elements:

1. Hands: Performers use arm and hand movements to tell a story, creating sharp, angular lines or soft, circular motions – or a quick-fire combination of the two.

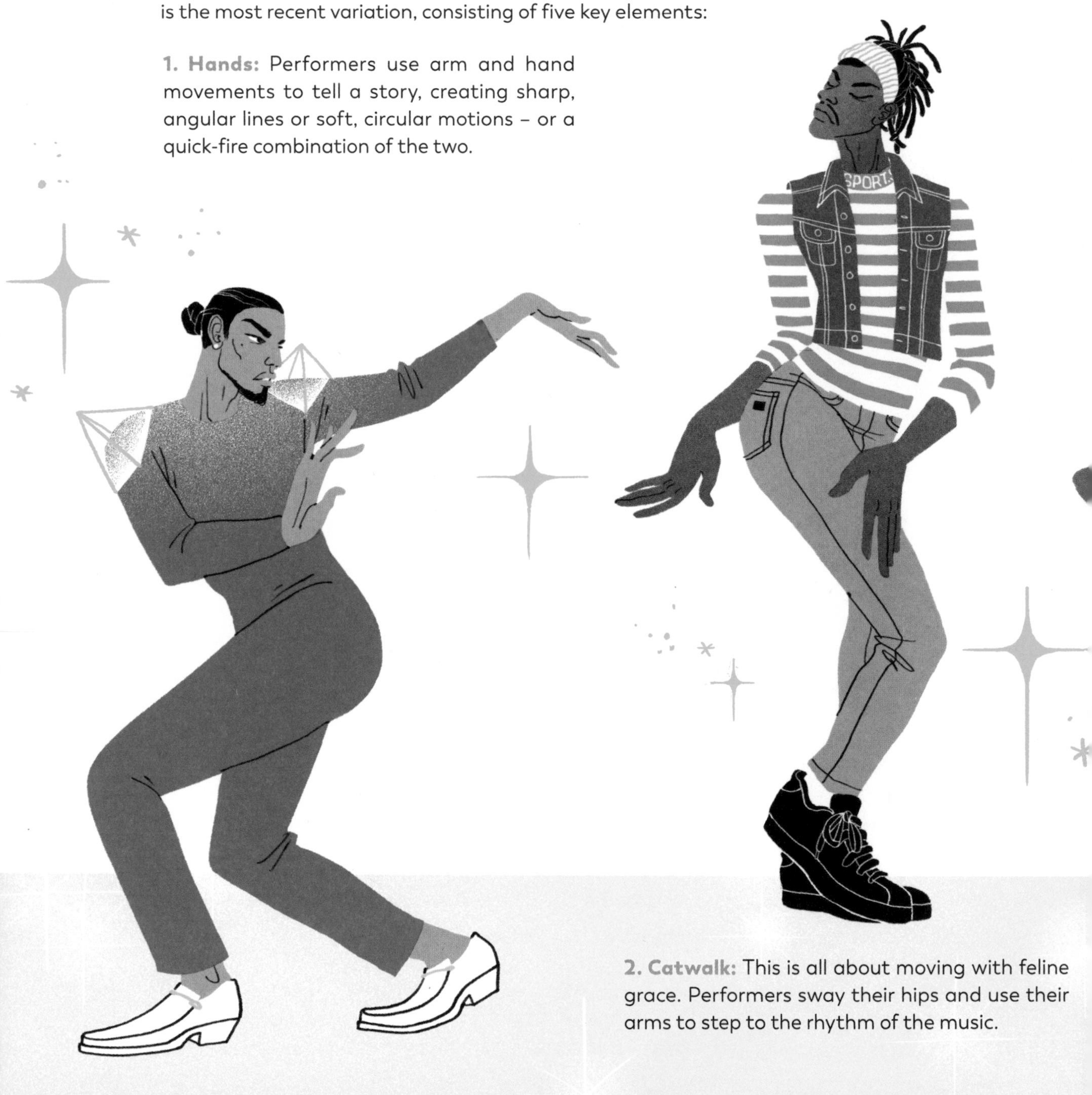
SPORTS

2. Catwalk: This is all about moving with feline grace. Performers sway their hips and use their arms to step to the rhythm of the music.

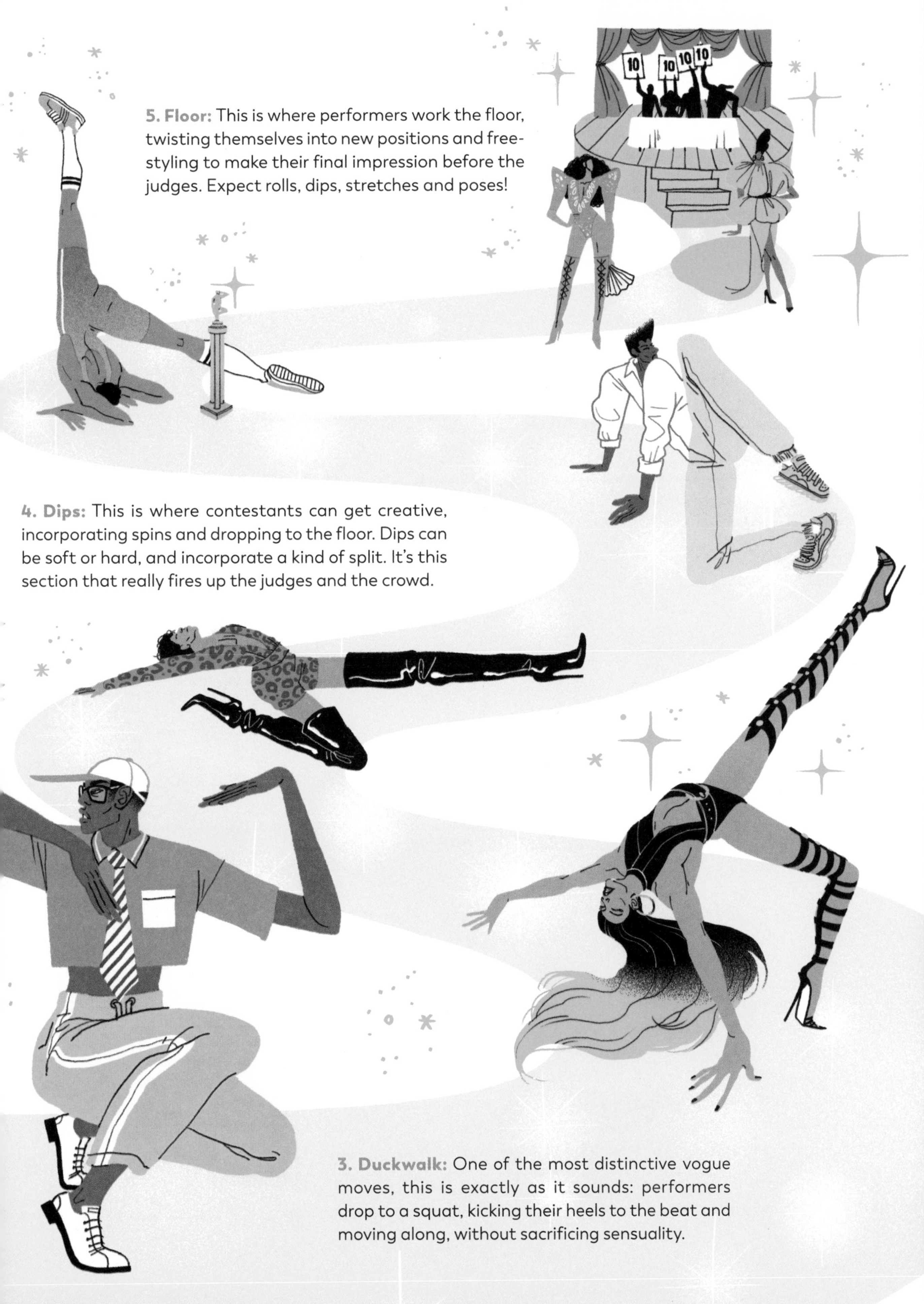
10
10
10
10

5. Floor: This is where performers work the floor, twisting themselves into new positions and free-styling to make their final impression before the judges. Expect rolls, dips, stretches and poses!

4. Dips: This is where contestants can get creative, incorporating spins and dropping to the floor. Dips can be soft or hard, and incorporate a kind of split. It's this section that really fires up the judges and the crowd.

3. Duckwalk: One of the most distinctive vogue moves, this is exactly as it sounds: performers drop to a squat, kicking their heels to the beat and moving along, without sacrificing sensuality.

RUPAUL

RuPaul is arguably the world's most famous drag queen. Born and raised in San Diego, Ru fled to Atlanta at fifteen years old, where he struggled to make a living first as a musician and then a filmmaker. As the years went by, Ru found his calling: drag.

His earliest attempts were gloriously, deliberately messy – Ru's aesthetic was part confrontational, part tongue-in-cheek. This changed in the early 1990s when, after years of wild punk looks, Ru dug out a platinum blonde wig for his most famous character: the six-foot-tall 'glamazon', as seen in the music video for his 1992 breakout hit 'Supermodel', an infectious house track. With this pedigree, it's unsurprising that designers like Jean Paul Gaultier and Thierry Mugler have cast him to walk in their shows.

Within months of 'Supermodel', RuPaul was walking the red carpet at the MTV Video Music Awards. He would go on to make memorable cameos on shows like *Sabrina, The Teenage Witch*, and in 1996 he was given his own talk show, *The RuPaul Show*. Now, he's best-known as the creator of the hit reality show *RuPaul's Drag Race* (see p. 103), which borrowed from shows like *America's Next Top Model* to find 'the next drag superstar'. In 1994, MAC launched its first ever Viva Glam lipstick with RuPaul as its ambassador, kickstarting an initiative which has since raised more than $500 million for HIV research.

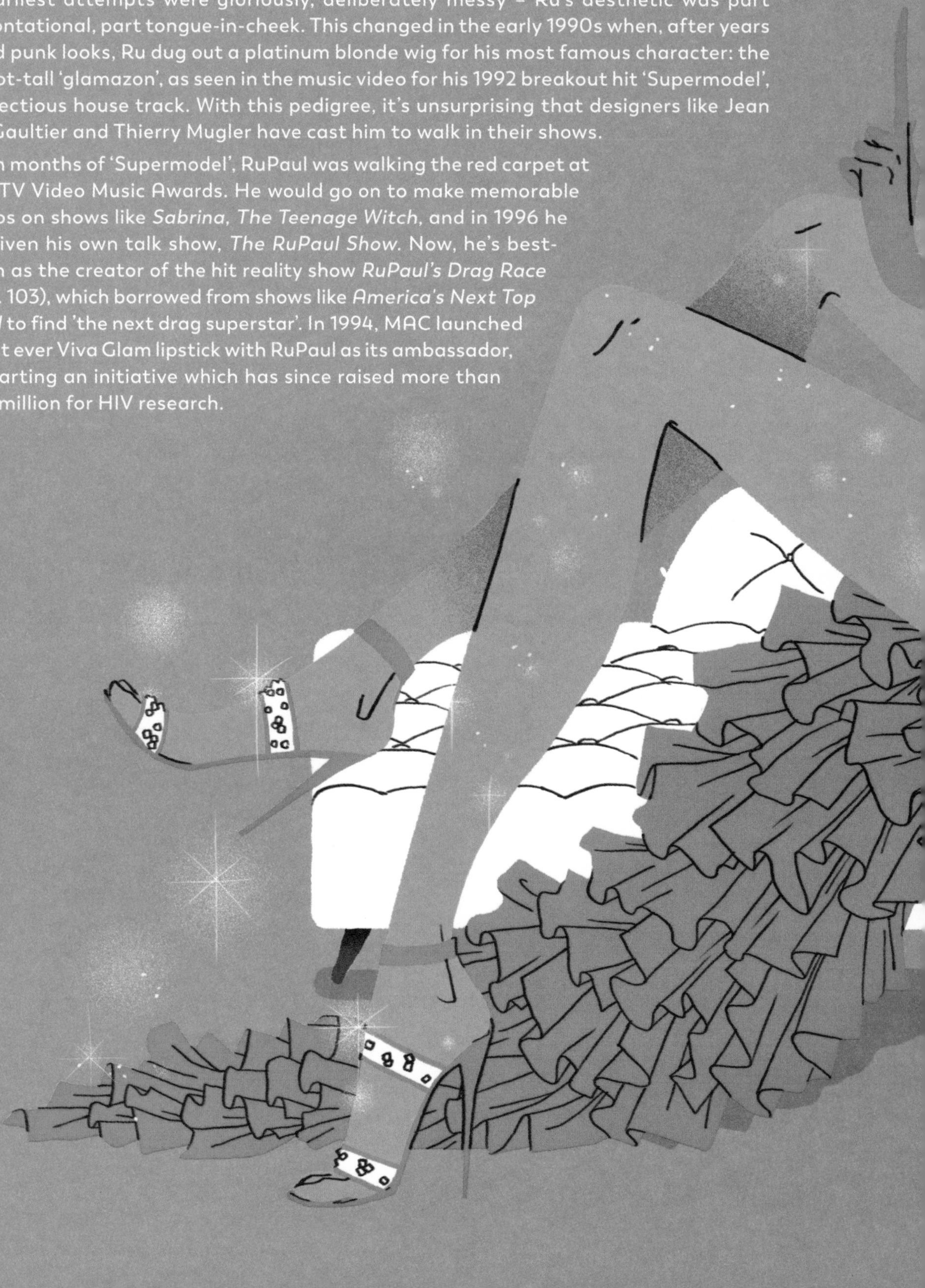

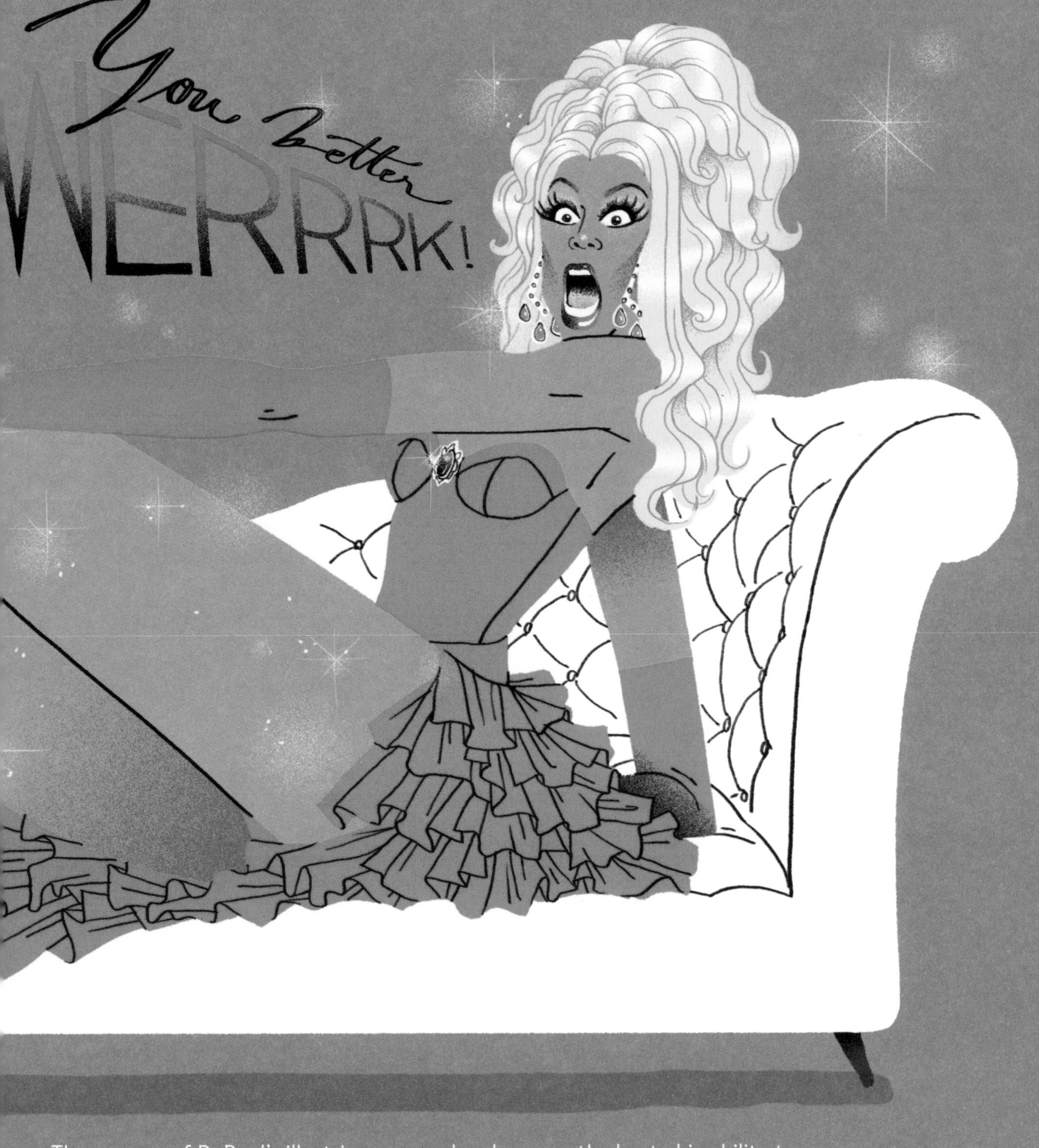
You better
WERRRK!

The success of RuPaul's illustrious career has been partly due to his ability to engage with his audience. He gave guests drag makeovers on the *Ricki Lake Show* and distilled academic queer theory into accessible catchphrases such as "We're all born naked and the rest is drag", which alludes to the idea that we all 'drag up' on a daily basis using clothes, make-up and mannerisms. With his charm, humour and message of self-love, RuPaul brought drag as we know it now to a global audience, making him a poster child for drag queens everywhere.

LADY BUNNY & WIGSTOCK

In 1984, bored of nightclubs and desperate for new distractions, drag queen Lady Bunny and a group of her friends traipsed over to New York's Tompkins Square Park with crates of beer in hand. As the alcohol flowed and the night wore on, they gradually came up with an idea: to create Wigstock, the world's first day-long drag festival. Twelve months later, Bunny was cutting the metaphorical ribbon and welcoming the world into her fabulously zany brainchild.

Bunny curated a line-up of performers who ranged from the iconic to the avant-garde, proving her reputation as one of New York's best-connected queens. For the first time, drag artists nationwide could show off their most extravagant outfits during the day without fear of harassment. The first festival's anti-capitalist, punk ethos attracted around a thousand attendees, which only swelled over the years. Wigstock's legendary status was cemented with the release of a documentary in 1995.

Although it seemed the festival had run its course by 2001, this wasn't to be the case. Bunny remained hugely popular as a cult drag legend and in 2018, there was a Wigstock revival. This spawned the 2019 documentary *Wig*, a thorough retelling of the festival's history, littered with previously unseen footage.

Even from this heightened platform, Bunny remains true to drag's DIY origins. At the 2018 Wigstock, she boldly proclaimed to the crowd: "Baby, look at me. Listen to my foul mouth. Do you think I'm ever going to go mainstream?"

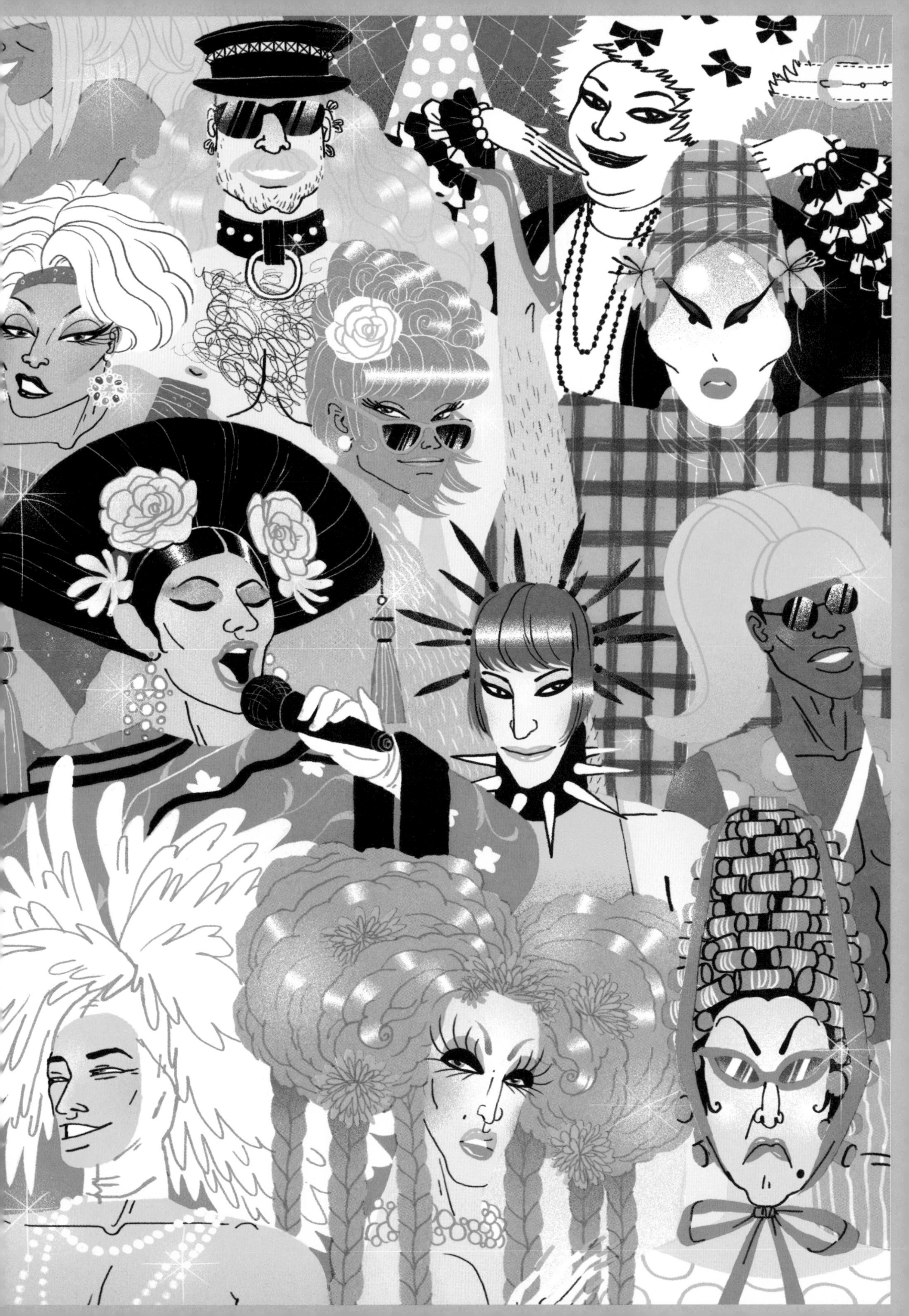

VISUAL KEI

Glam rockers have never been afraid to experiment with their style. This is no different in Japan, where 'visual kei' – a rock genre defined by androgyny – continues to thrive. The earliest pioneers were 1980s bands like Buck-Tick, XJAPAN and Malice Mizer (pictured), who teamed often effeminate, Victoriana clothes with heavy black eye make-up and enough hairspray to penetrate the ozone layer. Throw in a sprinkle of Lolita-style ruffles and you have the recipe for one of Japan's most enduring styles.

Similar to Bowie or Prince, '80s visual kei artists gravitated towards femininity and wholly embraced a New Romantic style, wearing frills and elaborate, gothic looks. Whether or not this can be classed as drag is debatable but these artists were undeniably creating new definitions of masculinity. The movement remains popular today, thanks to acts like Mana (centre), Kaya and Versailles – commonly referred to as bishonen, "beautiful youths" – attracting international fans with their off-kilter brand of romantic androgyny.

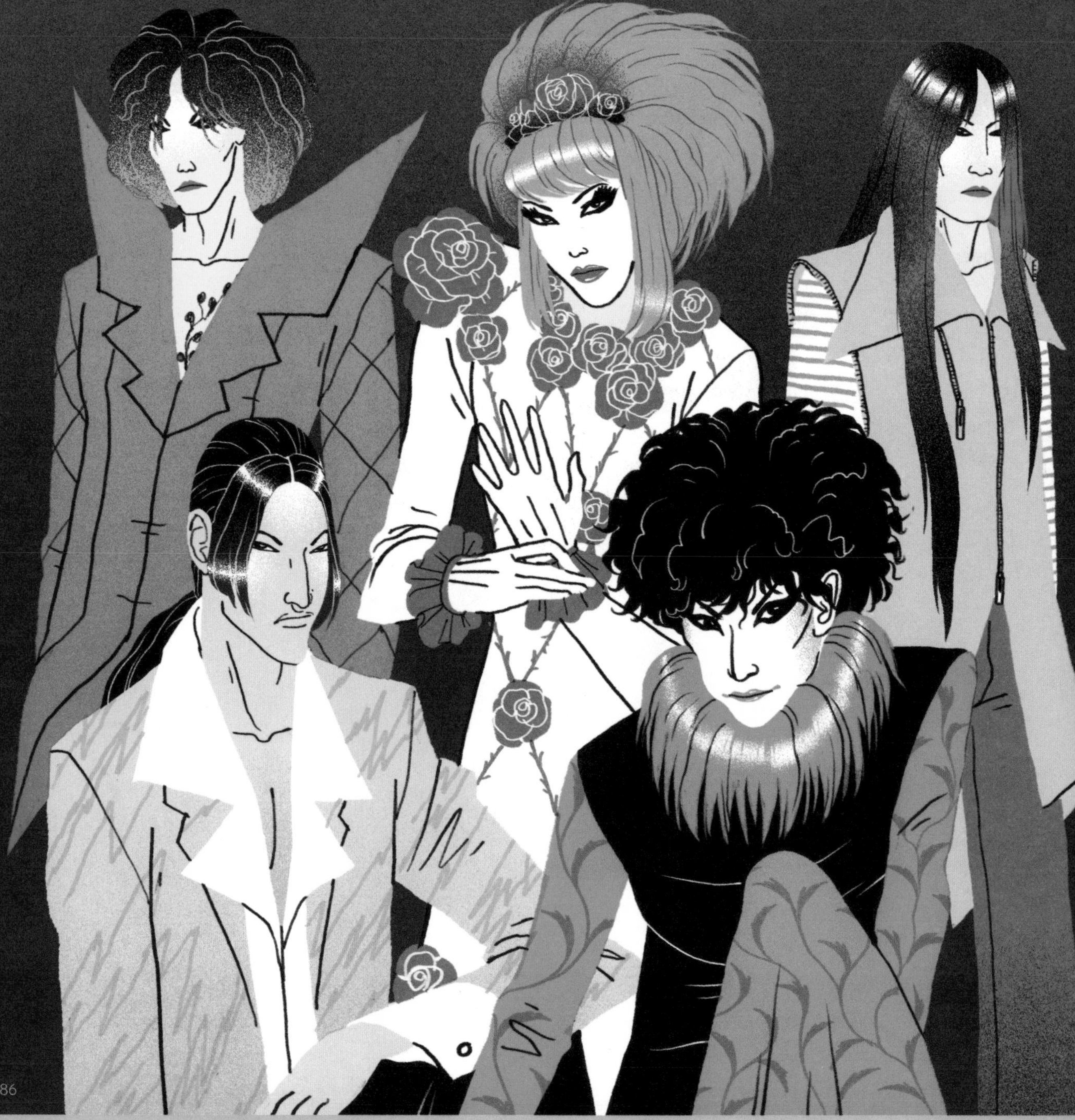

MISS TIFFANY'S UNIVERSE

In July of each year, hundreds of transgender women descend upon the picturesque coastal city of Pattaya, Thailand. Their annual pilgrimage is to attend Miss Tiffany's Universe, a beauty pageant dedicated to celebrating the beauty of trans women, promoting Thailand's culture of trangender acceptance and raising vital funds for humanitarian causes.

When the pageant first launched back in 1984, trans showgirls were commonly mistaken for sex workers and subsequently targeted by authorities. They had often been sidelined or fetishised; Miss Tiffany's Universe sought to counter this, adopting the conventional pageant format to put these women front and centre.

Like all pageants, the competition encourages the kind of hyper-glamorous femininity that enraptures audiences. But when combined with emotional backstories and an activist slant, this beauty contest becomes so much more: it's about creating resilient, charismatic spokeswomen who just happen to look breathtaking in a ballgown.

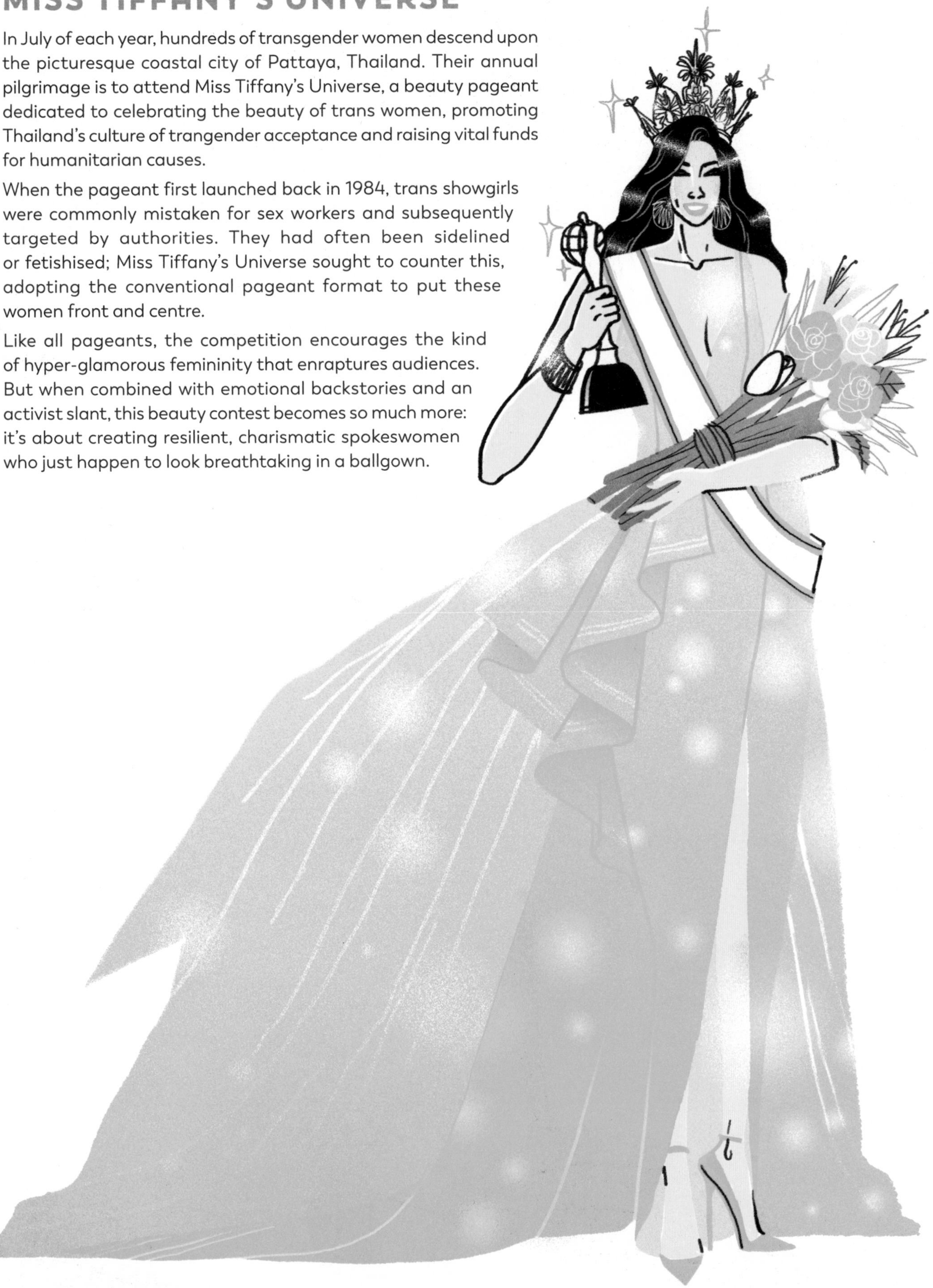

THE LEGEND OF LIP-SYNC

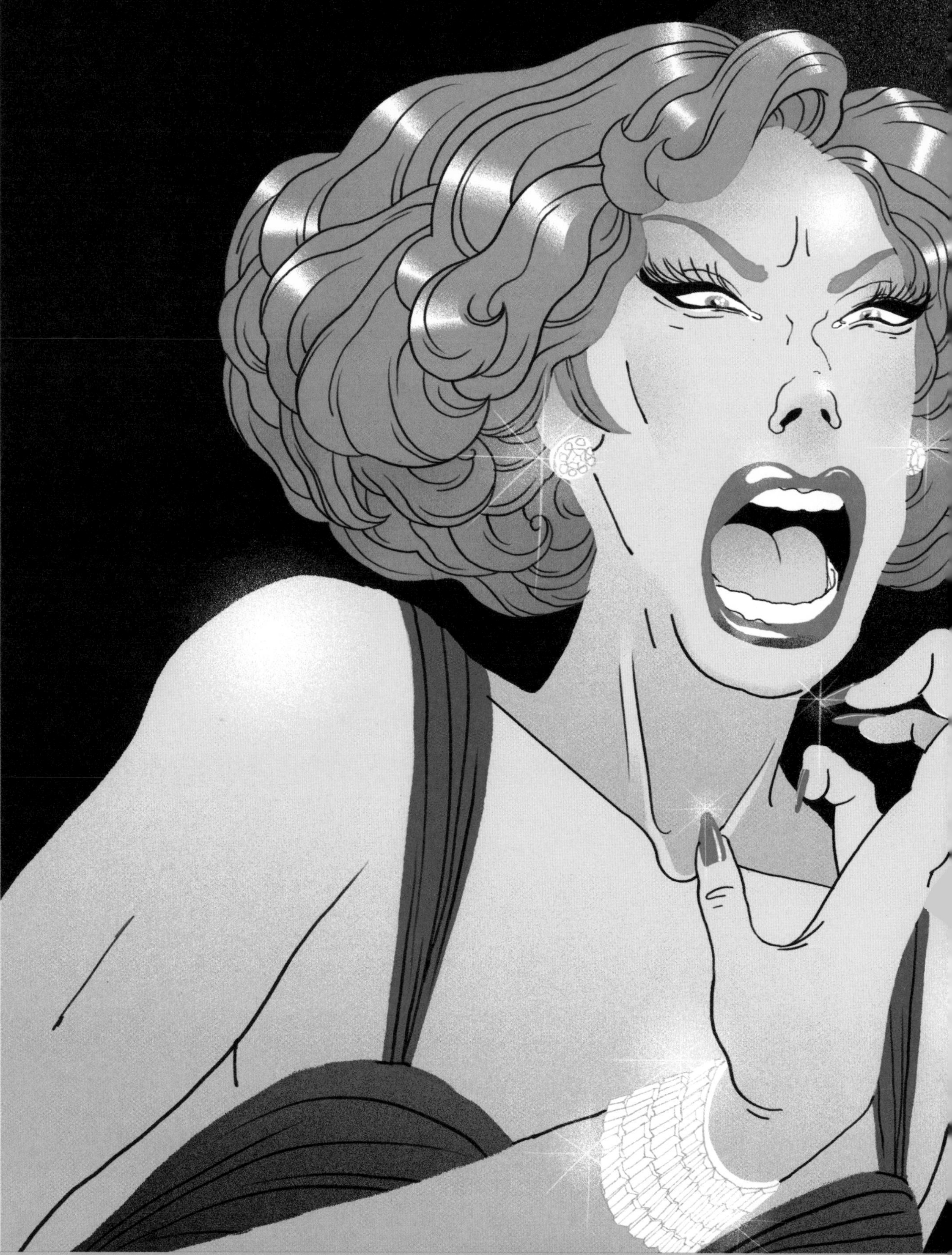

In reality show *RuPaul's Drag Race*, the two worst-performing queens each week are asked to 'lip-sync for their lives', performing iconic queer anthems while mouthing the lyrics. The show bills this as the main event; a drag staple. But when did lip-sync become such an integral part of the culture?

ORAL ORIGINS

Until the mid-20th century, drag artists would typically sing live while performing. This began to change with the increased availability of jukeboxes and portable record players and for another, obvious reason: not all queens can sing. Flat vocals can ruin even the most convincing impersonation, so a series of 'record acts' turned lip-sync into their trademark. This created a kind of drag hierarchy – the accessibility of lip-sync led to record acts being stereotyped as street queens, often disrespected or looked down upon by their more seasoned, vocally-talented counterparts.

However, lip-sync allowed performers to more convincingly impersonate their idols. Drag queens across the USA in particular began bringing their own records to gigs, unleashing carefully rehearsed tributes to spellbound crowds. As time went by, these lip-sync artists, initially written off as low-skilled performers and paid accordingly, started to gain respect.

LYPSINKA

John Epperson – better known as 'Lypsinka' – is widely credited for elevating the art of lip-syncing to new heights. His acts were choreographed around witty, old-school film monologues delivered by glamorous, charismatic women and often featured the kind of audio collages that are now commonplace in drag performances. Telephone conversations became his signature; he could switch at the blink of an eye from conversation to song, all the while wrapping his mouth around the syllables and darting his eyes manically.

Before long, Lypsinka captured the attention of French designer and couturier Thierry Mugler, who asked him to perform in spectacular couture shows no fewer than three times throughout the 1990s. The affiliation with high fashion is fitting: Epperson chose the name Lypsinka after becoming fascinated by the one-word names of 1960s supermodels like Twiggy and Veruschka.

Arguably the most famous Lypsinka performance came in 1992 at Mugler's Los Angeles show, where Epperson performed in a curled red wig, ripping away outfit on top of outfit, revealing layers to the performance in more ways than one. The grandiose routine, performed on such a global stage, is still regarded as one of the best lip-syncs in history. While Epperson prefers to be called a 'surrealist' rather than a drag queen, Lypsinka has now undeniably shaped drag culture in his own glamorous image.

CLUB KIDS

Throughout the 1980s and 1990s came 'genderfuck' drag. As the name suggests, this radical brand of drag throws out gender norms completely by deliberately clashing 'masculine' and 'feminine' looks, topping them off with elements of the monstrous or otherworldly. Its popularity was driven in no small part by New York's club kids. These young, fashion-savvy artists used extreme costumes, outlandish face paint and prosthetics to create looks which were barely human, let alone gendered. In their eyes, nightclub dancefloors were their own private runways.

Word spread quickly, and soon the club kids found themselves the main attractions of the city's most popular venues. Club owners began paying these fabulous freaks to host nights, while chat show hosts sought out the flamboyant, self-described 'weirdos' as guests. Club kids fast became a cultural phenomenon, but there was a dark side to the party culture.

The chaos of the New York scene was recreated in the film *Party Monster* (2003), based on an autobiography by club kid leader James St. James (far right). He spoke candidly about the rise and fall of his friend Michel Alig, who made global headlines for the murder of Angel Melendez. Stories of drug addiction and violence soon trickled out, yet the club kids' hedonistic embrace of excess still inspires designers and drag artists today.

LEIGH BOWERY

Legendary club kid Leigh Bowery (bottom right) is considered the most iconic and experimental of any club kid worldwide. His signature performance saw him simulate giving birth to his 'wife' (their marriage was thought to be performance art), a scene decorated liberally with sausages – a makeshift umbilical cord – and fake blood. Aesthetically, his shaven head became a trademark: along with his face, he often covered it with elaborate, painted patterns. Even his body became artistic material, with folds of flesh and fat taped and pinned into new configurations.

Bowery's legacy has lived on since his death in 1994. Creatives from Lady Gaga to Vivienne Westwood have paid tribute to the artist, whose looks were as conceptual as they were political. His famous 'dot-painted' face is said to mimic the facial lesions of Kaposi's sarcoma, a cancer which disproportionately affected AIDS victims during the crisis. In Bowery's eyes, pain, hedonism and his outsiderness were all creative inspirations. It's this unique outlook that keeps his influence alive today.

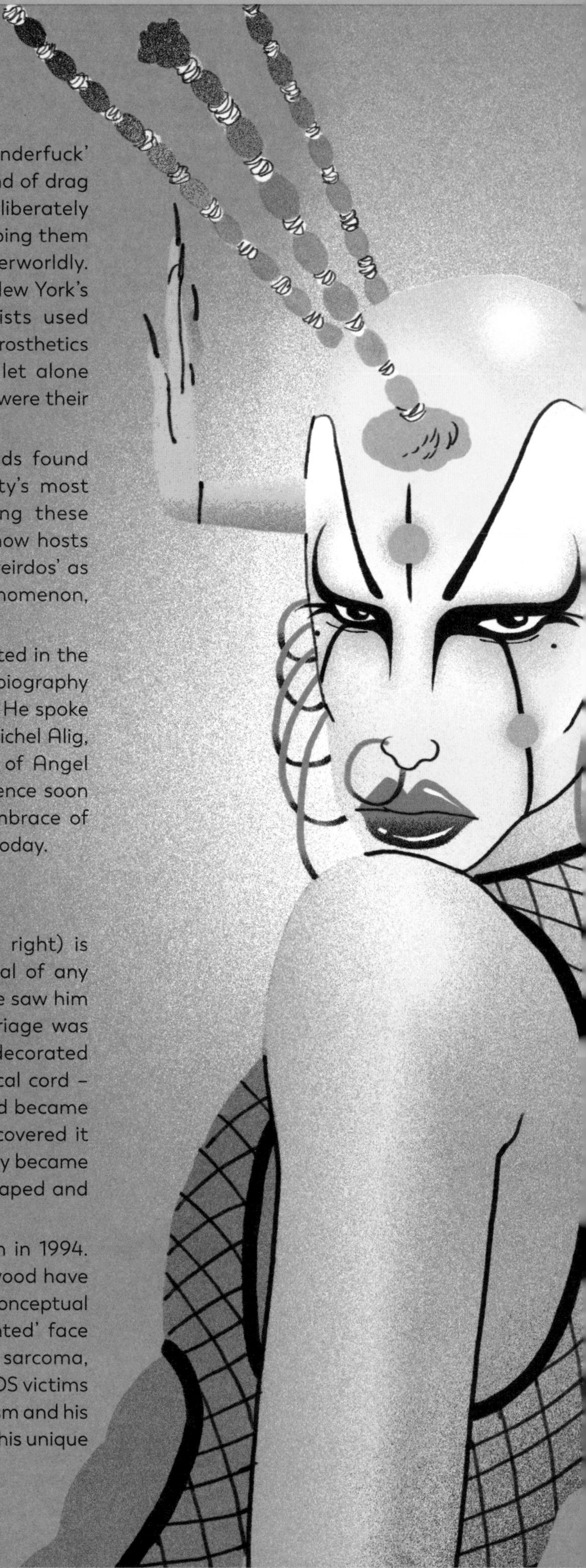

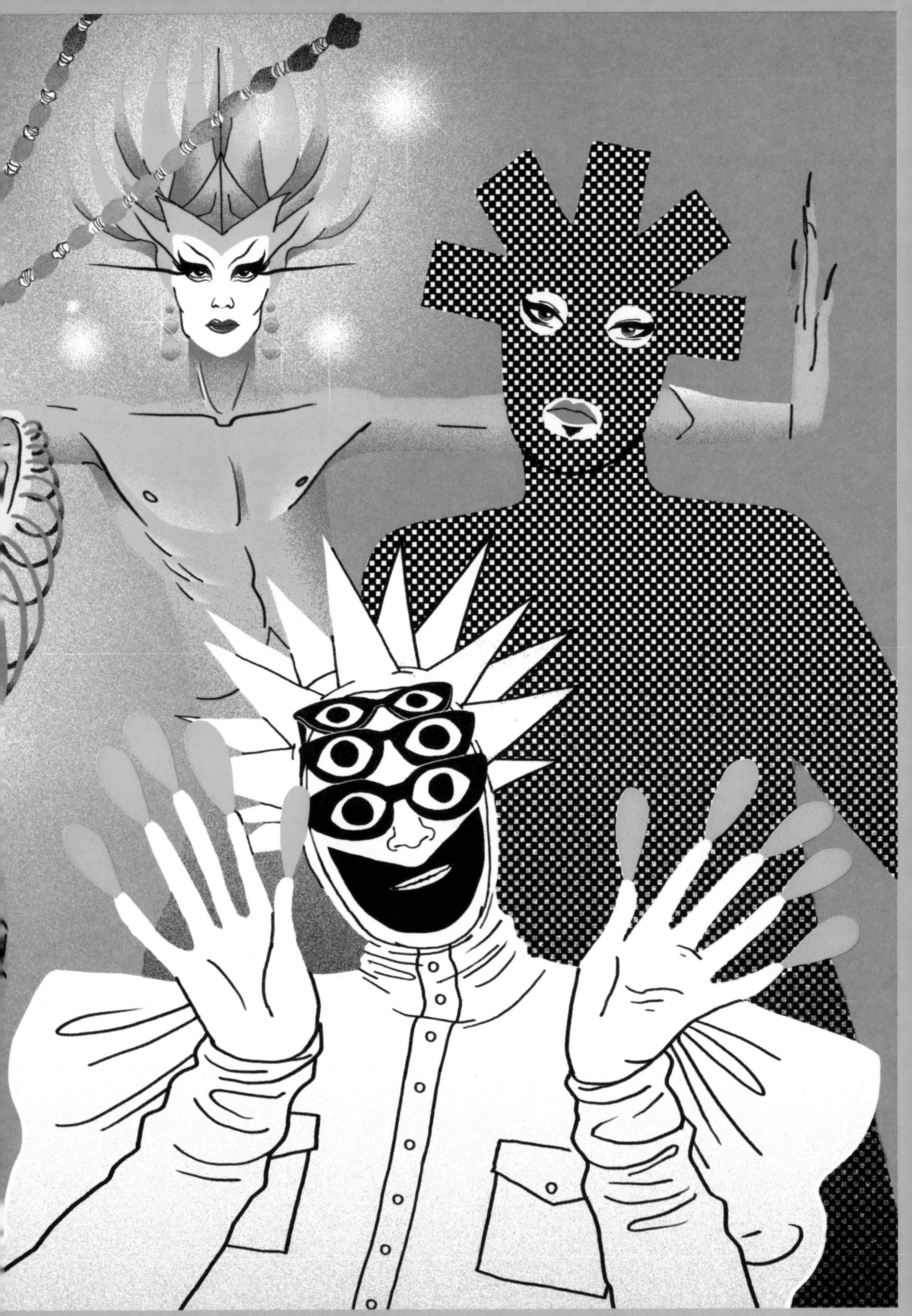

AMANDA LEPORE & DAVID LACHAPELLE

Amanda Lepore was working as a dominatrix in a New York S&M club on the night that changed her life. Despite having already earned a name for herself as a glamorous club kid and, in her own words, "the world's most famous transsexual", it wasn't until she met legendary fashion photographer David LaChapelle that she was catapulted into the spotlight, birthing an influential creative partnership. Of course, Amanda was already well-known in her own right, with a string of chat show appearances throughout the 1980s under her garter belt. With her impossible proportions, bee-stung lips and carefully coiled blonde hair, she was cartoon perfection – the pin-up in a sea of club kids. It was only a matter of time before she became a muse.

Together, Lepore and LaChapelle created art: in one image, Amanda became a hyper-saturated, exaggerated replica of Warhol's Marilyn Monroe; in another, a naked blonde starlet hoovering up diamonds like cocaine from an upturned mirror. Through projects for high-profile magazines and brands, most famously MAC and Absolut, the duo took Amanda's unique beauty to an international audience.

Along the way, she has spoken candidly about undergoing gender affirmation surgery on prime-time television shows and raised awareness of what it meant to be a transgender woman in an era when transgender visibility was the exception, not the rule. Amanda readily acknowledges that trans women can do drag, but her appeal transcends labels. Her blend of hyper-femininity and infectious charisma, combined with maximalist glamour, make her a drag icon in her own right.

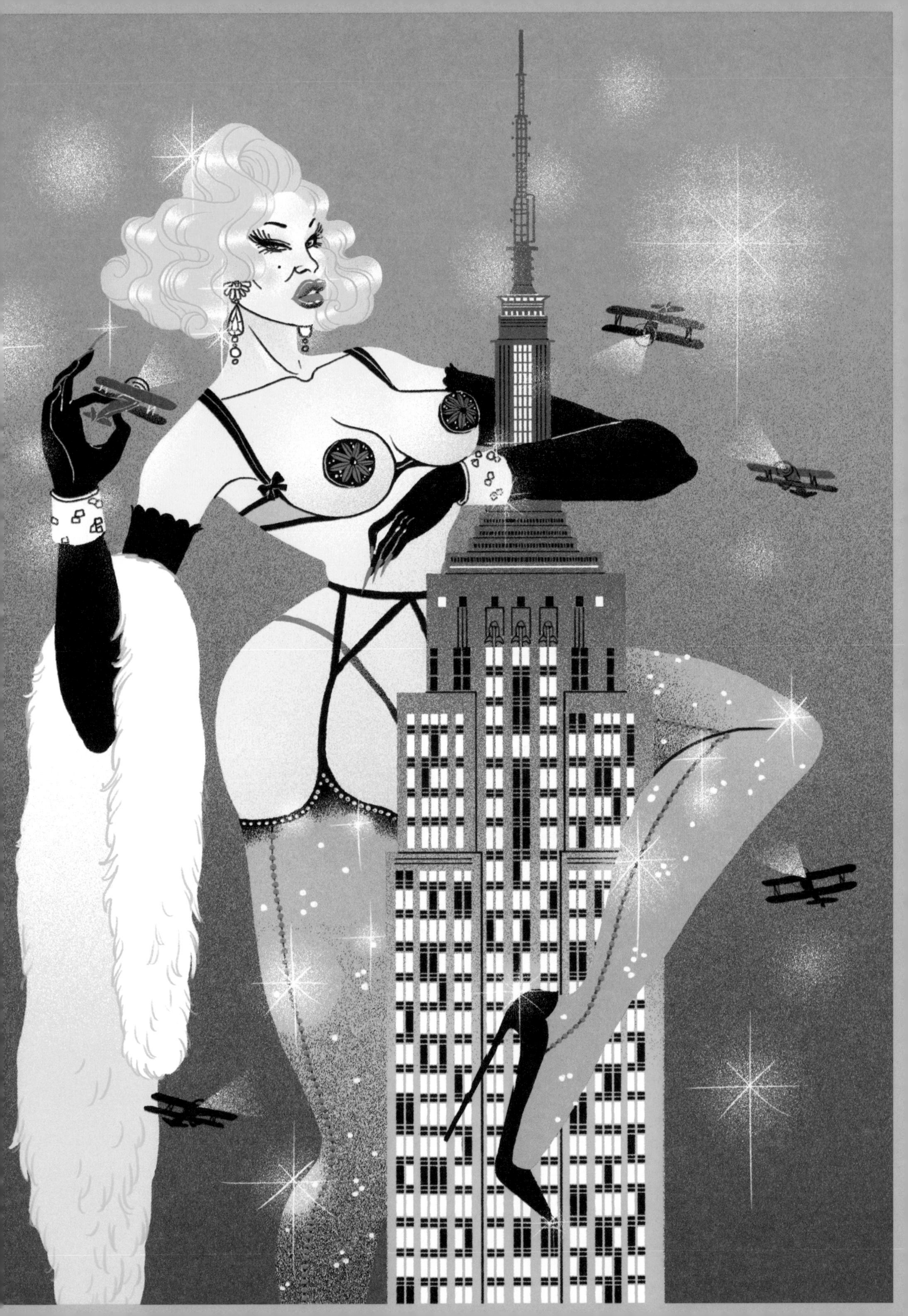

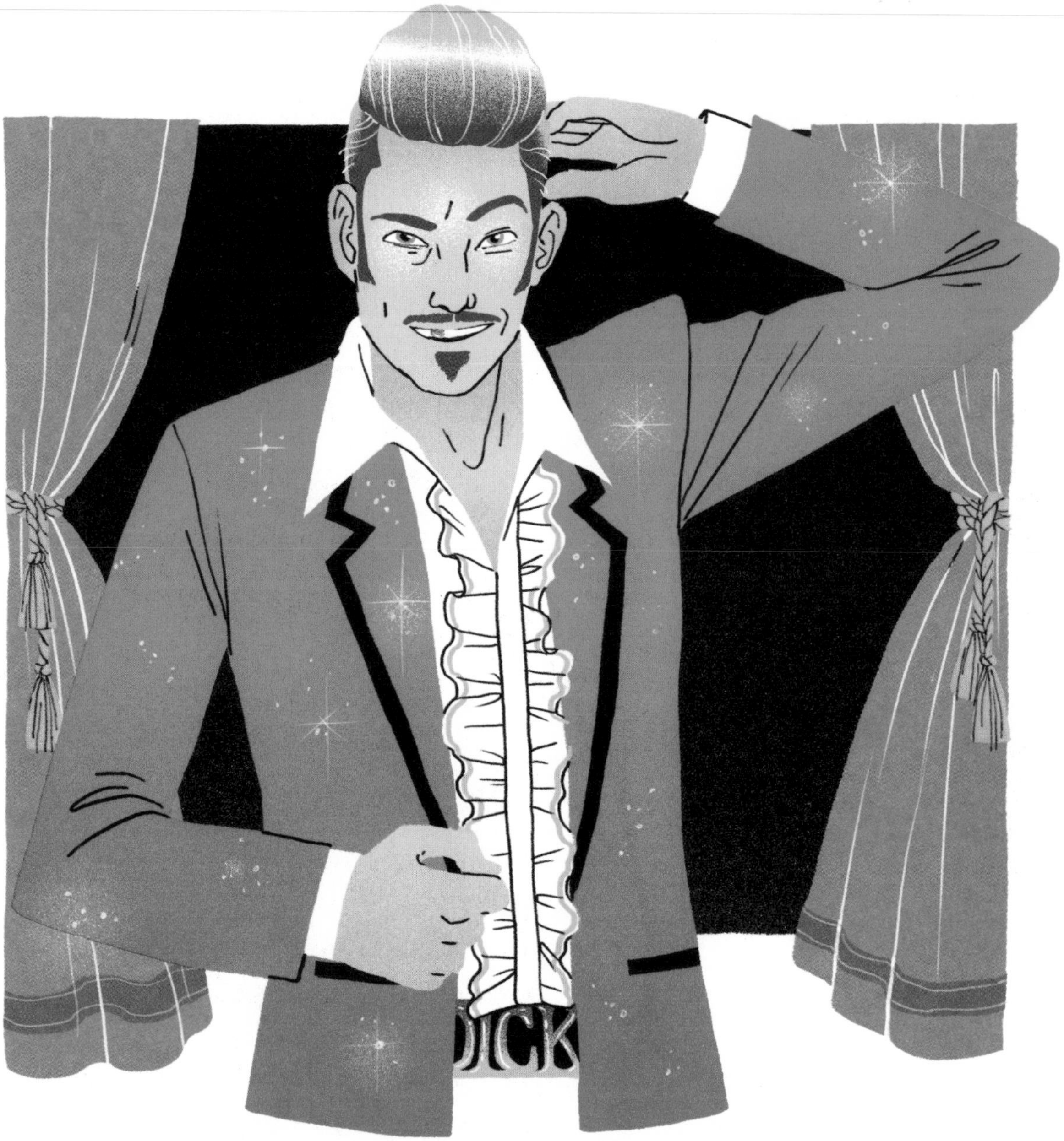
DICK

MO B. DICK & CLUB CASANOVA

The mainstream visibility of drag queens soared throughout the 1990s, but drag aficionados still had to scour underground scenes to find drag kings. Perhaps in response to this lack of visibility, Mo Fischer – otherwise known as Mo B. Dick – founded Club Casanova, the world's first weekly drag king party, in 1995.

Held in clubs across Manhattan, New York, Club Casanova showcased talented performers like Murray Hill, Diane Torr and Dréd, some of whom starred in the groundbreaking documentary *Venus Boyz*, which features scenes of the action at Casanova. At the helm was Mo B. Dick himself, whose distinctive aesthetic of sharp suits, a gold tooth and signature pompadour won over the likes of cult filmmaker John Waters, who cast Fischer in his 1998 film *Pecker*.

At the same time, trouble was brewing. Then-mayor Rudy Giuliani – or Ghouliani, as he was known by locals – revived an archaic law against dancing, which led to regular visits from the police. In December 1997, Fischer chose to shutter the night and embark on a series of successful Casanova tours, sparking a mid-90s drag king revolution.

EXPERIMENTAL QUEER THEATRE

In the more avant-garde nooks of 1990s queer culture, theatre performers were making groundbreaking work on their own terms. Just as drag artists pushed beyond the gender binary with genderfuck, and activists reclaimed the word queer to mean 'radical and disruptive', the world of theatre saw a shift towards a more avant-garde approach to telling queer stories.

Tony Kushner debuted his two-part epic *Angels in America* in 1991, a complicated story of a gay couple in Manhattan trying to navigate the devastating AIDS crisis. The play sent a strong political statement by cutting through AIDS stigma to expose the racism and homophobia at its heart.

Then there was Ethyl Eichelberger, an underground drag icon determined to retell theatre history through a queer lens. From *Hamlet* to *King Lear*, no classics were off-limits. Eichelberger played both male and female roles, from sleepy villager Rip Van Winkle to Lucrezia Borgia, a Renaissance-era noblewoman cast often – and perhaps innacurately – as a femme fatale. These characters populated Eichelberger's zany, politically charged universe, which relied on a number of impressive tricks such as acrobatics, fire-breathing and even accordion solos.

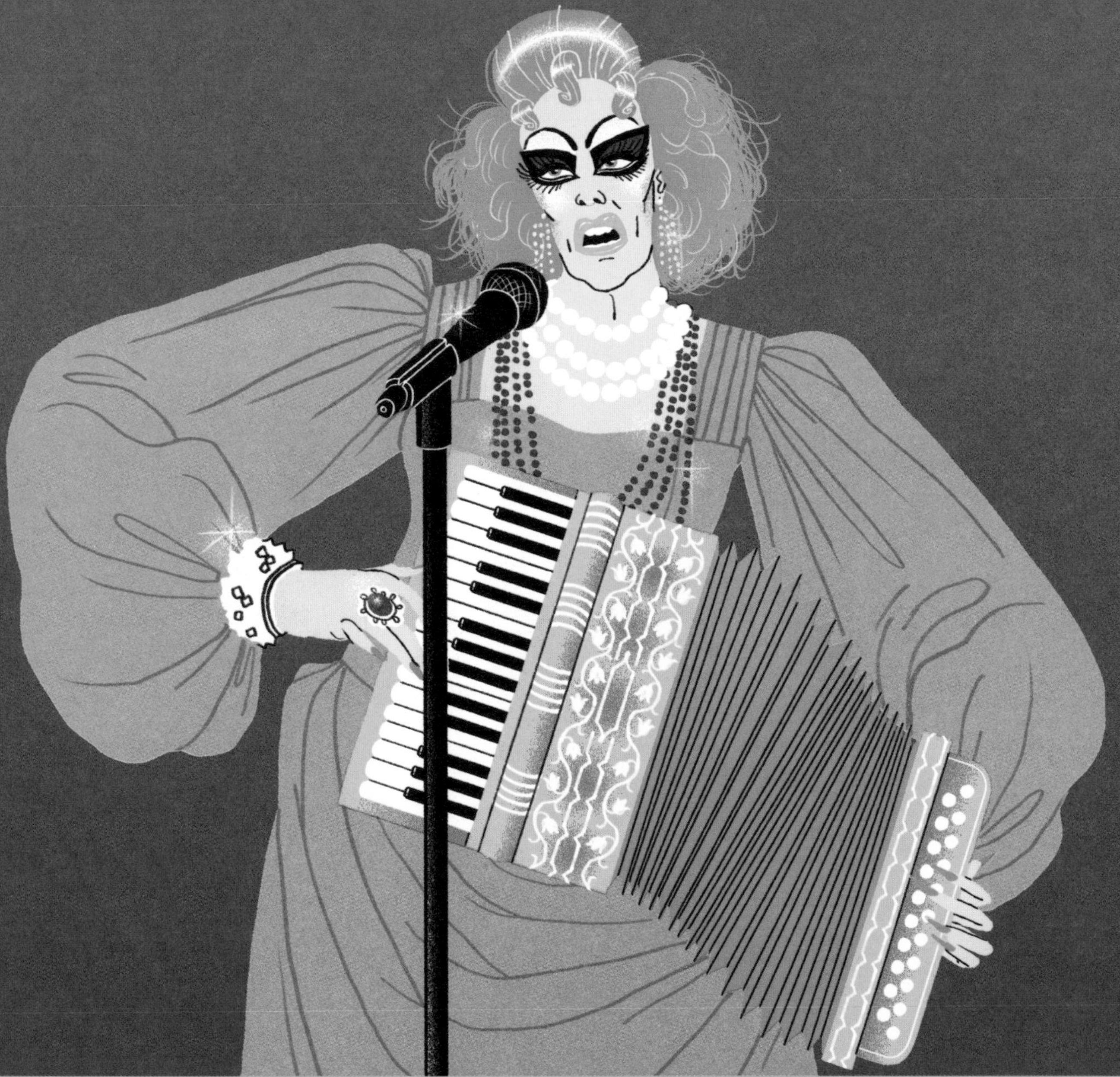

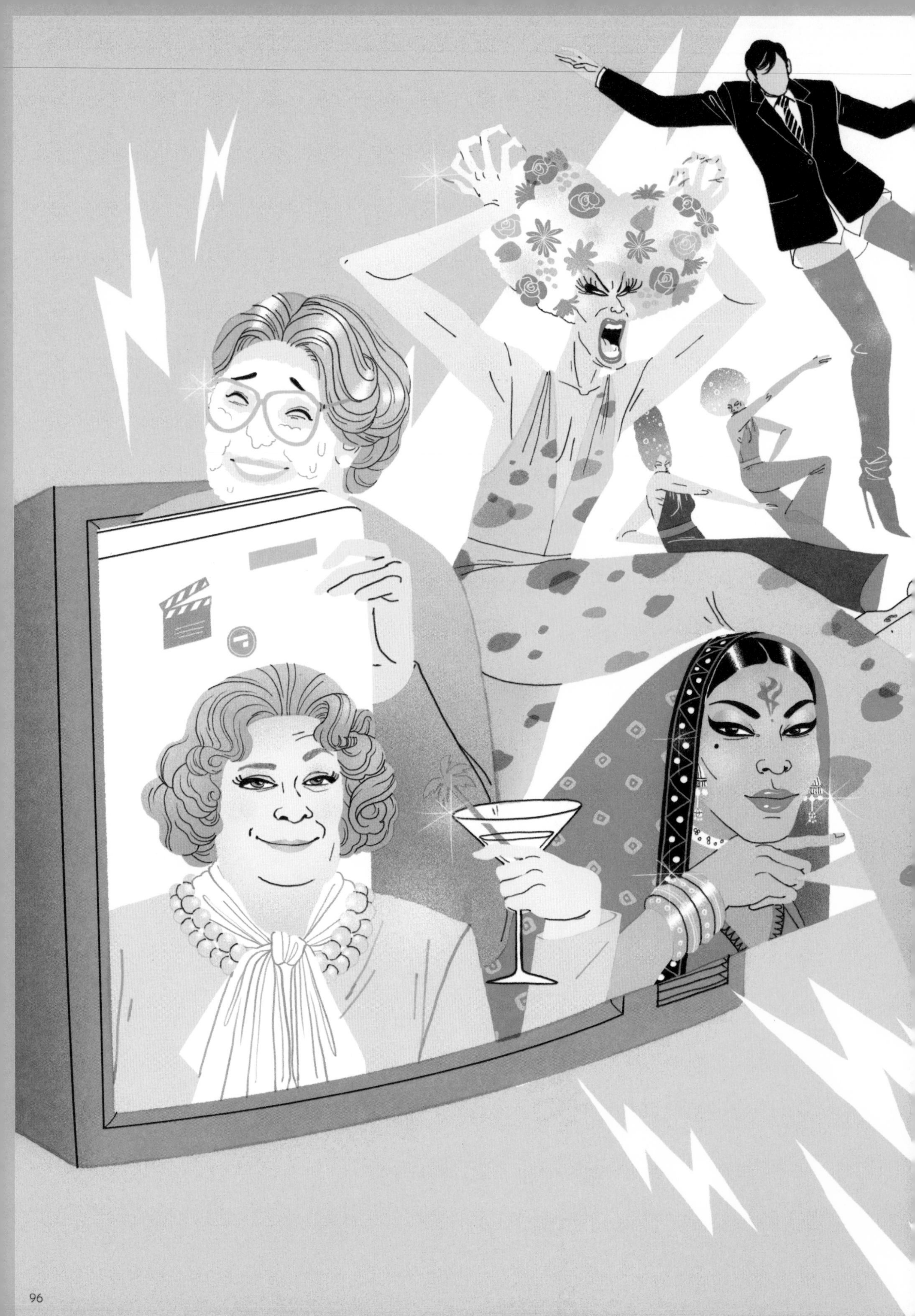

DRAG AT THE MOVIES

As the popularity of drag increased, film studios became unable to ignore the phenomenon – and unable to keep rehashing the same clichéd portrayals of drag artists. As a result, the 1990s saw a wave of more nuanced on-screen depictions of drag.

MRS DOUBTFIRE (1993)

With Robin Williams in the title role, this heartwarming comedy put a new spin on the trope of drag as disguise. By tapping into his feminine side, an unreliable father patches up a messy custody battle, creating one of film history's most loveable drag matriarchs in the process.

THE ADVENTURES OF PRISCILLA, QUEEN OF THE DESERT (1994)

Drag queens cracking lewd jokes on an action-packed desert road trip – what more could you want? With its sharp humour and sensitive portrayals of homophobia and transphobia, this surprise hit teamed camp comedy with real issues to achieve worldwide success.

TO WONG FOO, THANKS FOR EVERYTHING! JULIE NEWMAR (1995)

This film made a huge splash by feminising muscle men Wesley Snipes and Patrick Swayze, who adopt their own 'drag daughter'. Naturally, hilarity ensues, but the film's resounding message of unity and acceptance has done wonders for drag representation.

THE BIRDCAGE (1996)

This story of a gay nightclub owner whose son falls in love with the daughter of an ultra-conservative politician proved to be timely – by the time of its release, Mayor Giuliani was decimating New York nightlife. A light-hearted exploration of political conflict, *The Birdcage* sees a straight-laced family warm up to the idea of drag.

KINKY BOOTS (2005)

An unlikely international hit, *Kinky Boots* tells the story of a struggling shoe factory owner who teams up with a charismatic drag queen called Lola to save his business. What starts as a solution to financial difficulty becomes a journey of acceptance – which ends with Lola's iconic rendition of 'These Boots Are Made For Walkin''.

THE PINK MIRROR (2006)

Despite attempts at censorship, Indian director Sridhar Rangayan released his award-winning film *The Pink Mirror*, acclaimed for its sensitive portrayals of queer and transgender characters. The film explores the still-stigmatised subject of HIV through a tender, considerate lens.

THE ART OF

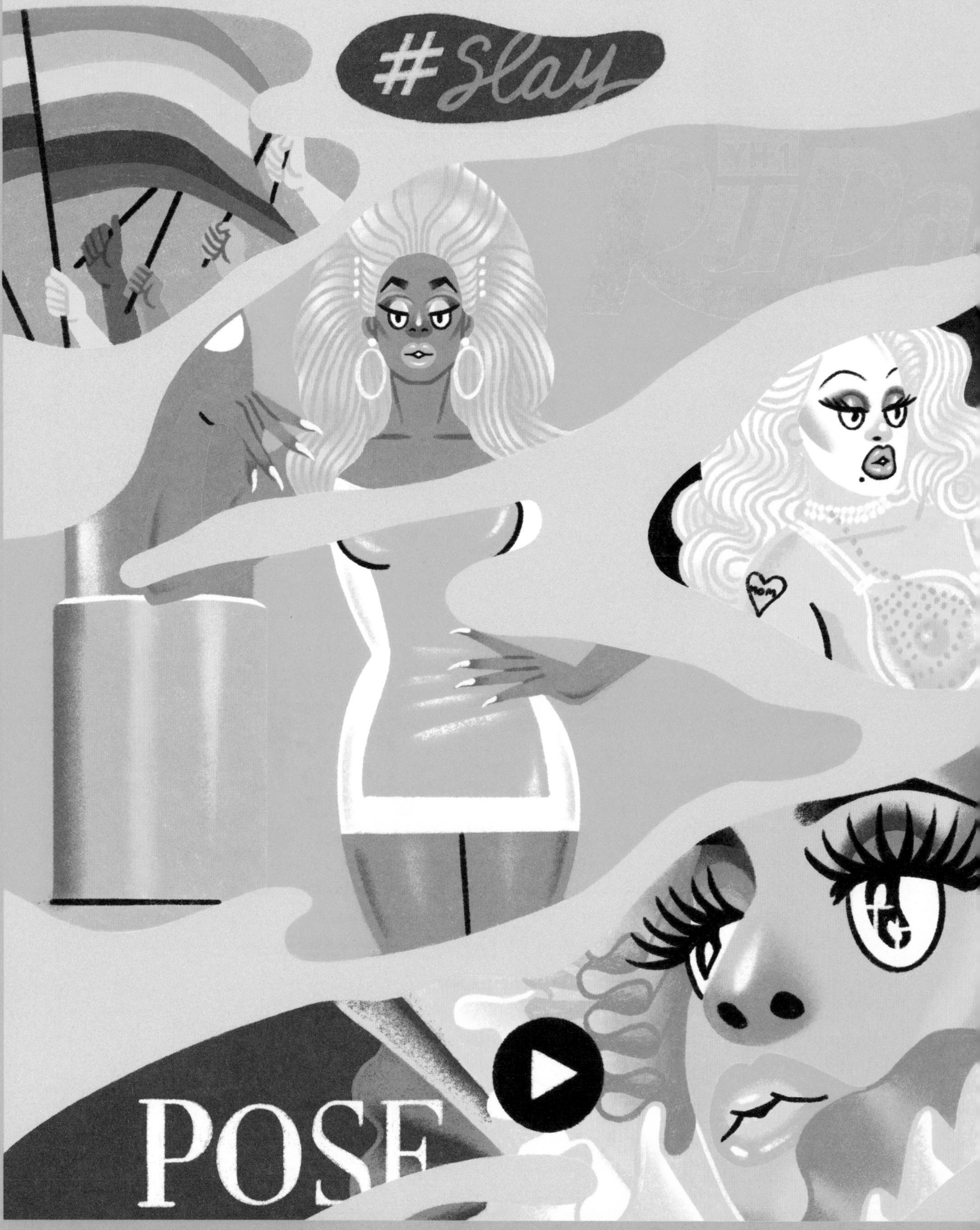
#Slay
MOM
POSE

INFLUENCE

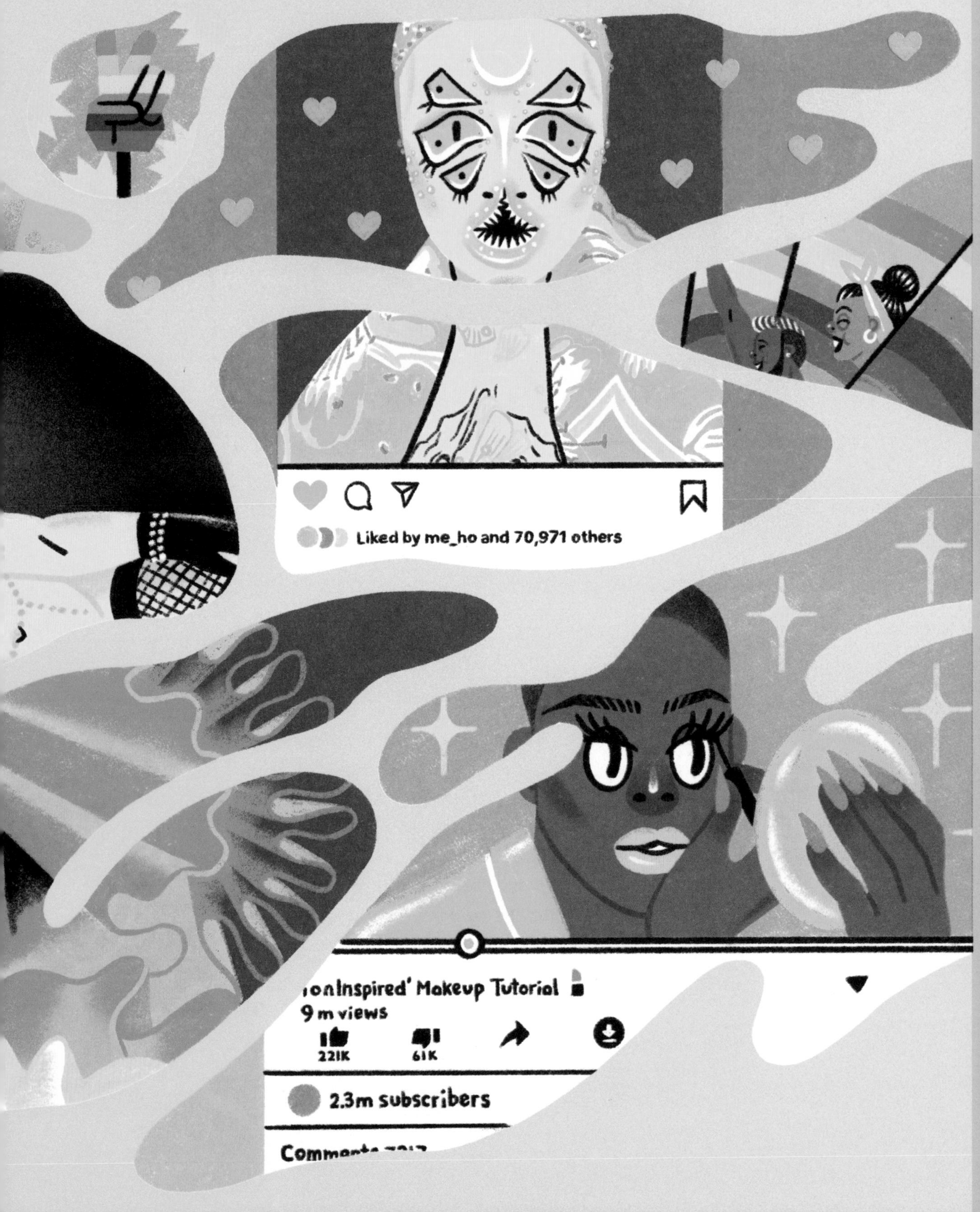

Liked by me_ho and 70,971 others
onInspired' Makeup Tutorial
9 m views
221K
61K
2.3m subscribers

2000s-2010s

There was a time that drag artists were only seen in nightclubs or brief television cameos. But things have changed rapidly and irreversibly over the last decade. Thanks to the rise of *RuPaul's Drag Race*, social media, and a growing number of celebrity fans, drag has become more influential than ever.

Although still subversive at its heart, drag has seeped into mainstream culture. Not only do drag queens have prime slots in music videos, ad campaigns and corporate parties, a handful of muses work closely with designers and make-up artists to shape cultural standards in a way that once seemed impossible. Shows like *Pose* have brought the Harlem ballroom scene to an international audience; elsewhere, the rise of video-sharing platforms has brought classic documentaries to new, younger viewers and given local queens a platform to showcase their talents.

This rise in popularity has also led to debate. Drag is arguably more commercial than ever – too commercial for some – but this substantial increase in visibility has helped to advance LGBTQ+ rights worldwide. What's clear is that drag queens aren't just underground provocateurs any more: they're high-profile activists, magazine cover stars and queer role models for the next generation.

RUPAUL'S DRAG RACE

The initial success of reality TV show *RuPaul's Drag Race* hinged on the popularity of its star host. If anyone could take drag mainstream, it was RuPaul. He promised camp humour, extreme glamour and emotional storylines – and he delivered.

Despite a shaky start, creases in the show's early format were ironed out, and more high-profile drag queens started auditioning for the show. For mainstream audiences unfamiliar with drag, the diversity of talent was impressive: there were comedy queens, pageant acts and spooky, oddball performers quite unlike the campy, high-glamour drag acts they were already familiar with.

Now the show has more than a dozen seasons under its rhinestoned belt, as well as spin-offs like *Drag U* and backstage bonus show *Untucked*. Each episode draws in hundreds of thousands of viewers. Then there's DragCon, a mammoth convention which takes place biannually in New York and Los Angeles – the first of its kind. The convention is a clear testament to *Drag Race*'s position as a cultural phenomenon, as die-hard fans (both kids and adults) queue for hours to be photographed with their favourite queens.

Naturally, a handful of international spin-offs have also been released. Although it only premiered in 2018, *Drag Race Thailand* has already been praised for putting its own spin on the show. The hallmarks of Thai drag culture – the extravagant historical costumes, the mixture of traditional and modern pop music and the unreserved embrace of trans queens – all prevail. After just a few seasons, the Thai version has also been seen as a victory for diverse representation, having crowned a plus-size winner in its first season and a trans winner in its second, which as of 2020 has never happened on the US show. →

The international popularity of *Drag Race* is showing no sign of slowing down, with UK and Australian versions now also airing. But like any reality show, *Drag Race* has drama and controversy aplenty. The show primarily favours more conventionally feminine queens over their kookier counterparts, and isn't generally inclusive of trans or non-binary contestants, though it looks to be getting better.

Overall, the show succeeds in striking a difficult balance, delighting mainstream newcomers and die-hard drag fans alike. Tricky on-screen discussions have also shed light on various issues within the queer community, including conversion therapy, racism in the drag scene, gender affirmation and familial acceptance.

With nothing more than a good idea, a slew of charming queens and a choice selection of high profile contacts, RuPaul has turned drag into a global phenomenon, elavating its influence to previously unreachable heights.

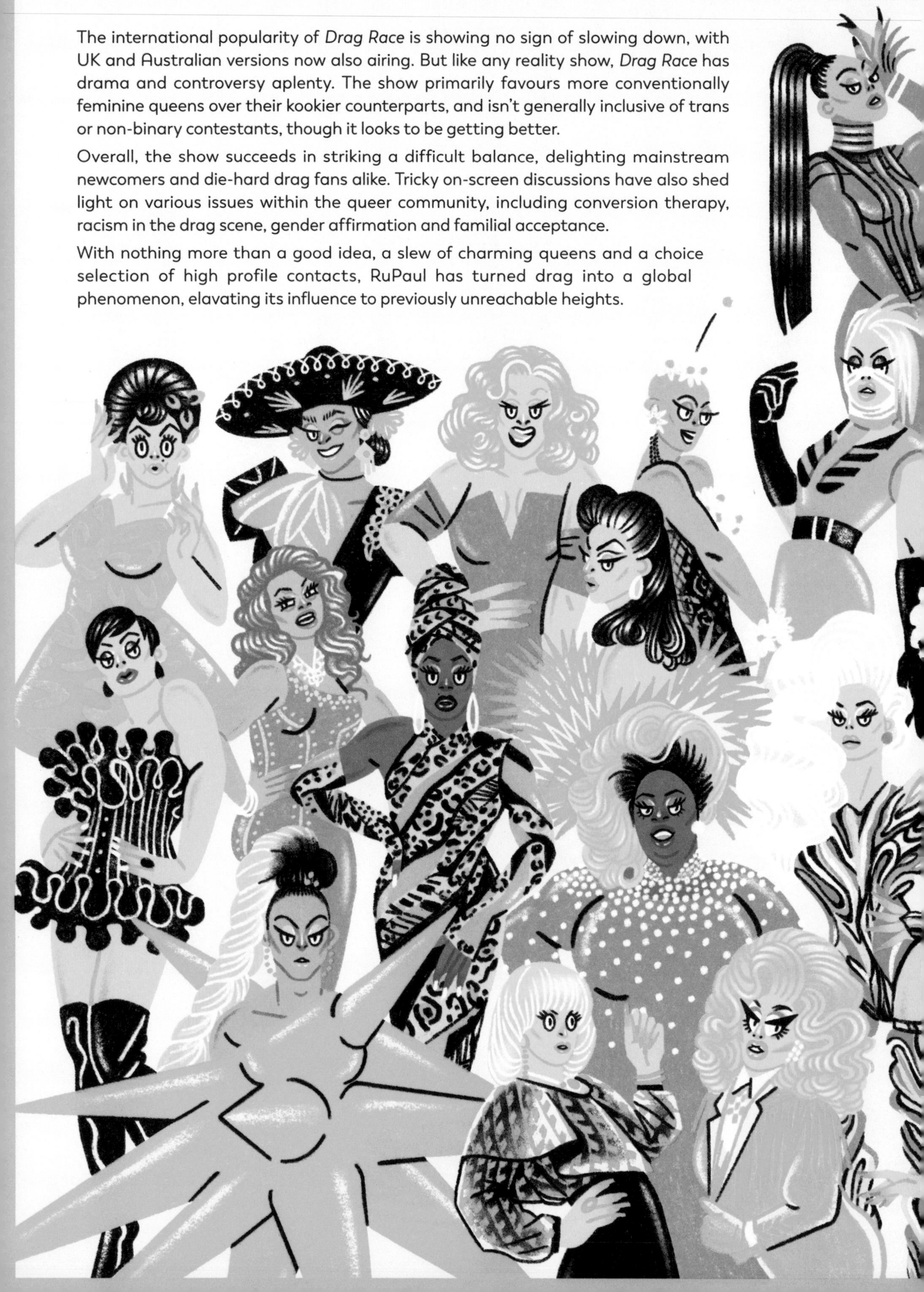

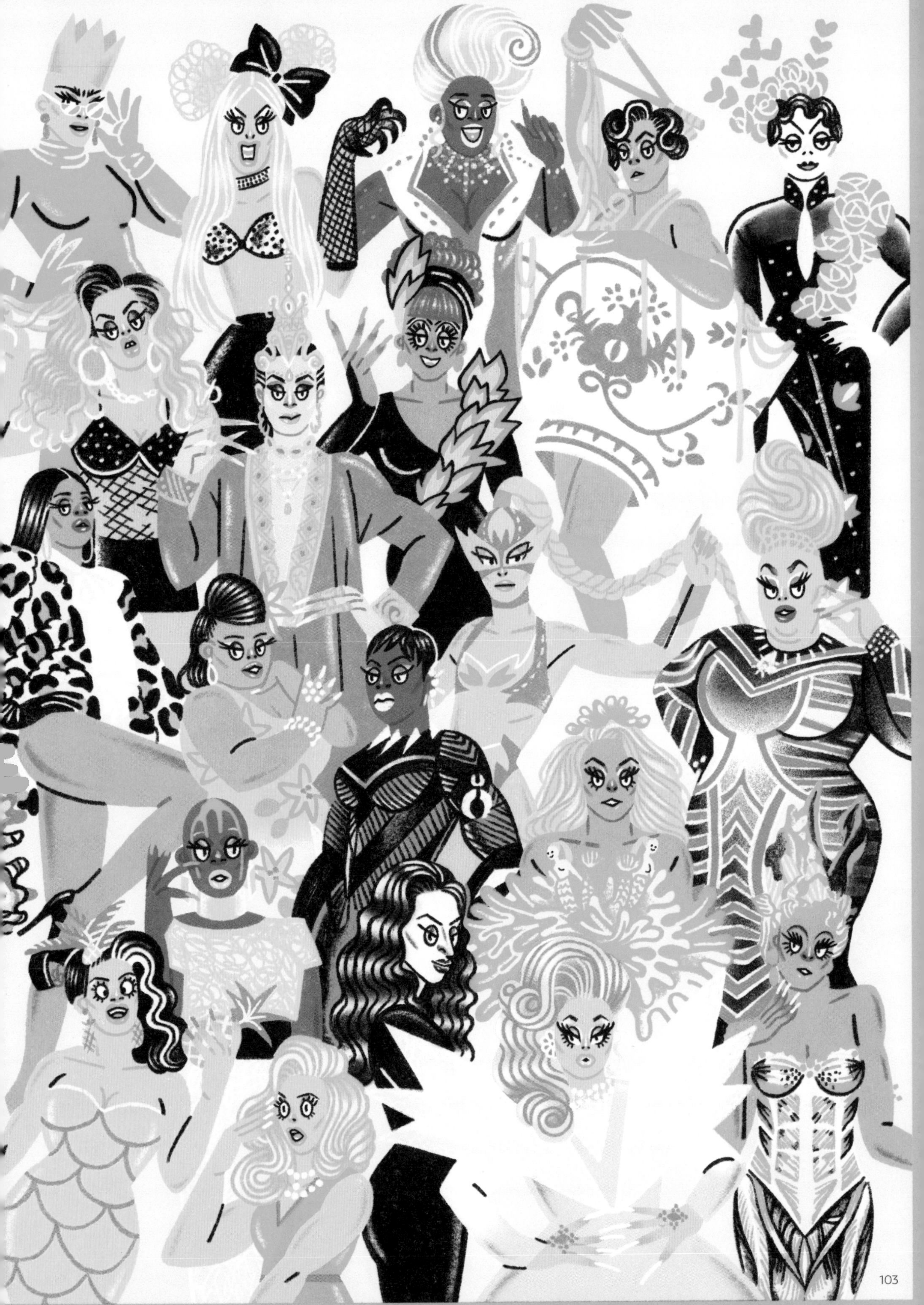

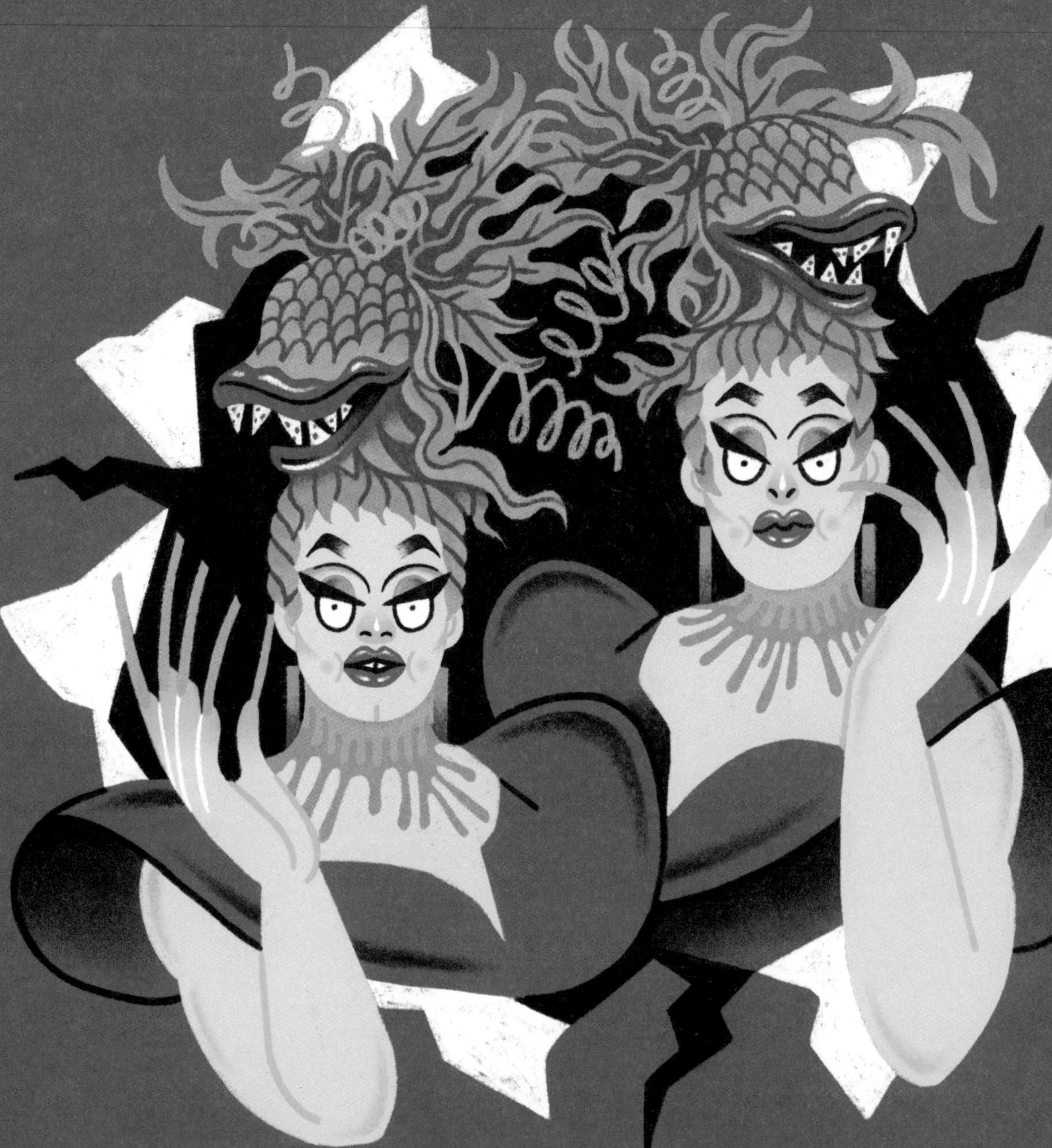

THE BOULET BROTHERS & DRAGULA

It's unrealistic to expect *Drag Race* to represent the entire spectrum of drag, so a handful of equally entertaining alternatives have emerged in response. *Dragula*, the horror-themed drag competition created by LA's eerie, glamorous Boulet Brothers, is a prime example. In its first episode the sultry hosts, Swanthula and Dracmorda, strut through a graveyard in skintight latex before descending into a lair to meet the contestants. It's the perfect start to a series with campy scares and a freaky drag aesthetic, aiming to find a 'supermonster' instead of a superstar.

The format does share similarities with *Drag Race* – there are backstage segments, a main challenge (called the floor show) and a weekly 'extermination' – but a strong stomach and a high pain threshold are also required, as the lowest-scoring competitors face weekly challenges ranging from jumping out of planes to eating animal intestines. Twists like these prove that even as the art form creeps into the mainstream, drag is still a filthy, fun freakshow.

DRAG FOR ALL

Even as we see more varied representation in drag, there's still a common myth that it's a male-only art form. But this isn't true, anyone can do drag! In the 21st century, drag simply means using aesthetic and artistic tricks to disrupt our idea of what it means to look like a man, a woman, or even just a person. It's the art of playing with gender.

Nightclubs worldwide have long housed talented trans and non-binary performers, as well as cisgender women. Social media has helped tremendously with the scouting of these talents, allowing drag artists who might normally be denied gigs a platform to showcase their skills.

Trans and non-binary drag artists have always been leaders in the queer and drag communities. They continue to push conversations around the mainstreaming of drag into new realms, shedding light on how an artform created by outsiders can still be guilty of gatekeeping. Queens including (below, l-r) Victoria Sin, Glamrou, Imp Queen and Peppermint – who in 2017 became the first *Drag Race* contestant to be open about her trans identity from the start of the competition – aren't just creating beautiful art. They're also proving that drag is not, and never has been, the exclusive domain of men.

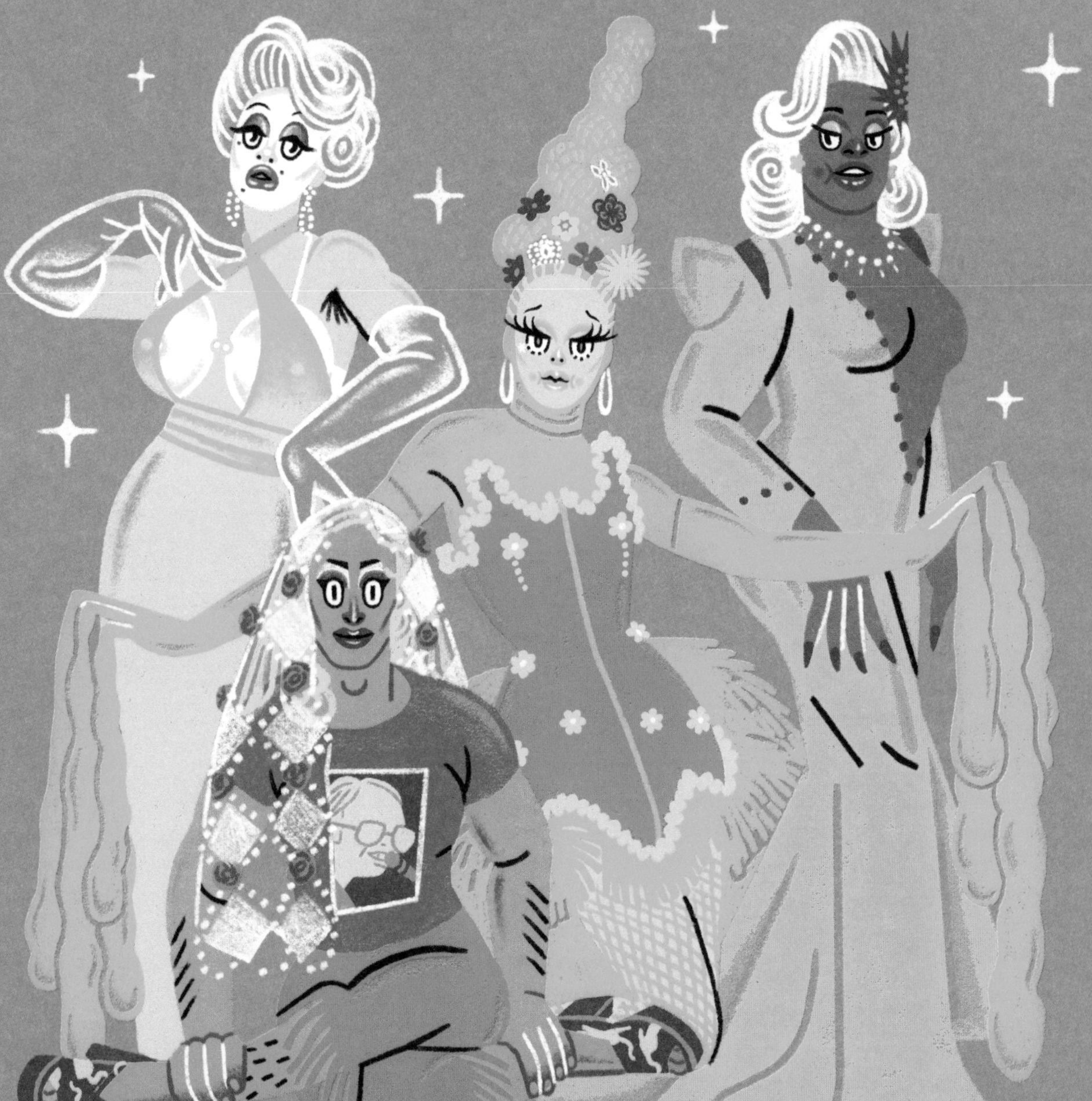

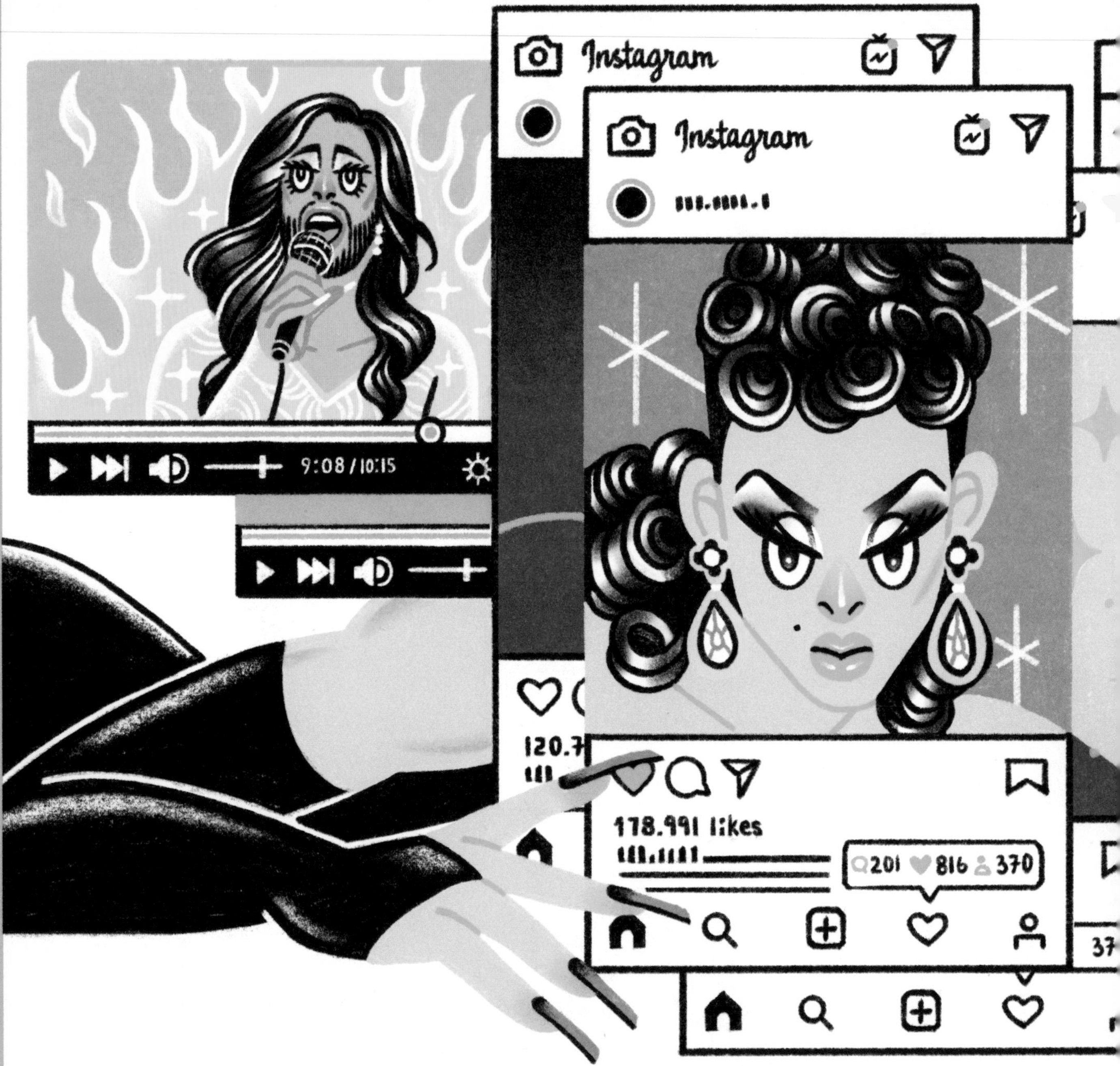
Instagram
Instagram
9:08 / 10:15
120.7
178.991 likes
201 816 370
37

A GLOBAL TAKEOVER

Once upon a time, drag was seen as a niche practice. Now, drag artists aren't just part of the zeitgeist; they play a role in actively shaping it.

The fashion industry was one of the earliest to fully embrace the aesthetics of drag and now queens like Violet Chachki, Milk and Miss Fame are designer muses, starring in advertising campaigns and walking the red carpet at prestigious fashion events like the Met Gala. Even pop heavyweights like Taylor Swift, Katy Perry and Lady Gaga have handpicked queens to feature in their music videos.

The visual focus of social media platforms like YouTube and Instagram has made it easier for queens to gain popularity through make-up tutorials, and as a result, drag techniques like 'contouring' and 'baking' (setting your look with powder as you go along) have crept into everyday beauty looks. Video content also provides another place to perform for a whole

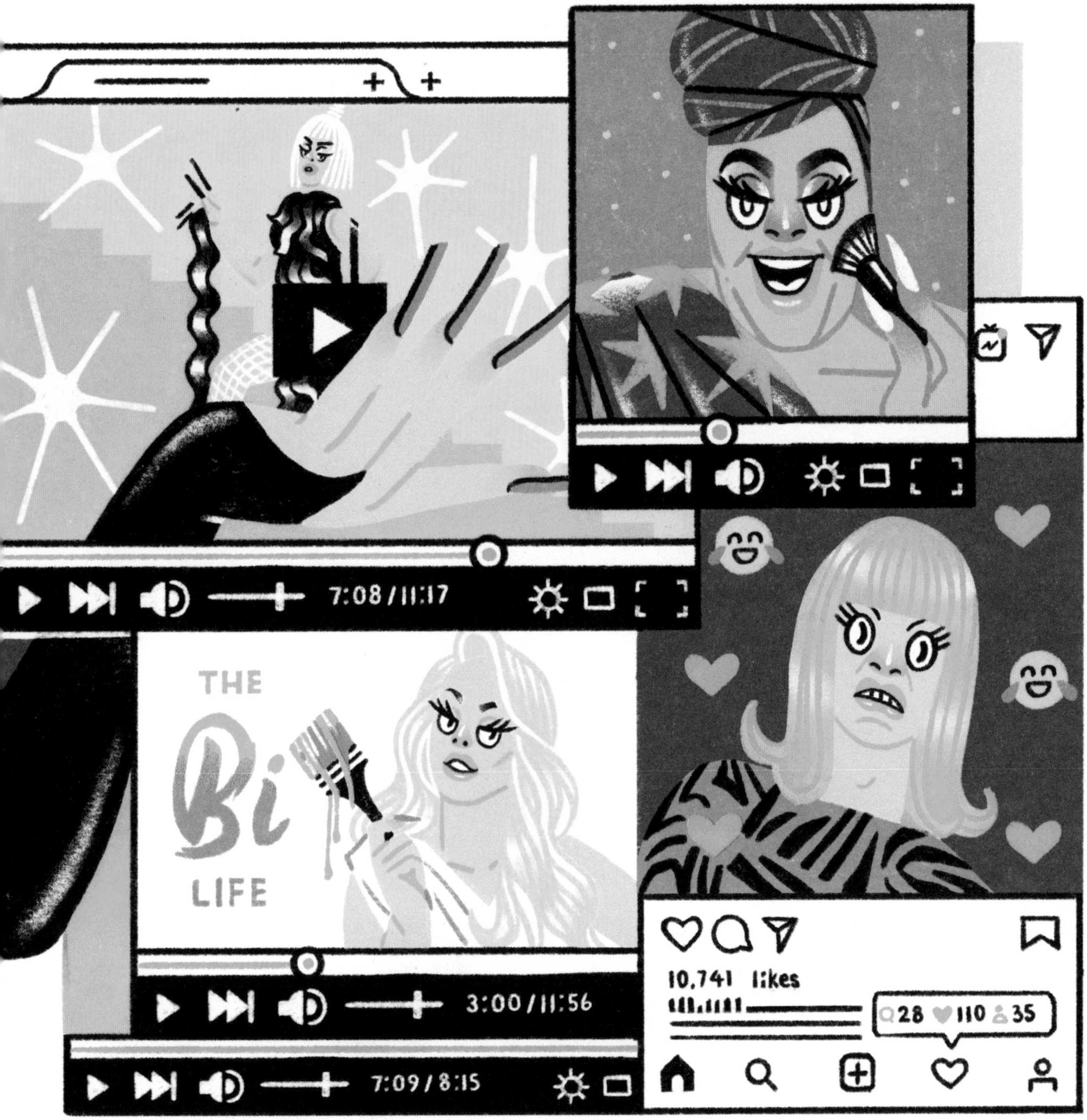
7:08 / 11:17
THE
Bi
LIFE
3:00 / 11:56
7:09 / 8:15
10,741 likes
28
110
35

new audience. Comedy veteran Coco Peru's sarcastic rants about herbal teas, supermarket layouts and overpriced panettone have earned her hundreds of thousands of followers, most of whom probably don't know anything about her 1990s one-woman comedy show.

The influence of drag can be felt broadly across mainstream media: reality shows feature lip-sync battles and queens are popping up on primetime makeover shows. Conchita Wurst teamed a floor-length gown with a neat, brunette beard in 2014 to become the first drag winner of the Eurovision Song Contest. Former *Drag Race* contestant Courtney Act similarly won over the UK public in 2018 when she was crowned the winner of *Celebrity Big Brother*. By combining charisma and kindness with glimpses of her drag expertise, she charmed her housemates and became a TV personality in her own right, going on to present primetime bisexual dating show *The Bi Life*. More of these historic moments look set to happen in the near future, as drag superstars continue to spark cultural shifts worldwide.

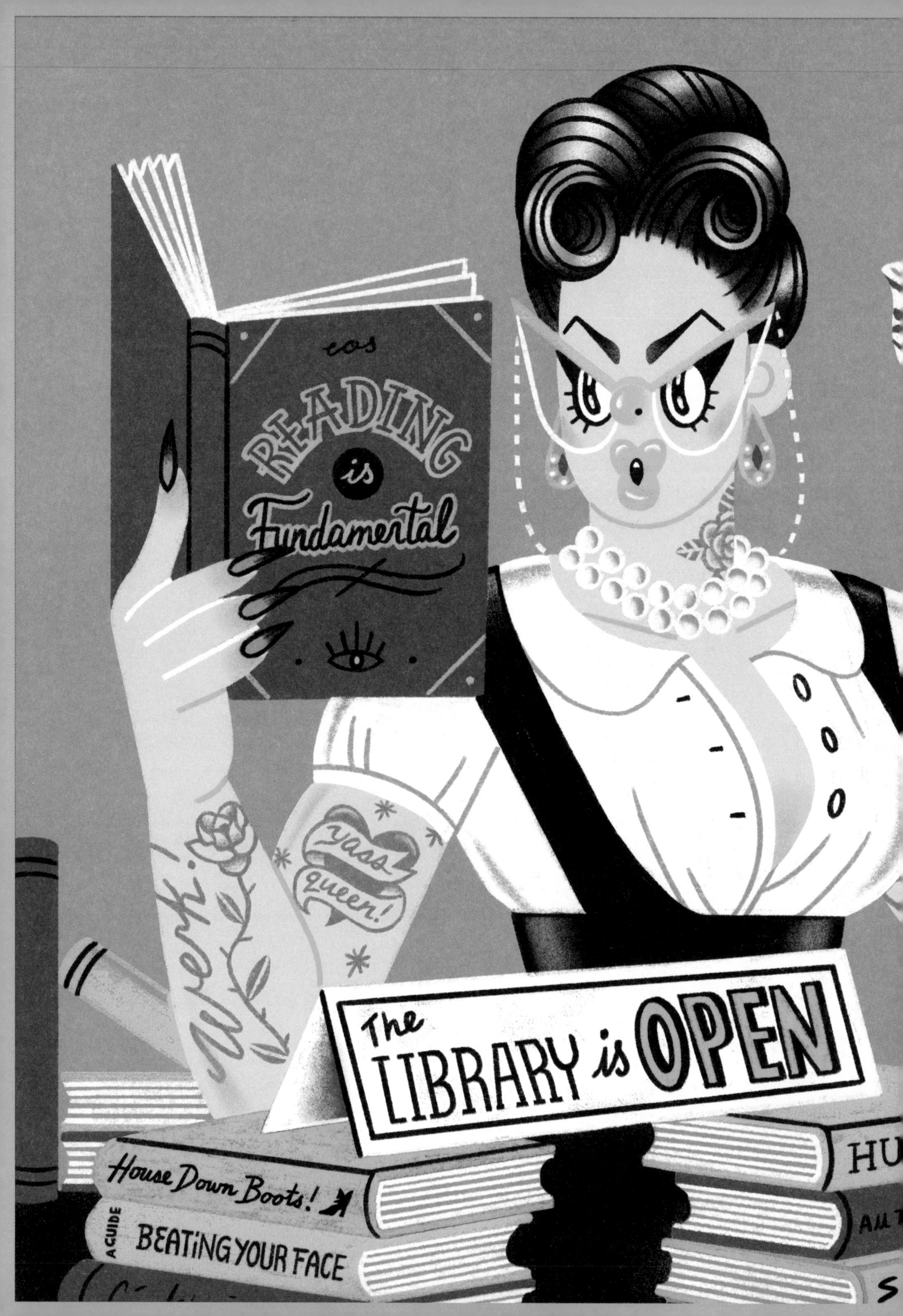
READING is Fundamental
yass queen!
Werk!
The LIBRARY is OPEN
House Down Boots!
A GUIDE BEATING YOUR FACE

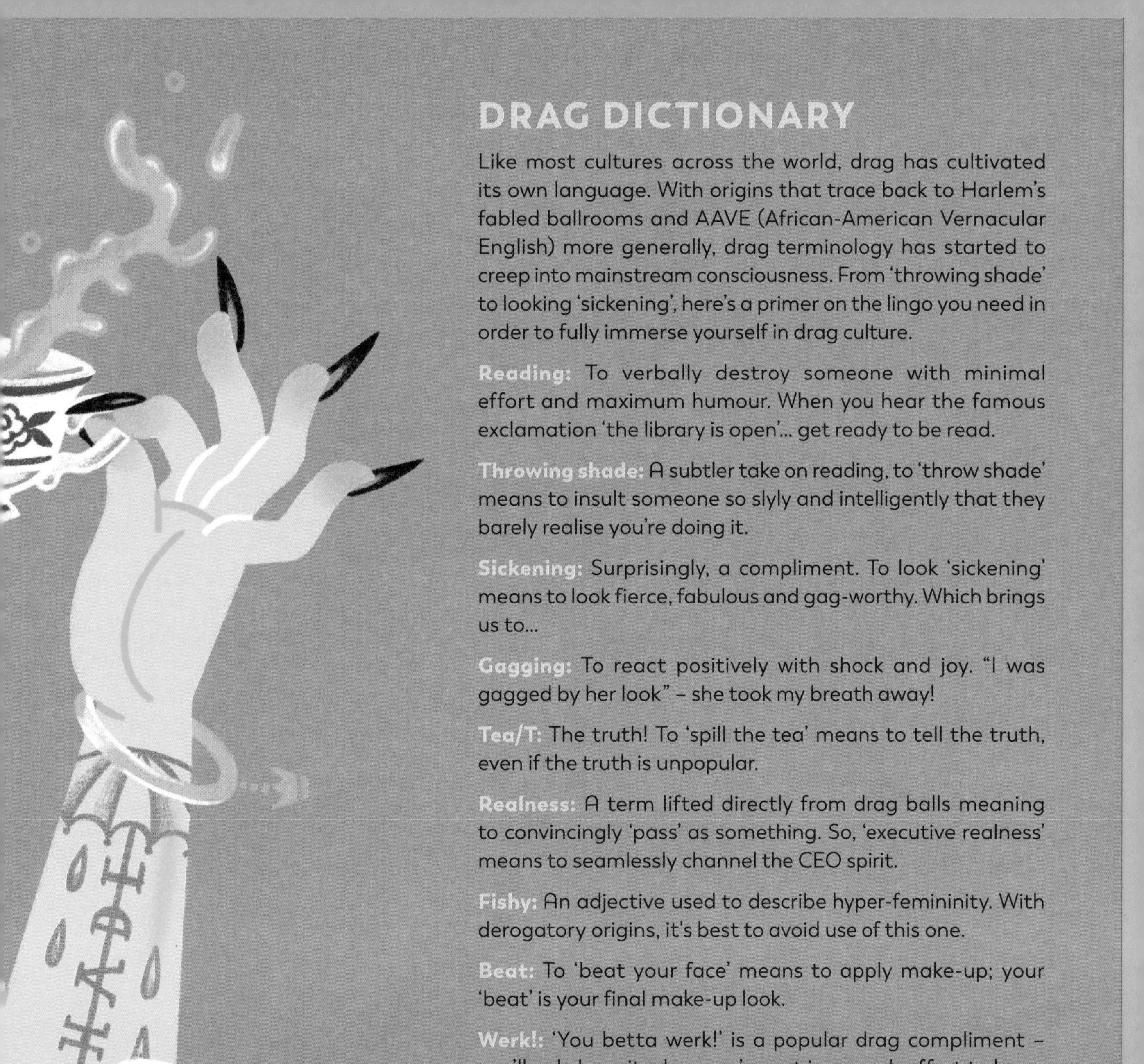
SHADE

DRAG DICTIONARY

Like most cultures across the world, drag has cultivated its own language. With origins that trace back to Harlem's fabled ballrooms and AAVE (African-American Vernacular English) more generally, drag terminology has started to creep into mainstream consciousness. From 'throwing shade' to looking 'sickening', here's a primer on the lingo you need in order to fully immerse yourself in drag culture.

Reading: To verbally destroy someone with minimal effort and maximum humour. When you hear the famous exclamation 'the library is open'... get ready to be read.

Throwing shade: A subtler take on reading, to 'throw shade' means to insult someone so slyly and intelligently that they barely realise you're doing it.

Sickening: Surprisingly, a compliment. To look 'sickening' means to look fierce, fabulous and gag-worthy. Which brings us to...

Gagging: To react positively with shock and joy. "I was gagged by her look" – she took my breath away!

Tea/T: The truth! To 'spill the tea' means to tell the truth, even if the truth is unpopular.

Realness: A term lifted directly from drag balls meaning to convincingly 'pass' as something. So, 'executive realness' means to seamlessly channel the CEO spirit.

Fishy: An adjective used to describe hyper-femininity. With derogatory origins, it's best to avoid use of this one.

Beat: To 'beat your face' means to apply make-up; your 'beat' is your final make-up look.

Werk!: 'You betta werk!' is a popular drag compliment – you'll only hear it when you've put in enough effort to leave your audience gagged.

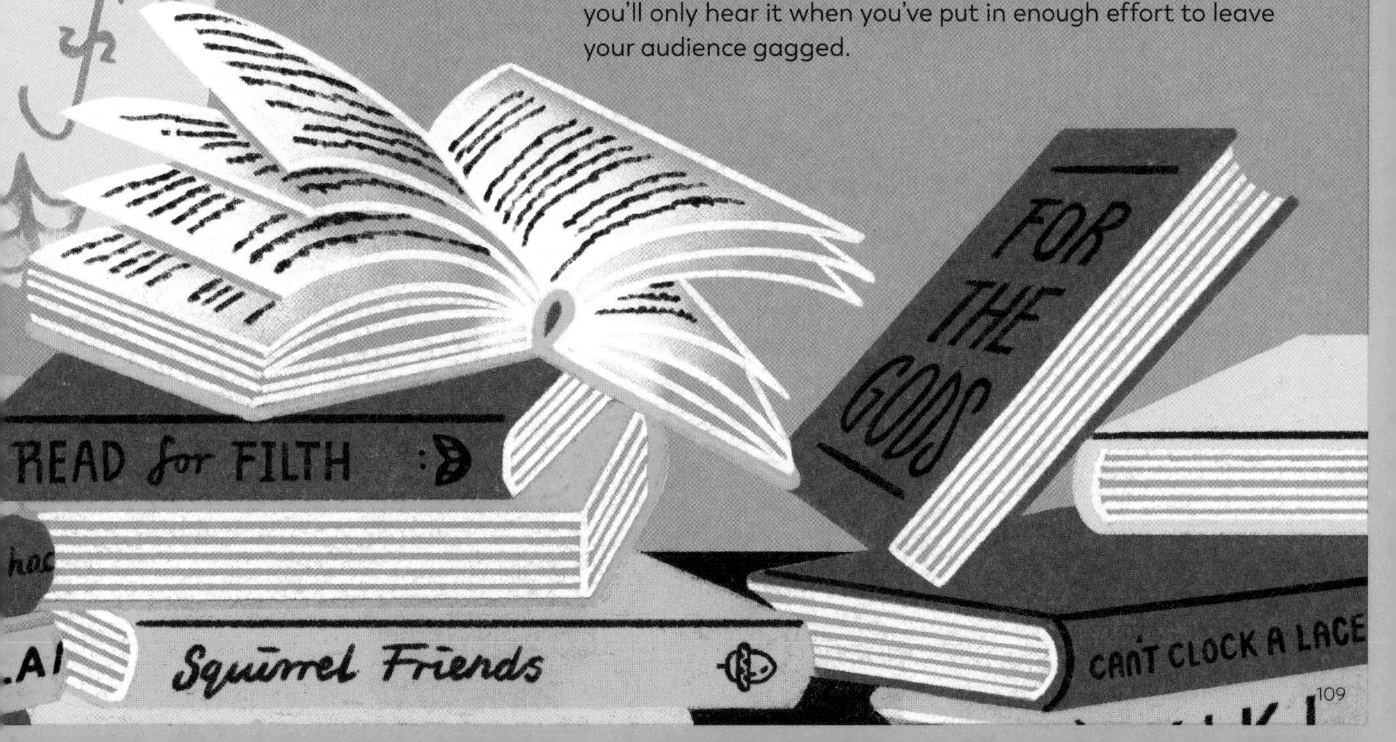
READ for FILTH
FOR THE GODS
Squirrel Friends
CAN'T CLOCK A LACE

FIGHT FOR THE RIGHT

A lot has changed since the Stonewall Riots, and drag has paved the way for more progressive attitudes towards homosexuality and cross-dressing, both of which have largely been decriminalised around the world. But there's still to work to be done.

Almost 70 countries still have laws that target people for being LGBTQ+, but within them, a series of underground drag circuits have started to emerge. In countries like Russia, Turkey and Malaysia, drag queens like Kamilla Crazy White (Moscow), Matmazel Coco (Istanbul) and Shelah (Kuala Lumpur) have learned to blend glamour and theatricality with politics and activism. In an environment which could see them killed for practising their art, even leaving the house in drag is an act of resistance.

Even in apparently progressive countries, drag queens are still fighting discrimination. Technology has made activism easier: high-profile performers can now curate social media feeds that team selfies with messages of support for activists worldwide. Thanks to crowdfunding and petition websites, today's drag stars have more tools to make global change.

The influence of drag on mainstream culture is also having a positive impact on the next generation. Conventions like DragCon attract thousands of young fans desperate to dress up and snap selfies with their idols, whereas the newfound fame of 'drag kids' and the rise of child-friendly drag events proves that attitudes are slowly changing. There's still progress to be made, but with drag stars using their profiles to effect international change and today's youth growing up with queens as their role models, drag continues to play an important role in pushing for LGBTQ+ rights.

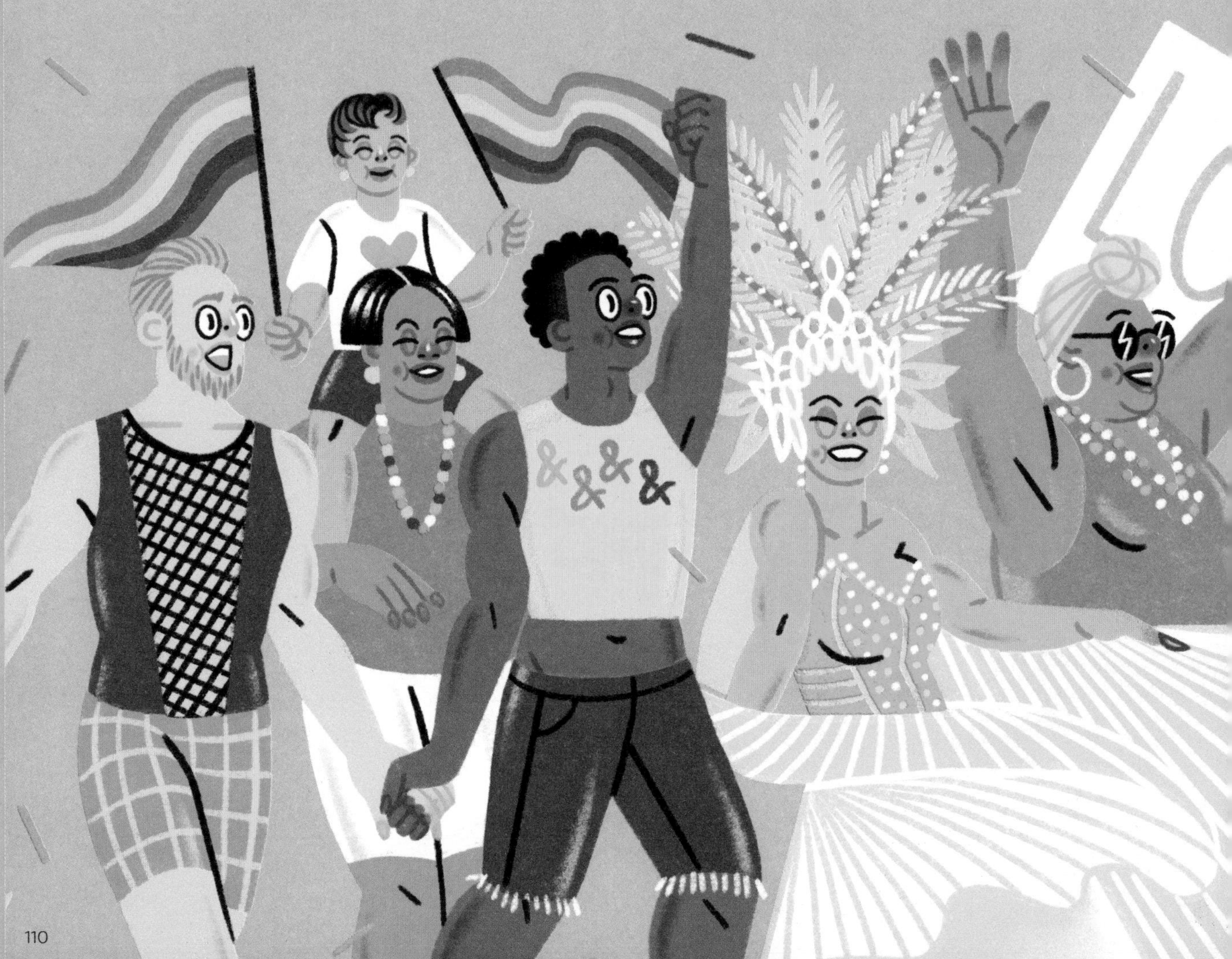

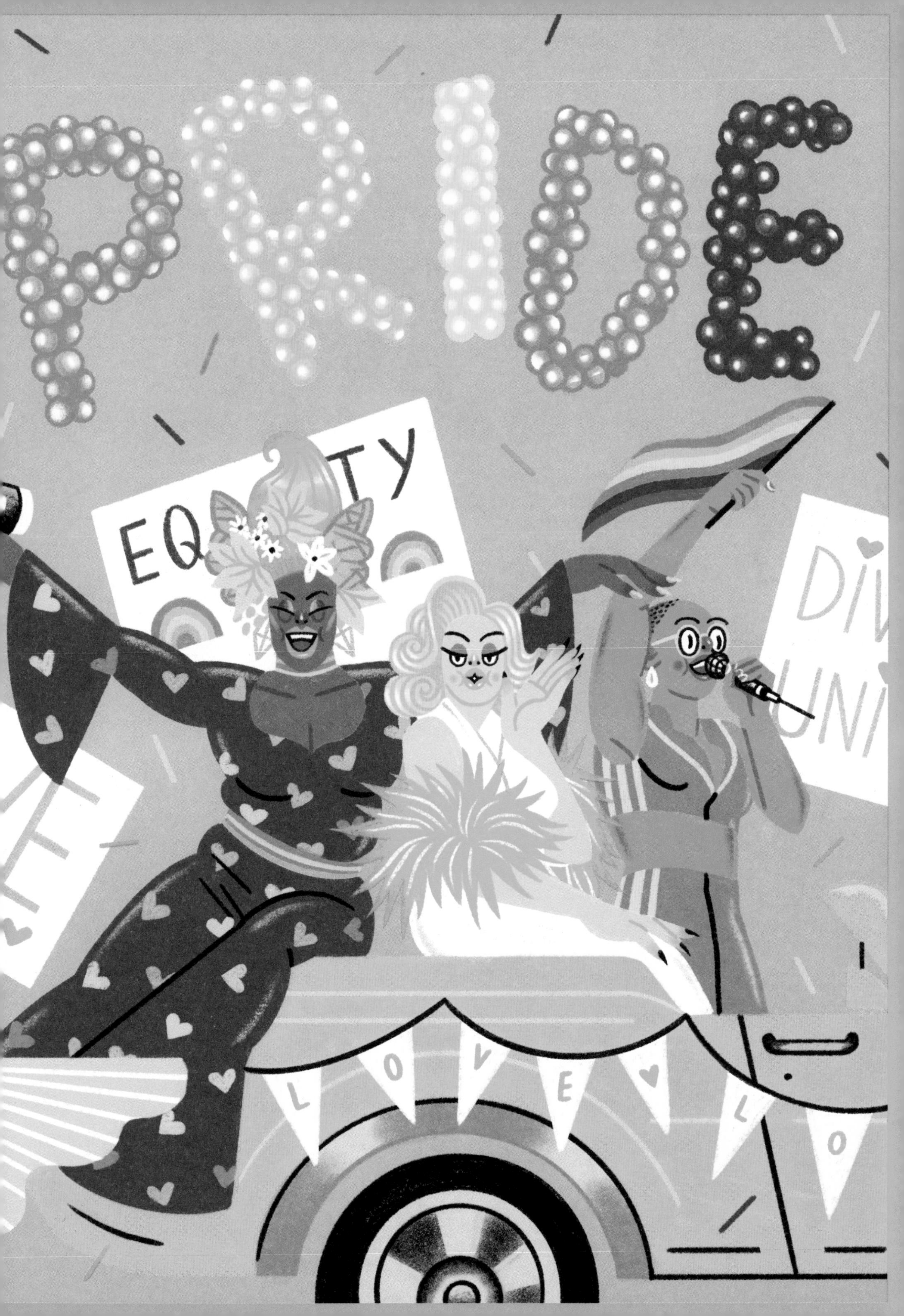
PRIDE
LOVE

DRAG: THEN & NOW

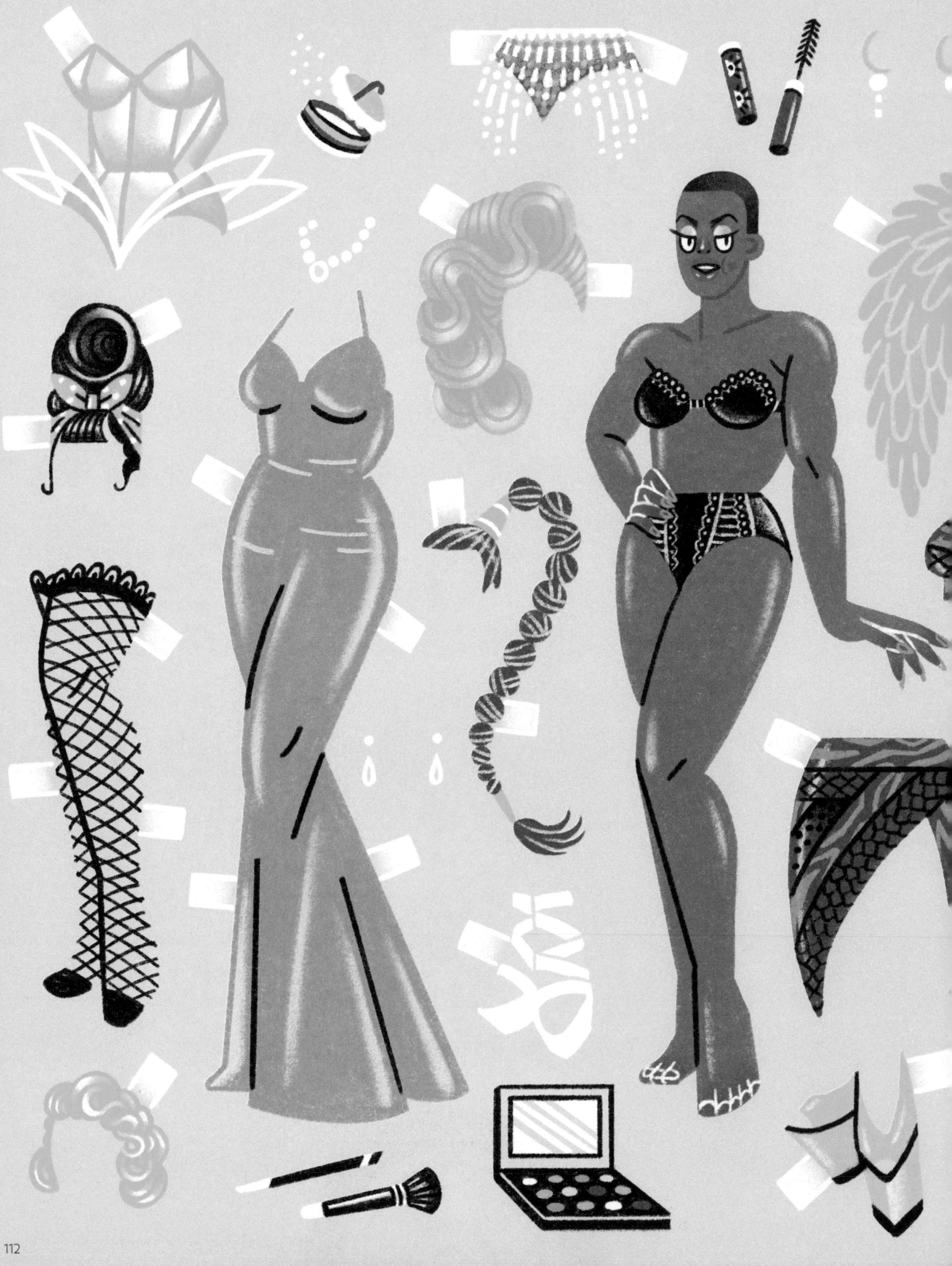

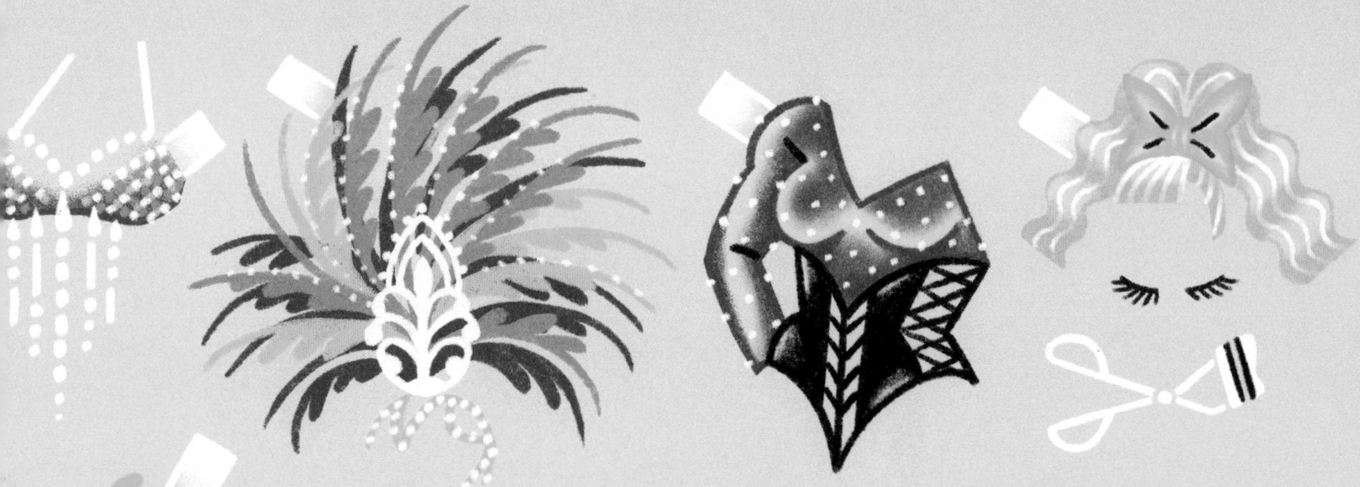

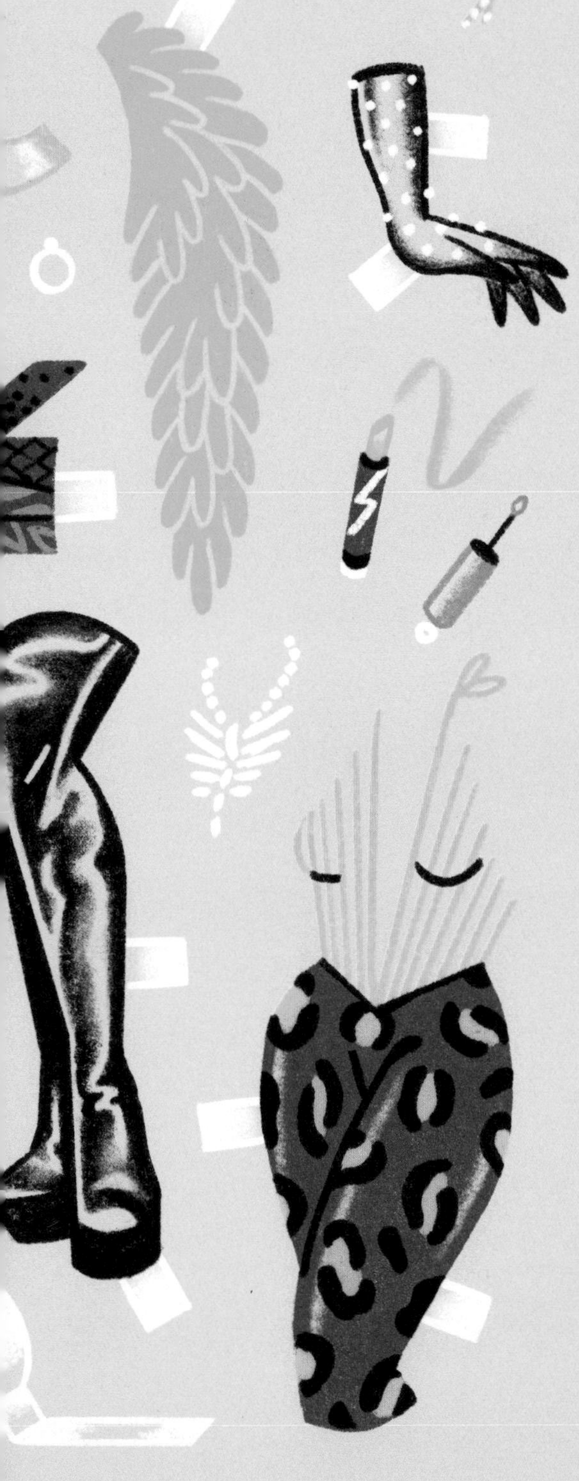

...THEN

As with beauty and fashion trends, the aesthetics of drag have changed hugely over time. The early theatre variations – like kabuki, Kathakali and mime – were usually tied to distinctive make-up styles because they were linked to specific cultures. But as the years went by and the number of drag artists worldwide increased, the array of different drag looks multiplied.

The role of drag queens more generally changed too. For centuries, their primary aim was either to make audiences laugh or provide a glamorous illusion. So pantomime dame or flawless female impersonator were the two options, often with little room for variation.

Early stage pioneers went for exaggerated silhouettes, pairing sky-high wigs with an hourglass figure. Make-up consisted of thin, feathery brows drawn in high arches, heavy eyeshadow and lips painted bright: an amped-up aesthetic which ensured that audiences paid attention. But whatever the look, drag has always required time, effort and expertise.

...NOW!

Fast-forward a few decades, and things are completely different and yet very much the same. Now we're just as likely to see a queen on social media as on stage.

The most widely seen face of drag today is taped back to a smooth finish, shaded carefully with powder and highlighted to create the illusion of a delicate bone structure. Lips are subtly overdrawn, while eyes have become a cosmetic testing ground, with looks from cut-creases to 'halo eyes'.

The real beauty of drag is that it will always be diverse: for every pageant queen with a flawless beat, there's a club kid around the corner with a face full of prosthetics and paint. From the self-professed weirdos and rebels to the polished cabaret performers and high-femme pageant queens, there's room in drag for everyone's sparkle.

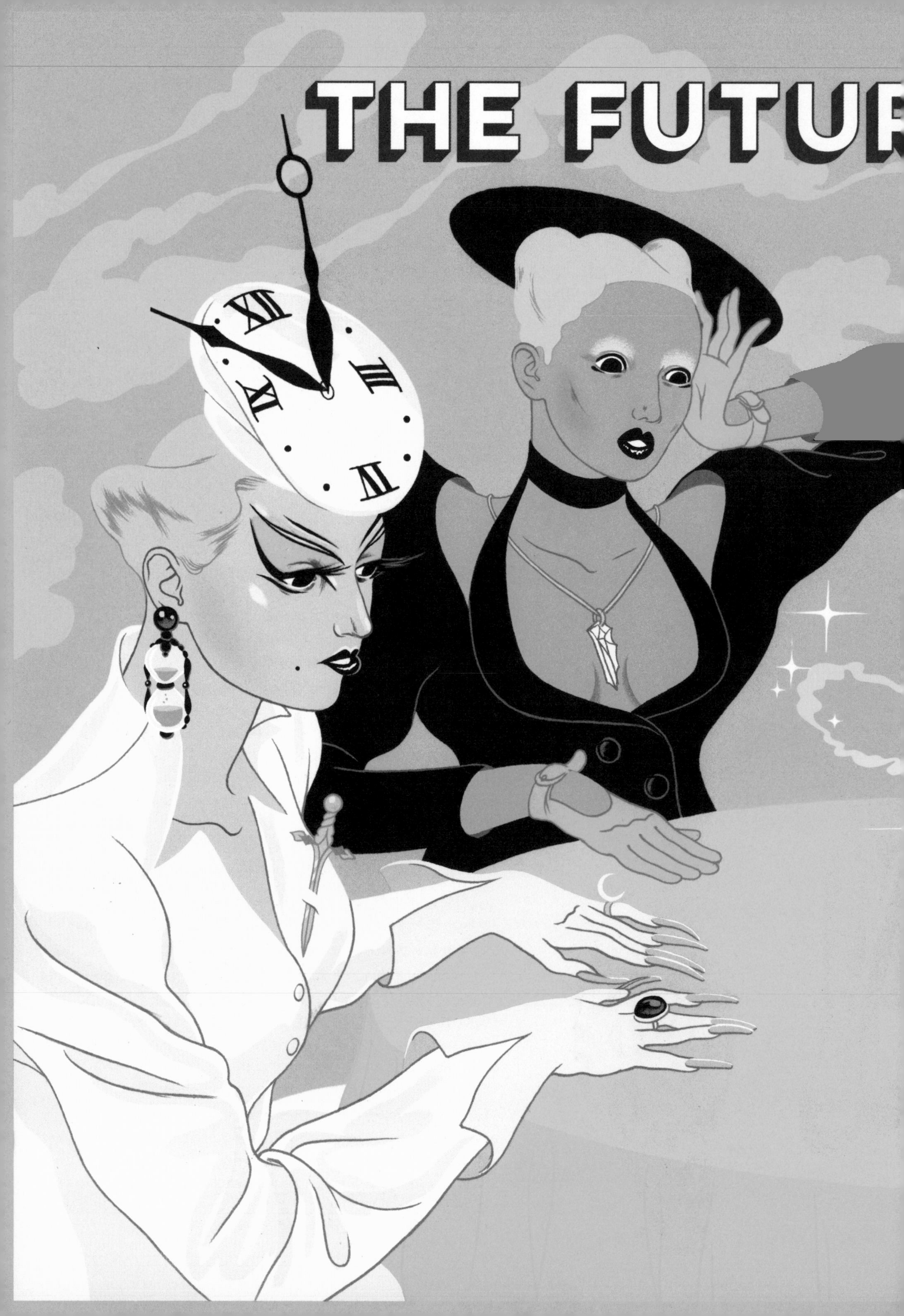
THE FUTUR

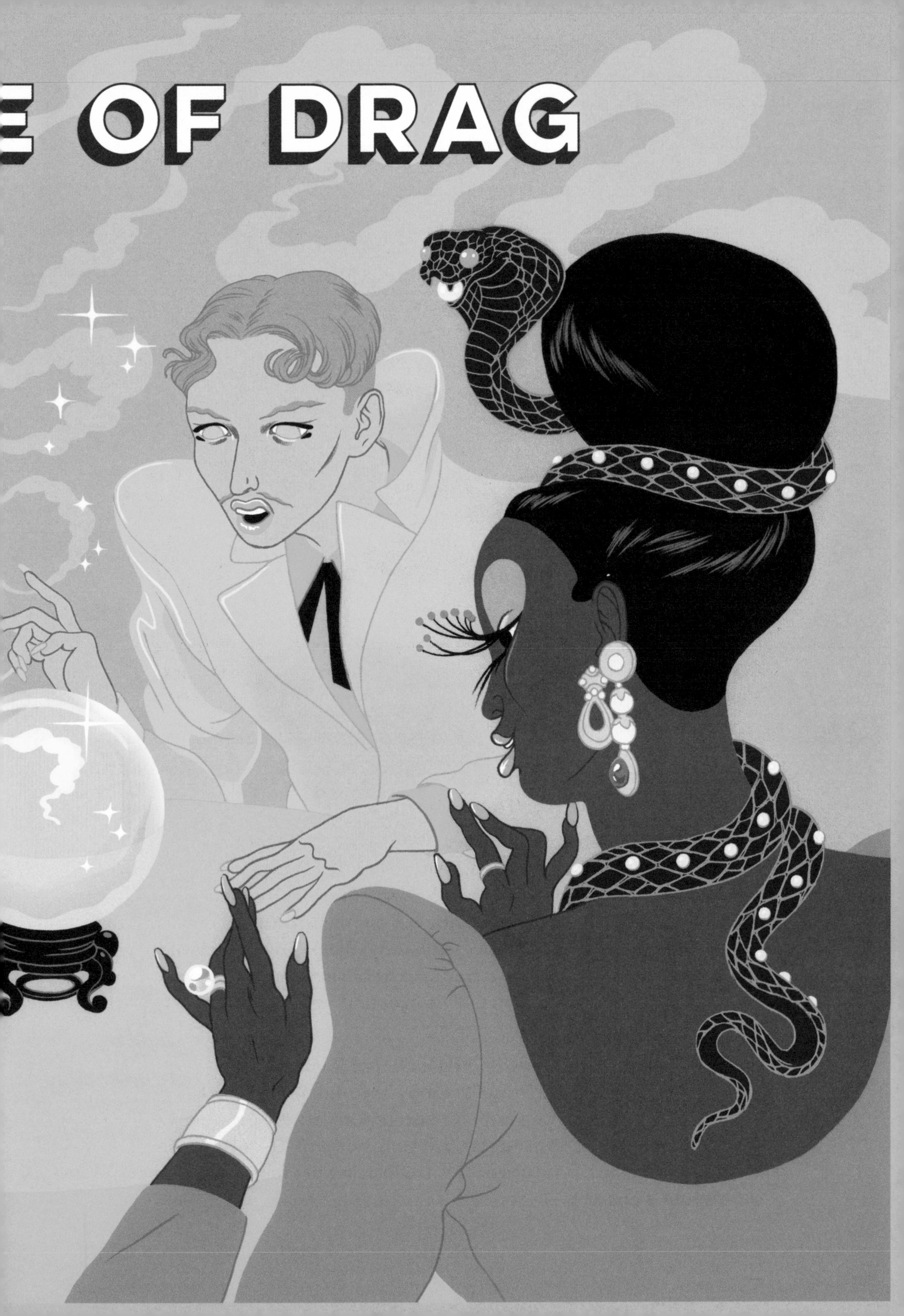
E OF DRAG

2000s & BEYOND

In today's world, drag artists have an arsenal of new tools at their disposal: from trippy filters and virtual make-up to advanced prosthetics, today's superstars use technology to create surreal imagery that distorts the idea of what it even means to look human. Thankfully, conversations around gender are becoming more progressive, too. The world is beginning to understand that anyone can do drag, and increasingly we're talking less about kings and queens and more about drag *creatures*.

The artists on the following pages are just a handful of the shining stars pushing drag into the future. Crystal Rasmussen pairs her razor-sharp wit with a fabulous, glitter-strewn beard; The Vixen teams a comic-book aesthetic with a willingness to bluntly call out racism in drag, and a desire to uplift fellow Black queens with her trailblazing Black Girl Magic; Sweatmother trawls the streets of London to capture the brilliance of their community on film; while Birmingham's Don One is injecting humour and heart into the UK's drag king scene.

Each represents a new breed of drag: one that is unashamedly political. The rise of shows like *RuPaul's Drag Race* may have opened up a certain blueprint of drag to global audiences, but underground artists are constantly working to show that drag has no gender and fits into no norm. This ethos of inclusivity is what underpins the future of this trailblazing art form. Needless to say, that future is dazzling.

"The future is uncertain, but for as long as society is intact then drag will exist, dissent, diverge, and grow. I hope that the more critical, punk, political voices will gain hold of the centre of it – that those who aren't prioritised will be both uplifted and treated as the oracles they are. That they will be listened to as people who are already surviving the apocalypse, when the apocalypse comes. Personally, in my drag, I hope to one day be seen as more than a superficial accessory. I hope that people can come and hear me sing, and speak, and make them laugh, and they can see more than the artifice of drag. More than all this, I hope the future will be predicated less on gender and so much more on what somebody has to say. Make-up or not. "

– CRYSTAL RASMUSSEN

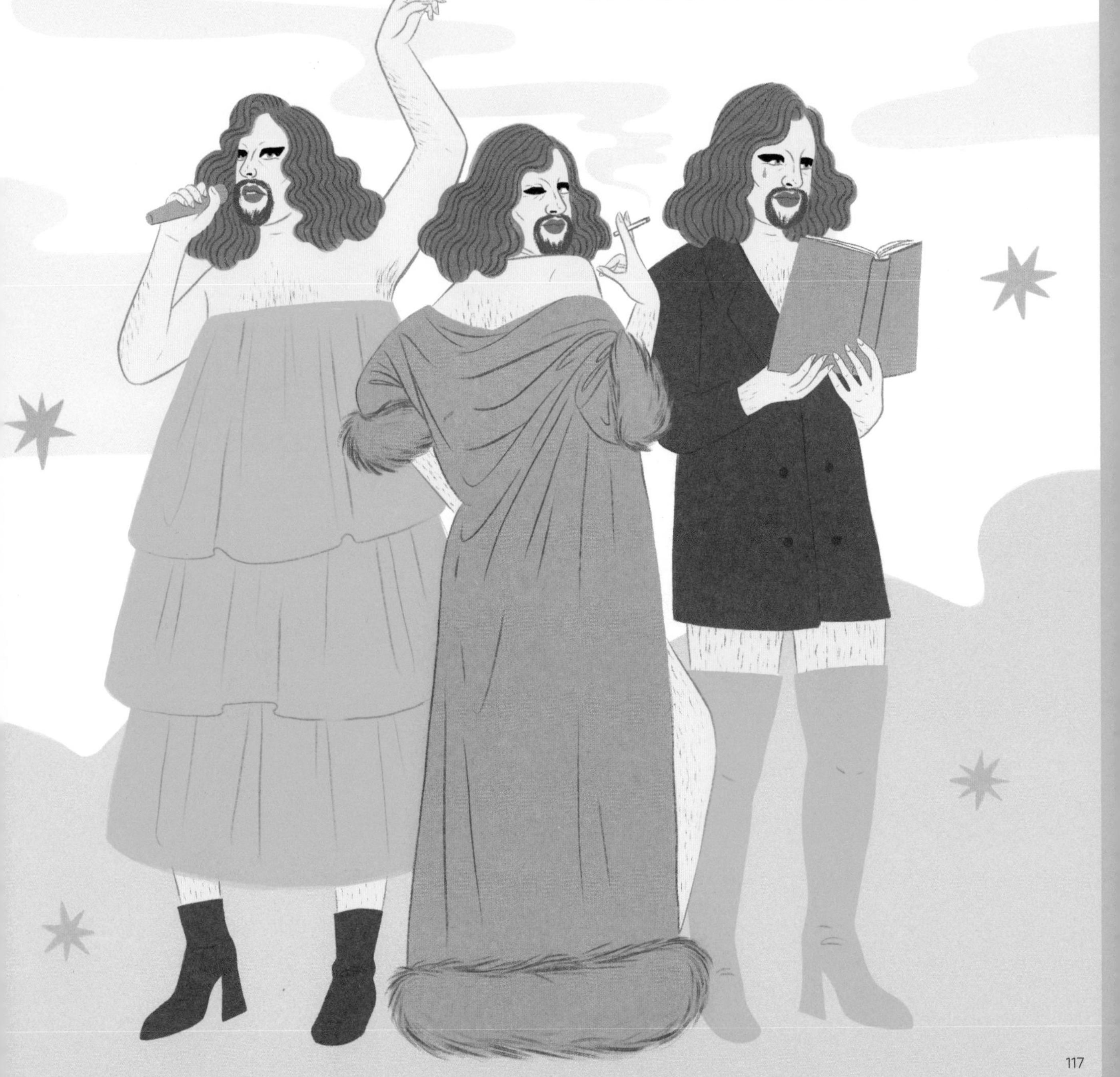

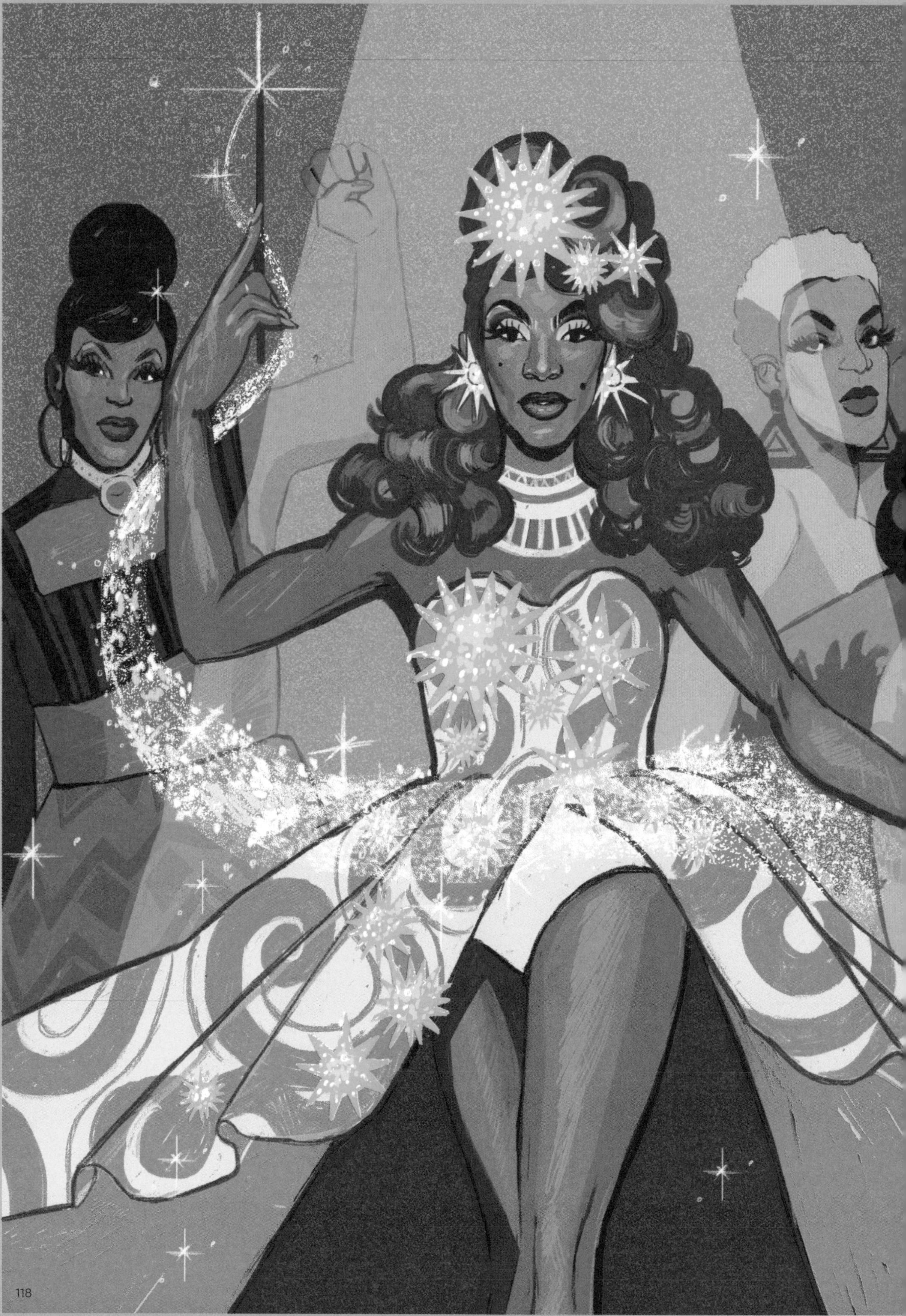

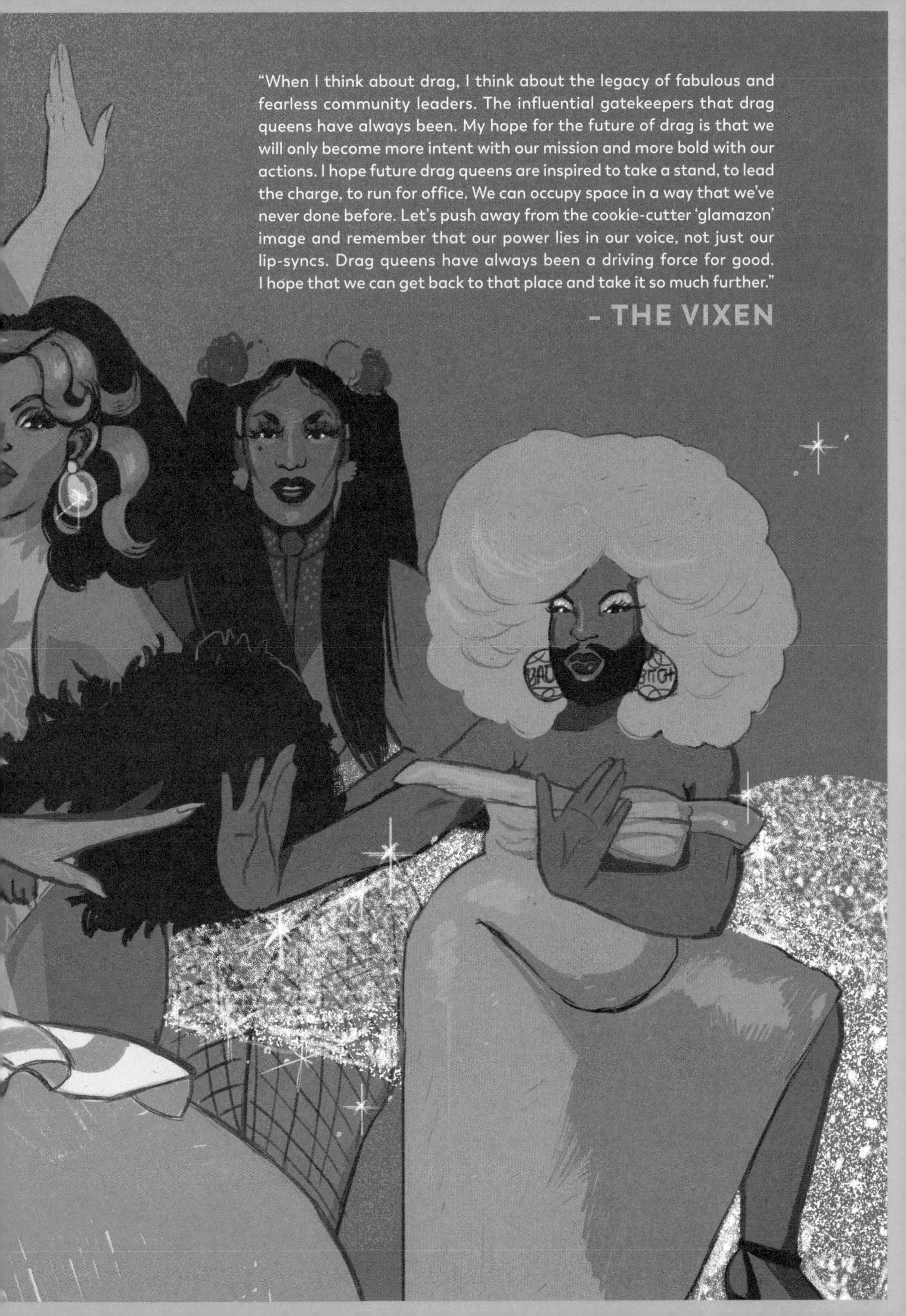

"When I think about drag, I think about the legacy of fabulous and fearless community leaders. The influential gatekeepers that drag queens have always been. My hope for the future of drag is that we will only become more intent with our mission and more bold with our actions. I hope future drag queens are inspired to take a stand, to lead the charge, to run for office. We can occupy space in a way that we've never done before. Let's push away from the cookie-cutter 'glamazon' image and remember that our power lies in our voice, not just our lip-syncs. Drag queens have always been a driving force for good. I hope that we can get back to that place and take it so much further."

- THE VIXEN

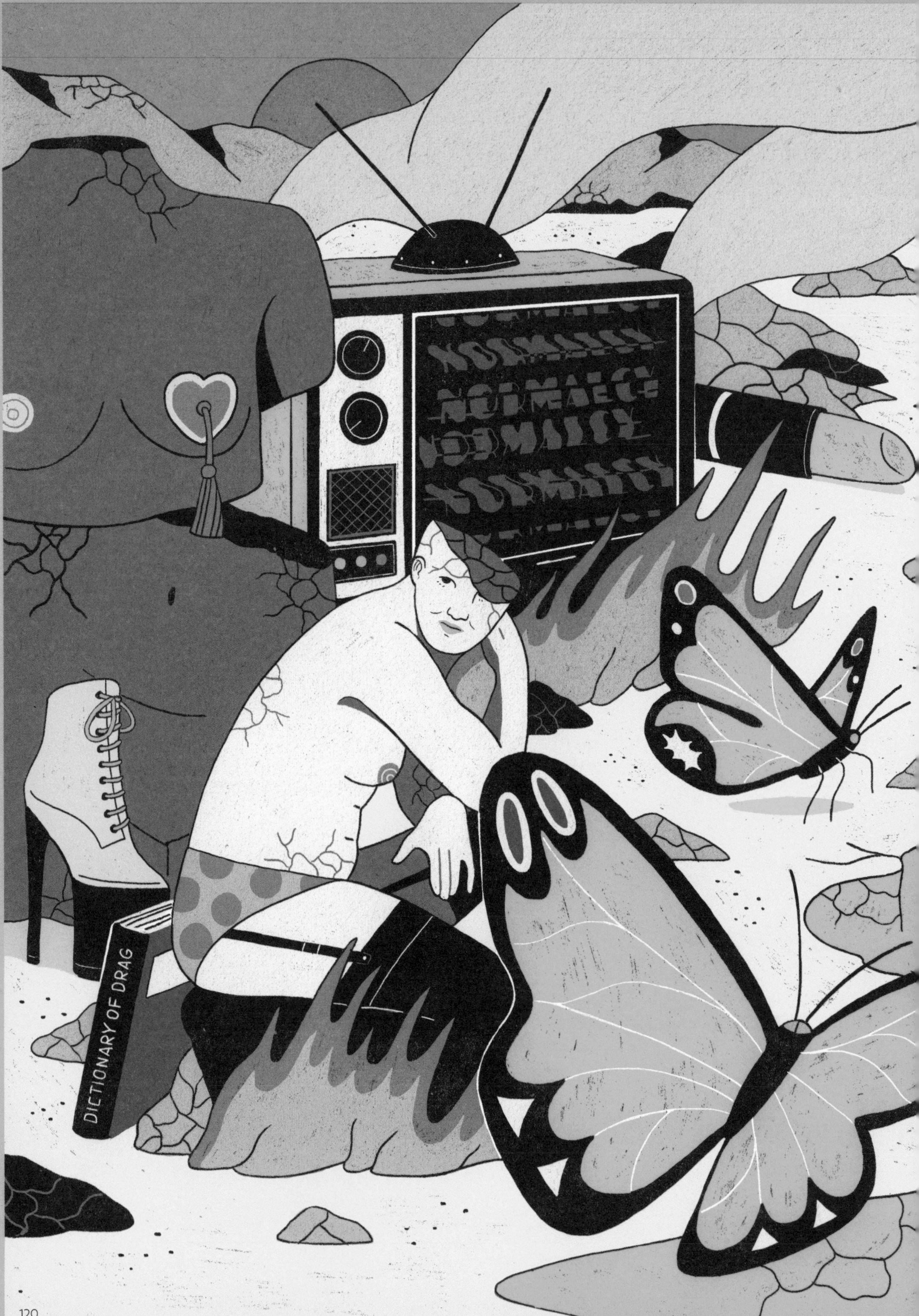
DICTIONARY OF DRAG

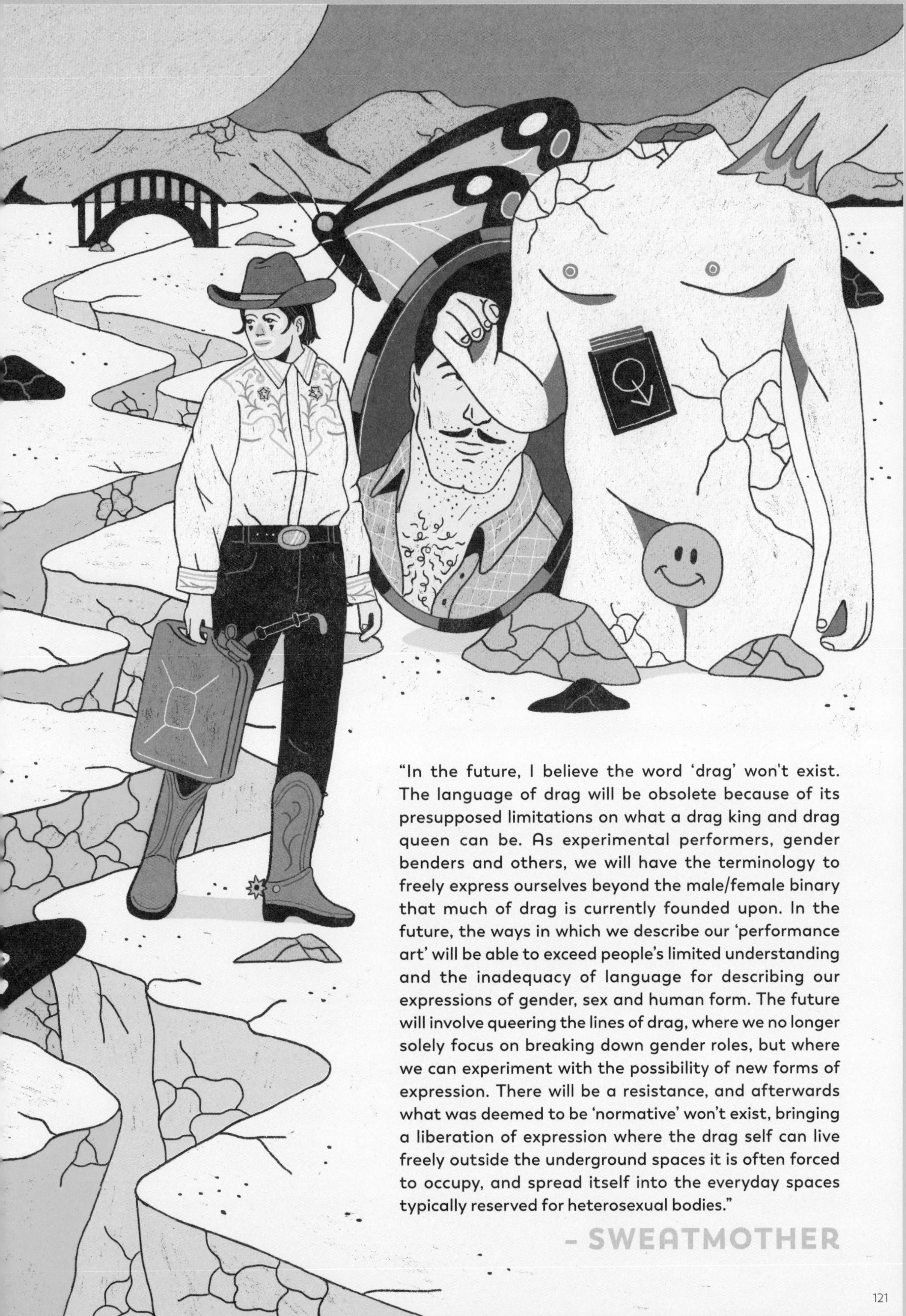

"In the future, I believe the word 'drag' won't exist. The language of drag will be obsolete because of its presupposed limitations on what a drag king and drag queen can be. As experimental performers, gender benders and others, we will have the terminology to freely express ourselves beyond the male/female binary that much of drag is currently founded upon. In the future, the ways in which we describe our 'performance art' will be able to exceed people's limited understanding and the inadequacy of language for describing our expressions of gender, sex and human form. The future will involve queering the lines of drag, where we no longer solely focus on breaking down gender roles, but where we can experiment with the possibility of new forms of expression. There will be a resistance, and afterwards what was deemed to be 'normative' won't exist, bringing a liberation of expression where the drag self can live freely outside the underground spaces it is often forced to occupy, and spread itself into the everyday spaces typically reserved for heterosexual bodies."

– SWEATMOTHER

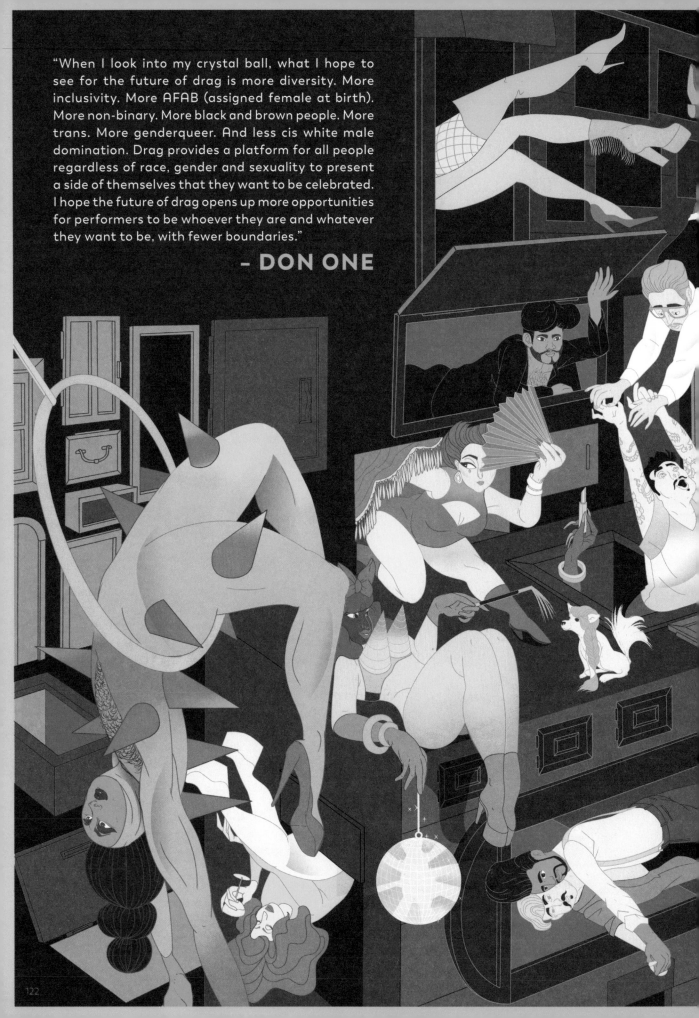

"When I look into my crystal ball, what I hope to see for the future of drag is more diversity. More inclusivity. More AFAB (assigned female at birth). More non-binary. More black and brown people. More trans. More genderqueer. And less cis white male domination. Drag provides a platform for all people regardless of race, gender and sexuality to present a side of themselves that they want to be celebrated. I hope the future of drag opens up more opportunities for performers to be whoever they are and whatever they want to be, with fewer boundaries."

– DON ONE

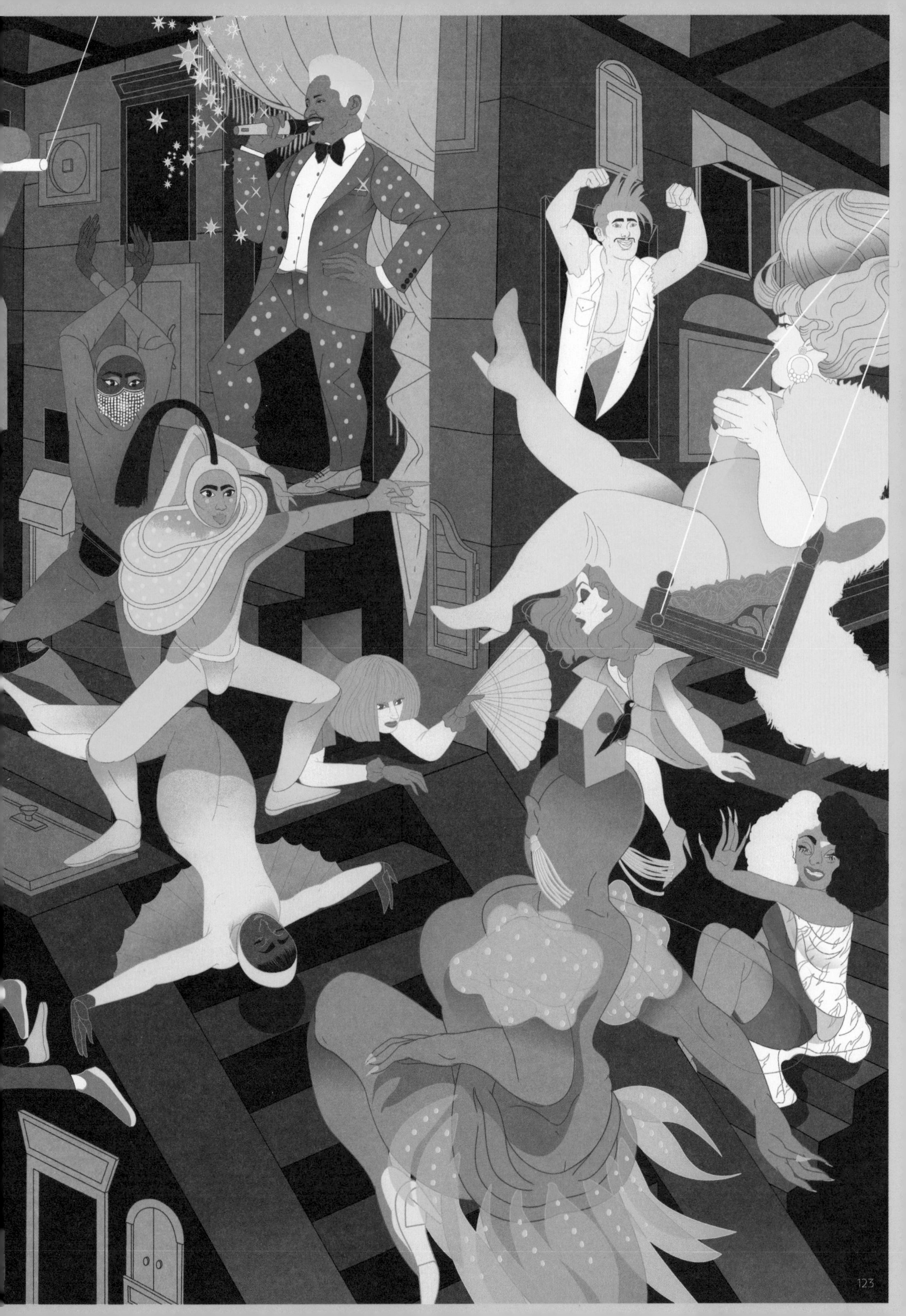

BIBLIOGRAPHY

THE ART OF PERFORMANCE

Port Out, Starboard Home: The Fascinating Stories We Tell About The Words We Use, Michael Quinon.

From the Greek Mimes to Marcel Marceau and Beyond: Mimes, Actors, Pierrots and Clowns: A Chronicle of the Many Visages of Mime in the Theatre, Annette Lust.

"Secret lives of women who broke taboo to act in Shakespeare", https://www.theguardian.com/culture/2016/apr/10/secret-lives-of-women-shakespeare.

"Shakespeare and gender: the 'woman's part'", https://www.bl.uk/shakespeare/articles/shakespeare-and-gender-the-womans-part.

The Corset: A Cultural History, Valerie Steele.

Yoshiwara: The Glittering World of the Japanese Courtesan, Cecilia Segawa Seigle.

Sex, androgyny, prostitution and the development of onnagata roles in Kabuki theatre, Sara K. Birk.

Kathakali, the Dance Theatre, Kalamandalam Govindan Kutty.

Sounding Roman: Representation and Performing Identity in Western Turkey, Sonia Tamar Seeman.

Peking Opera, Chengbei Xu.

The Encyclopedia of Vaudeville, Anthony Slide.

"themstory: This Black Drag King Was Once Known As The Greatest Male Impersonator Of All Time", https://www.them.us/story/themstory-florence-hines.

Arresting Dress: Cross-Dressing, Law, and Fascination in Nineteenth-Century San Francisco, Clare Sears.

THE ART OF GLAMOUR

Film Censorship: Regulating America's Screen, Sheri Chinen Biesen.

Dorothy Parker: Complete Broadway, 1918-1923, Dorothy Parker & Kevin C. Fitzpatrick.

Sing Out! Gays and Lesbians in the Music World, Boze Hadleigh.

Harlem Renaissance Lives from the African American National Bibliography, Henry Louis Gates & Evelyn Brooks Higginbotham.

Takarazuka: Sexual Politics and Popular Culture in Modern Japan, Jennifer Robertson.

"Pansy Craze: the wild 1930s drag parties that kickstarted gay nightlife", https://www.theguardian.com/music/2017/sep/14/pansy-craze-the-wild-1930s-drag-parties-that-kickstarted-gay-nightlife.

THE ART OF WAR

"5 LGBTQ Protests That Set the Stage for Stonewall", https://www.vice.com/en_us/article/d3nenv/lgbtq-protests-before-stonewall.

Stonewall: The Riots That Sparked The Gay Revolution, David Carter.

Stonewall: The Definitive Story of the LGBT Rights Uprising that Changed America, Martin Duberman.

"Ian Berry: Cape Town Moffie Drag", http://makingafrica.net/2015/04/featured-workian-berry-cape-town-moffie-drag/.

"Meet Kewpie, The Rediscovered Daughter of District 6", https://afropunk.com/2019/05/kewpie-cape-town-south-africa-queer-trans-gay-photo-archive/.

"50 Years of Chosen Family", https://www.thecut.com/article/the-house-of-labeija.html.

THE ART OF FREAK

The Black Hole of the Camera: The Films of Andy Warhol, J.J. Murphy.

Love Saves the Day: A History of American Dance Music Culture, 1970–1979, Tim Lawrence.

Black Performance on the Outskirts of the Left: A History of the Impossible, Malik Gaines.

"Drag Herstory: The Wild Life and Untimely Death of Divine, Drag Queen of the Century", https://www.them.us/story/drag-herstory-divine.

"How T. Rex's 'Get It On' Launched Glam Rock", https://www.wsj.com/articles/how-t-rexs-get-it-on-launched-glam-rock-11554827860.

Grace Jones interview on *Day by Day*, 1985. https://www.youtube.com/watch?v=vuW4TcZWeLl.

"20 Crazy Details Behind The Making Of The Rocky Horror

Picture Show", https://screenrant.com/rocky-horror-picture-show-behind-scenes-details-making-trivia/.

"Is It a Male or Female?; Danny La Rue Winning New Fans in London", https://www.nytimes.com/1970/08/31/archives/is-it-a-male-or-female-danny-la-rue-winning-new-fans-in-london.html.

Danny La Rue live at the 1972 Royal Variety Performance. https://www.youtube.com/watch?v=qAmB5AGI8so.

World Heritage Encyclopedia entry on Invasion of the Pines. http://community.worldheritage.org/articles/eng/Invasion_of_the_Pines.

"A 1968 police raid on Fire Island led to one lawyer making LGBT history", https://www.nbcnews.com/feature/nbc-out/1968-police-raid-fire-island-led-one-lawyer-making-lgbt-n903716.

THE ART OF CHARISMA

"It's Neither a Death Drop Nor a Shablam: Celebrating the Art of 'The Dip'", https://hornet.com/stories/death-drop-shablam-dip/.

"Voguing 101 with Cakes Da Killa", https://www.teenvogue.com/story/voguing-101.

"A short history of voguing – an art, a sport, a way of life", https://www.spectator.co.uk/2017/07/how-voguing-came-back-in-vogue/.

"'Paris is Burning' Goes Global", https://www.nytimes.com/2019/06/29/style/paris-is-burning-queer-ballroom-culture.html.

MAC Viva Glam Timeline. https://www.maccosmetics.com/vivaglam-timeline.

"Lady Bunny Shaped Drag As We Know It – And She's Just Getting Started", https://www.them.us/story/lady-bunny-profile.

An Introduction to the World of Visual Kei, Aimee Mariko Kanemori.

"A Developing Legacy", https://www.bangkokpost.com/life/social-and-lifestyle/1717839/a-developing-legacy.

Mother Camp: Female Impersonators in America, Esther Newton.

"Lypsinka Speaks: Interview With A Surrealist", https://www.slantmagazine.com/features/lypsinka-speaks-interview-with-a-surrealist/.

"Sex, sin and sausages: the debauched brilliance of Leigh Bowery", https://www.theguardian.com/artanddesign/2018/aug/13/sex-sin-and-sausages-the-debauched-brilliance-of-leigh-bowery.

"Amanda Lepore on Tr*mp, trans progression and why she's such a f*cking legend", https://www.gaytimes.co.uk/originals/120799/amanda-lepore-on-trmp-trans-progression-and-why-shes-such-a-fcking-legend/.

Doll Parts, Amanda Lepore.

"She's King of the Road", *The Advocate*, 25th September 2001.

Visual AIDS: Ethyl Eichelberger. https://visualaids.org/artists/ethyl-eichelberger.

THE ART OF INFLUENCE

Gender Trouble, Judith Butler.

"How RuPaul's Drag Race Fueled Pop Culture's Dominant Slang Engine", https://www.wired.com/story/rupauls-drag-race-slang/.

"Talking Race and Intersectionality with Victoria Sin", https://i-d.vice.com/en_uk/article/3kb87v/talking-race-and-intersectionality-in-drag-with-victoria-sin.

"Defying State Conservatism, Russia's Drag Queens Strut On", https://www.themoscowtimes.com/2017/02/17/russian-drag-queens-a57177.

"Where Love Is Illegal: Shelah", https://whereloveisillegal.com/shelah/.

"Matmazel Coco, the drag queen aiming to transform Turkey", https://www.efe.com/efe/english/destacada/matmazel-coco-the-drag-queen-aiming-to-transform-turkey/50000261-4009530.

INDEX

CONTRIBUTORS

Jake Hall | Author

Jake is a freelance journalist and postgraduate student of Gender & Sexuality with a relentless interest in all things queer. Their work over the years has covered everything from sex workers' rights and climate change to fashion subcultures and – of course! – the past, present and future of drag. Their clients include *Dazed*, *i-D*, *VICE*, *British Vogue* and *Playboy*, and their spare time is usually spent watching wrestling, scrolling through dog memes and eating their own body weight in sushi.

Acknowledgements

Thanks to my mum and grandparents for always making me believe I could turn my passion into a living, to my closest friends for putting up with my stressed-out rants, and to my editor Ayoola Solarin, for being the most understanding and encouraging partner-in-crime I could have hoped for. Without you, this process would have been twice as stressful – for that reason alone, I'm incredibly grateful!

Helen Li | Cover, Art of Freak & Influence

Helen is an Australian illustrator currently residing in Warsaw, Poland. She has an MFA in Illustration from the School of Visual Arts and has enjoyed collaborations with Google, Dropbox, Adobe, Redbull, *The Wall Street Journal* and more. In between client work and personal projects you'll find her tattooing, and exploring nature with her spouse and dog.

Acknowledgements

Special thanks to Ayoola Solarin for bringing me onboard and guiding me through this wild journey, to Lilly Gottwald for her direction, to Sofie and Jasjyot for their dedication and inspirational drive, to Cynthia and Francesca for their generous insight and advice, to Shin and Eugenia for lending an ear in times of need, to Pawel for his unwavering belief and to my family for their earnest support.

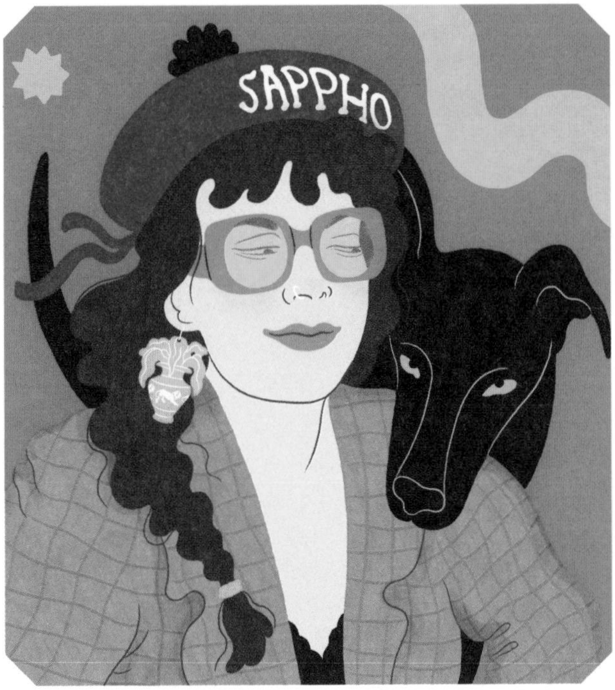
SAPPHO

Sofie Birkin | Art of Performance & War

Sofie is a British illustrator living in Denver with her wife Erika and dog Arthur, who are both very tall and very smart. She creates bright, playful images which prioritize inclusive representation, encourage daydreams, and above all aim to empower. Sofie uses her work to promote the gay agenda whenever possible, and has created queer and trans inclusive illustrations for *Cosmopolitan* and *Playboy*. She is currently working on an installation for *Meow Wolf* Denver. When she's not attached to her drawing tablet, she's probably getting emotional at an estate sale or telling ghost stories.

Acknowledgements

A huge thank you to Erika for your unwavering support, motivation and endless cups of tea at all times of night, to Helen and Jasjyot for your incredible talent and solidarity, to Ayoola and Lilly for your guidance and compassion, to my mum for always picking up the phone and my dad for 30 years of art direction, and to more friends than I could list for being a tonic at my most stressed-out moments.

Jasjyot Singh Hans | Art of Glamour & Charisma

Jasjyot is an illustrator from Delhi, currently based in the US. He is unendingly inspired by an explosive neon mix of fashion, music and pop culture. He has a constant regard for things past and a voracity for all that is current.

His work chronicles themes of body image, sexuality and identity. His clients include Google, *The New York Times*, *Vogue India* and Adidas.

Acknowledgements

Thank you Maa & Paa, for always checking on me and keeping me in check! Parveer, thank you for being my sounding board.

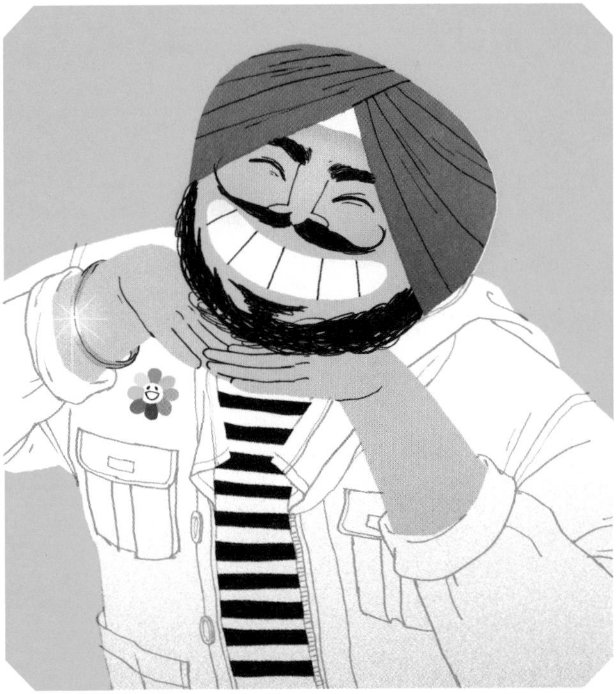

Eero Lampinen is a Berlin-based illustrator who loves clean lines and dreamy pastel palettes. His work blends elements of traditional storytelling and contemporary fashion to create an adjacent reality populated by melancholic characters. His current obsessions include plants, his local drag scene, sad memes and jazzy, speculative technology.

Crystal Rasmussen Look up the term 'Global Phenomenon' in the dictionary and you will simply find a picture of Crystal's face. She's beautiful. She's a model. She forms one fifth of DENIM, the drag supergroup, and is adored by fans for her lazy demeamour and her powerful falsetto. When out of drag, Tom Rasmussen is a Northerner based in London who regularly contributes to publications including The Independent, Dazed & Confused, i-D, LOVE Magazine and Refinery29. In 2018 they were named an LGBT trailblazer by The Dots, and one of i-D's 'Voices of Now'. Tom also forms half of the radical queer punk bank ACM.

Salome Papadopoullos is an illustrator based in London. Inspired by feelings of nostalgia in music, fashion and film, her work involves portraits and typography using gouache, glitter and colour pencils, all encapsulating girl pop culture.

The Vixen is a multi-talented performer dedicated to making the world a better place. Growing up on Chicago's South Side, her art has always been intertwined with social justice and activism. An accomplished drag queen, songwriter, fashion designer and dancer, she credits her creative family for her love of the arts. Since turning 21, The Vixen has perfected a combination of excellent make-up skills and athletic performance, which quickly made her a key name in Chicago's drag scene. She is also the founder of BlackGirlMagic, a drag concert where queens of colour can celebrate their unique experiences through storytelling and performance. The Vixen lives by her grandmother's belief that helping others makes life worthwhile.

Noa Denmon is a Philadelphia-based artist and illustrator. Growing up in Pittsburgh, she was heavily influenced by the industrial landscape and how that contributed to her identity. Today, she works to bring these bright colors and patterns into stories uplifting the underrepresented; she hopes to create work that displays humanity and all of its differences.

Sweatmother is a London-based filmmaker and artist. Their moving image work re-evaluates cinematic conventions and explores alternative narratives to queer identities, feminisms and womxn-identifying representations. Their work more generally reclaims the often misplaced voice, body and gaze by repurposing femme and gender non-conforming identities in spaces where objectification is removed, and the agency and difference in otherness is celebrated. Presently they work as a video artist in London's DIY/club scene. They are also an active member of Transmissions, a liberation collective for trans/gender non-conforming identities, a Contemporary, a queer feminist collective.

Nada Hayek is an illustrator, graphic designer and musician based in Vancouver, BC. Inspired by retro imagery, dark humor and the knick-knack section of your local thrift store, she aims to create work that is equal parts playful and unexpected.

Don One from Bir-ming-ham (now based in east London) is one of the most entertaining drag kings on the scene right now and they're on a mission to spread a special kind of Brummie love all over the land! Don is silky-smooth vocalist with a wide repertoire of songs and also has a huge stage presence having performed to over 35,000 people. Along with having a fantastic singing voice, Don hosts, MCs and raps - there really isn't much they cannot do!

Marcos Chin is an award winning Illustrator whose work has appeared as surface and wall designs, on book and CD covers, and in advertisements, fashion catalogues, and magazines. Marcos has given lectures and workshops throughout the US and abroad, and currently lives in New York where he teaches Illustration at the School of Visual Arts.

READ for FILTH
Squirrel Friends

Joe E. Jeffreys | Consultant

Joe E. Jeffreys is a multi-platform drag historian. He has published on the subject in encyclopedias, book anthologies, academic journals and the popular press. Jeffreys has been interviewed about drag by media outlets including *Time*, *The New York Times*, *The Guardian* and *L'Obs* as well as featured on Entertainment Tonight and BBC Radio 4. His drag-happy video work has screened at galleries, festivals and museums internationally including Tate Modern.